I0766947

AUTHOR'S PROFILE

Paul Baweja was born in Sydney, the Commonwealth of Australia. In 2007, Paul was awarded the New South Wales Higher School Certificate from LaSalle Catholic College (Sydney). The College of the former Australian Prime Minister, the Right Honourable Paul John Keating of the Commonwealth of Australia (r. 1991–1996). In 2012, Paul earned the Bachelor of Commerce Degree from Macquarie University (Sydney). Thereafter, in 2014, Paul attained the Graduate Diploma of Chartered Accounting from the Institute of Chartered Accountants Australia (Sydney). Furthermore, Paul is the recipient of numerous academic awards, including the prestigious 'Golden Key International Honour Society' Award (Atlanta, Georgia, the United States of America).

In addition, Paul completed postgraduate study within the Macquarie Business School at Macquarie University (Sydney), to obtain the Master of Business Administration Degree in 2016. Paul further completed research-based postgraduate study at the Australian National University (Canberra, the Australian Capital Territory), graduating with the Master of Diplomacy (Advanced) Degree in 2018. Paul's Master's Degree Thesis was completed under the auspices of the ANU College of Asia and the Pacific at the Coral Bell School of Asia Pacific Affairs. Paul's Thesis was titled 'International Conflict Mediation: A Diplomatic Analysis of the U.S. Camp David Talks (1978).'

On matters of theology, in 2022, Paul completed the Certificate of Catholic Theology at the Augustine Institute (Greenwood Village, Colorado, the United States of America).

Also, in the same year, Paul attained the Certificate in Biblical Studies from the Biblical Training Institute (Camas, Washington, the United States of America). Finally, also in 2022, Paul achieved the Certificate in the Catechism of the Catholic Church from Catholic Distance University (Charles Town, West Virginia, the United States of America).

Paul is an Australian author, intellectual, and scholar. Paul has authored several books on Philosophy, Women's History, English Literature, and English Poetry. Over the course of nine years, Paul has written and published the epic-length *A Philosophical Treatise of Reality*, a 500,000-word four-volume treatise released in 2021. Thereafter, Paul has authored *The Struggle of Women: Major Female Figures throughout World History* (2022), *A Commentary on Shakespeare's Plays* (2023), and *A Critique of Milton's Paradise Lost and Regained* (2024). Paul's book *The Struggle of Women* has been accepted into the Department of the Prime Minister and Cabinet Library (Brisbane, Queensland).

A CRITIQUE OF
MILTON'S PARADISE LOST AND REGAINED

FIRST EDITION

PAUL BAWEJA

MMXXIV

First published in Melbourne,
the Commonwealth of Australia, 2024

Published by Paul Baweja
APTOR2021_enquiries@protonmail.com

Copyright © Paul Baweja, 2024
First Edition 2024 (Hardcover Book)

A catalogue record for this
book is available from the
National Library of Australia

NATIONAL
LIBRARY
OF AUSTRALIA

ISBN: 978 0 6489818 6 2 (Hardcover Book)

Cover design and illustration by Ricardo Montaño Castro
(Bogotá, Colombia) via DesignCrowd (Sydney)
Cover image: *God watches, while the Serpent tempts Adam and Eve
with the Forbidden Fruit*
Text design and typesetting by Blue Wren Books (Melbourne)
Printed and bound by Ingram Spark

DEDICATION

Paul Baweja dedicates this book to the memory of Adeline Virginia Woolf (1882–1941). Adeline was an English writer. Some of Adeline's remarkable works include *Mrs. Dalloway*, *Orlando: A Biography*, *To the Lighthouse*, *A Room of One's Own*, and *The Waves*. Without question, Adeline is one of the most important and influential English writers of the twentieth century. Adeline's fascinating writing is important, not only in its historical context, however, its relevance in the contemporary era cannot be overstated. Adeline's writing gives voice to the inequality and disadvantage that women confront in modern society.

ACKNOWLEDGEMENT

Paul Baweja, of Sydney, the Commonwealth of Australia, acknowledges the original and true author of these sixteen books as the English poet and intellectual, John Milton (1608–1674) of London, the Kingdom of England. Milton's literary work is in the Public Domain. This critique augments and elucidates on the concepts, ideas, and themes advanced by the insightful and inquisitive English gentleman. All writing directly pertaining to Milton's sixteen books are appropriately referenced throughout this publication.

CONTENTS

PREFACE

This book proffers a contemporary critique of John Milton's grand work, *Paradise Lost and Regained*. Milton's phenomenal writing represents a profound contribution to English poetry and literature. In addition, Milton's literary work engages in a rigorous thematic analysis of Christian theology. This critique examines the Biblical narratives, theological principles, philosophy, and literature underlying Milton's magnificent work.

This book investigates the themes of blessing, damnation, death, defeat, devil, disobedience, evil, favour, forgiveness, free will, glory, God, good, grace, heaven, hell, hope, justice, justification, love, marriage, mercy, morality, mortality, obedience, passion, power, prayer, redemption, revelation, sacrifice, salvation, sanctification, sin, spiritual warfare, tragedy, and victory.

Milton's *Paradise Lost and Regained* is a fascinating text of English literature. This is true for a multitude of reasons. First, Milton's set of sixteen books; twelve books on *Paradise Lost* and four books on *Paradise Regained*, are written as a single and continuous poem. Second, this English poem is written in blank verse, also known as Miltonic verse. Third, Milton employs a personalised style of English spelling, grammar, and punctuation throughout the entire poem. This assists the learned English gentleman to create an original and striking effect on English phonetics and phonology. Fourth, Milton has made an original contribution to our understanding of the Old Testament and the New Testament. Last but not least, Milton's spellbinding style of poetry renders our engagement with complex doctrines of Christian theology as uncomplicated.

This critique explores the magnificent writing of John Milton. It examines the Biblical principles, themes, concepts, narratives, and stories contained within Milton's masterpiece literary work. With the passage of three and a half centuries, the grand importance of Milton's work has not diminished. The poetic writing of Milton constitutes a perennial contribution to English poetry and literature. The literary work of John Milton is second, in its originality and creativity, only to the Master English playwright and poet, William Shakespeare (1564–1616). The author trusts the reader finds this critique beneficial in reading and interpreting Milton's exceptional work.

Paul Baweja
Australian Author
Sydney
the Commonwealth of Australia
November 2024

KEYWORDS

Adam, Agency, Angel, Atonement, Chaos, Conflict, Conscience, Crucifixion, Damnation, David, Death, Decree, Defeat, Devil, Disobedience, Eternal Life, Eve, Evil, Faith, Fall of Man, Fate, Favour, Forbidden Fruit, Foreknowledge, Forgiveness, Free will, Garden of Eden, Glory, God, Good, Grace, Heaven, Hell, Husband, Jesus, Job, Joseph, Judge, Justice, Kingdom, Knowledge of Good and Evil, Love, Lucifer, Man, Mercy, Messiah, Milton, Obedience, Original Sin, Paradise, Paul the Apostle, Peace, Predestination, Punishment, Reconciliation, Redemption, Resurrection, Saint Michael, Salvation, Satan, Saul, Saviour, Serpent, Sin, Soul, Spirit, Temptation, Tree of Knowledge, Victory, War, Wealth, Wife, Will, Willpower, Wisdom, and Woman.

A CRITIQUE OF
MILTON'S PARADISE LOST AND REGAINED

INTRODUCTION

John Milton's *Paradise Lost and Regained* represents a remarkable work of English poetry and literature. Milton's incandescent writing is structured around major Biblical themes and stories. *Paradise Lost* constitutes the first half of Milton's epic two-part literary work. *Paradise Lost* is comprised of twelve interconnected books. Each of the twelve books narrate a specific event in the Biblical story of the Fall of Man, based on the conscious and free willed actions of Adam and Eve in the Garden of Eden. *Paradise Lost* masterfully portrays the inherent fallacy of human reason and the consequential effectuation of Original Sin in the Garden of Eden. Thereafter, humanity is to forever experience the negative consequences of Adam and Eve's free moral actions in contravening God's Sovereign Command.

God has complete foreknowledge of Adam and Eve's ill-intentioned actions in the Garden of Eden. God places complete confidence and total trust in Adam and Eve, leaving both of them with explicit instructions, as to what conduct is permissible and impermissible in the Garden of Eden. Beyond any doubt, as part of God's Divine Plan for Creation, God has granted Adam and Eve free will. Therefore, Adam and Eve possess the inherent capacity to make their own moral decisions. Unfortunately, Adam and Eve misappropriate their agency and improperly employ their natural reason. The serenity within picture-perfect Paradise is ruined.

The Devil in the seductive form of a serpent, employs empty rhetoric in his destiny-defining dialogue with Eve. The Devil utilises every trick in the book to persuade Eve to seek out the corrupt path of temptation and sin. The Serpent attempts to convince Eve to consume the Forbidden Fruit to acquire the knowledge of good and evil. Inaccurately, the Serpent narrates to Eve, that by consuming the Forbidden Fruit and contravening God's Eternal Word, she will attain a state of being that is far superior to her current condition. The Serpent gives voice to a false narrative, that Eve shall equal God, in the depth of her newfound knowledge of good and evil. Regrettably, Eve takes the bait.

Needless to say, Adam also consumes the Forbidden Fruit from the Tree of Knowledge of Good and Evil. Adam and Eve's immoral actions have now exposed them to the knowledge of good and evil. The two of them very quickly realise that the possession of this knowledge is not beneficial to their existence. Now, Adam and Eve find themselves in low spirits. Despondent and dejected, the duo attempt to apportion blame for their misgiving. As just punishment for their disobedience to God's Sovereign Command, both of them are escorted by Angels out of Paradise. As a consequence, an inferior world of sin, guilt, punishment, death, damnation, remorse, evil, and hell has been unleashed by the Devil.

Paradise Regained, as the title suggests, portrays the redemption and salvation of humankind. *Paradise Regained* is comprised of four interconnected books. In the second half of Milton's epic two-part literary work, humanity witnesses the Son of God, suffer the ultimate penalty for Adam and Eve's grave sins by the act of Crucifixion. As a result, the Son of God absolves humankind from God's eternal punishment of sin and death. Thereby, through the unrivalled power of intercession, the Son of God offers a new pathway to eternal life and into the Kingdom of Heaven. The sacrifice of the Son of God is the final and irreversible act, which forever atones humanity for the fundamental error of Original Sin.

The Crucifixion of the Father's beloved Son, in the human form, is deemed an acceptable sacrifice to God. This act of unconditional love by the *Messiah* wholly abrogates humanity from the inadequate method of constant atonement by way of animal sacrifices. God's True Justice is delivered to humanity vis-à-vis the saviour. The Crucifixion of the *Messiah* is the final atonement for humankind. The *Messiah's* sacrifice is perfect and complete in all respects. As a result, salvation is now near at hand for human civilisation. In upholding God's Eternal Word and submitting to God's Sovereign Will, the Son of God fulfils his divine mission pertaining to the redemption of humankind. Once again, human civilisation is shown God's Infinite Mercy. God has provided for the solution to humanity's problem of sin. By God's Grace, forgiveness has now been achieved for Adam, Eve, and the greater good of humankind.

Paradise Regained promotes reconciliation between God and humanity. By the voluntary act of Crucifixion of the Son of God, the adequate atonement for Original Sin is now satisfactorily and wholly complete. Milton concludes *Paradise Regained* by demonstrating the abject failure of the Devil to tempt the Son of God with private wealth, private property, riches, worldly kingdoms, territory, pleasure, gold, silver, pecuniary gain, prestige, fame, and the fleeting glory of the world. Milton very eloquently leaves his readers with the lasting impression, that all human endeavours to seek worldly praise, approval, fame, prestige, success, profit, pecuniary gain, and worldly glory, are all but trivial and fleeting objectives. In one sense, Milton's colourful writing expresses the vanity of all human aspirations and accomplishments.

In the final analysis, both in substance and form, all of Creation is to extol God's Creativity, Power, Goodness, Glory, Mercy, and Greatness. The profound theological wisdom contained in Milton's literary writing positions our life into perspective. In the end, what really matters is God. In as much as we centre our life around the construct of our being, and the insatiable demands of our ego, life is not all about us.

Human life is about bringing the Creator glory, honour, and praise. This lifetime is an unprecedented and finite opportunity for us to refine our character, strengthen our faith, love God, and cultivate our virtues. We must define our Earthly existence by adherence to the noble cause of peace, social justice, prosperity, community service, love, charity, equality, human dignity, respect, mercy, compassion, tolerance, freedom, benevolence, and forgiveness.

CHAPTER 1

PARADISE LOST: BOOK ONE

'The mind is its own place.
In itself can make a Heaven of Hell.
A Hell of Heaven.'

MILTON

BOOK ONE of *Paradise Lost* sets the opening scene and context for the Biblical story of Original Sin. In this book, Milton narrates the casting out of Lucifer from the Kingdom of Heaven. We witness Lucifer's ignorance and disobedience to God's Sovereign Command. Satan, who is now exiled from the Kingdom of Heaven is banished into the dark, disastrous, and dismal depths of Hell. Satan ignorantly inspires his legion of fallen Angels, with false hope to rebel against Almighty God. Satan has not learnt his moral lesson. Satan remains radically defiant in his illegitimate pursuit of evil and injustice.

At first, Satan considers a renewed second attempt to capture the Kingdom of Heaven. However, after much debate and discourse, Satan defers his ill-fated plan to commence war in Heaven. Instead, Satan is now determined to target God's newest Creation; Adam and Eve in the Garden of Eden. Satan cunningly reasons, that since he cannot gain victory over God's

Sovereign Kingdom in Heaven, he will fight a battle in the midst of Paradise. A battle against Adam and Eve. A battle in which Satan is more likely than not to secure a decisive victory. In the relentless pursuit of the fall of Adam and Eve, Satan now directs his time, energy, resources, and expertise. The epic battle for the Garden of Eden is on the horizon.

'Of man's first disobedience, and the fruit of the forbidden tree. Whose mortal taste brought death into the world, and all our woe, with the loss of Eden. Till one greater man restore us, and regain the blissful seat.'[1]

The intentional transgression of God's Sovereign Command and Sovereign Will brings forth misery, grief, suffering, pain, guilt, destruction, trauma, heartache, death, and loss into the world. Humanity is deluded by the false impression of the ego and the finite capacity of the intellect. Rationally speaking, the ego and the intellect seek to advance our self-preservation, self-interest, and self-determination, within the finite bounds of our temporal existence on Earth.

More often than not, humanity reasons itself to know better than God, on how to structure its personal affairs in society and state. We prematurely dismiss from our mind the supreme idea, that God's Plans are for humanity's prosperity, success, joy, abundance, and happiness. God's Desire is to bless humanity. Often times, we witness ourselves reject God's Superior Advice and Wise Counsel. Sometimes, we incorrectly perceive that we better fathom reality, and therefore, interpret our lives on the basis of our lived experience, limited knowledge, and exercise of natural reason.

With the benefit of hindsight, we learn to appreciate that we do not make the right decisions at the right time in our life.

---

1   Milton, John. (Darbishire, Helen, Ed.) (1958). *The Poetical Works of John Milton*. London: Oxford University Press, p. 5.

We do not possess complete foreknowledge of how future events will unfold. We do not fully comprehend the far-reaching consequences of our immediate actions, until well after we ascertain their effects upon ourselves. Unintended consequences, that are far beyond our understanding to conceive, comprehend, and conceptualise. Personal agency and free will are inherently good characteristics, however, their employment must be guided by virtuous and noble principles. We cannot escape the fixed reality, that the principles we observe and the actions we execute, ultimately determine our credibility, character, conviction, and conscience.

Encapsulating all material and living phenomena is divine providence—the ultimate guiding force in the Universe. No person, sovereign nation-state, power, energy, being, force, association, partnership, corporation, or entity, transcends God's Incomparable Power. God's Will is supreme and sovereign in all respects. Therefore, for humanity to voluntarily conform to God's Divine Plan, only functions to the overwhelming benefit and favour of humanity. We must shatter the ill-founded delusion of our ego, that undergirds our [present] state of being in the world. We must transcend [the fabrication of] the veil of our individuality.

Often times, the pursuit of the Self only leads us to misery, despair, despondency, guilt, anger, jealousy, trauma, loss, grief, depression, and regret. We must come to understand, that God's Spirit is far greater than the capacity of our mind to visualise, conceive, or imagine. We ought to align our spirit with God's Spirit. So that in times of adversity, we find courage. In times of despair, we find strength. In times of desperation, we find hope. In times of loss, we find contentment. In times of suffering, we find faith. In times of heartache, we find peace. In times of privation, we find gratitude. No matter the highs and lows that we experience throughout our life, so long as we maintain equanimity, we achieve spiritual progress.

'*Who first seduced them to that foul revolt? The infernal serpent. He it was, whose guile stirred up with envy and revenge. Deceived the Mother of humankind. What time his pride had cast him out from Heaven, with all his host of rebel Angels, by whose aid aspiring to set himself in glory above his peers. He trusted to have equalled the Most High. If he opposed; and with ambitious aim against the Throne and Monarchy of God, raised impious war in Heaven and battle proud with vain attempt. Him the Almighty Power hurled headlong flaming from the ethereal sky with hideous ruin and combustion down to bottomless perdition. There to dwell in adamantine chains and penal fire. Who darest defy the Omnipotent to arms?*'[2]

In all our hopes, endeavours, dreams, petitions, aims, and objectives, Satan is never to be trusted. It was Satan's evil plot to mislead and deceive the Mother of Humankind. That is to say, the Devil in the form of a serpent, schemed the downfall of Eve in the Garden of Eden. Lucifer fell foul of the priceless gifts that the Creator had bestowed upon him; lofty gifts of beauty, intelligence, wisdom, power, and position. All these God-given gifts were misappropriated. It was vanity and pride, which pre-empted Lucifer to seek the glory and honour that rightfully belongs to God. Forgetting his rightful place, Lucifer ignorantly challenged God for the Kingdom of Heaven.

Every person, being, or Angel must know its proper place in the Cosmic Order, and none are equal to God. As a lasting consequence of Lucifer's disobedience to God's Sovereign Will, he was banished from the Kingdom of Heaven. Lucifer was no longer permitted to remain within God's Everlasting Presence, Majesty, Favour, and Grace. Herein we witness the Devil, himself

---

2   Milton, John. (Darbishire, Helen, Ed.) (1958). *The Poetical Works of John Milton*. London: Oxford University Press, p. 6.

having been deceived by the endless entity of the ego. Lucifer has fallen for the superficial enticement of pride, the lust of power, the desire for glory, and the vanity of beauty. Thereafter, the Devil has been tirelessly at work to induce humanity to forget God's Blessing, Favour, Goodness, Grace, and Mercy.

We must always position God first place in our life. All the work that we perform on Earth must centre around furthering the cause of good over evil. For the incredibly brief period of time that we are situated on Earth, we remain consumed with our personal affairs, immediate challenges, and numerous life-changing priorities, all within the myriad and complex social, legal, medical, political, moral, and economic issues within the sovereign nation-state. All too often, we forget that the human condition is incomplete without God. Our spirit is incomplete without God's Spirit. The inner spiritual poverty of our existence is categorically affirmed without God's Presence in our life. It is only by God's Grace, that an individual attains reconciliation with God, and thereby transcends the sinful nature of humankind.

'As one great furnace flamed. Yet, from those flames no light. But rather darkness visible served only to discover sights of woe. Regions of sorrow. Doleful shades. Where peace and rest can never dwell. Hope never comes that comes to all. But torture without end still urges, and a fiery deluge, fed with ever-burning sulphur unconsumed. Such place eternal justice had prepared for those rebellious. Here their prison ordained in utter darkness, and their portion set as far removed from God and light of Heaven. As from the centre thrice to the utmost pole. O how unlike the place from whence they fell!'[3]

We cannot escape the consequences of our actions, both the intended and the unintended. If we seek to utilise our influence, time, energy, resources, talents, abilities, expertise, knowledge, experience, intellect, and power to promote evil in the world, then we are forced to contend with evil in our life. On the other hand, if we seek to utilise our influence, time, energy, resources, talents, abilities, expertise, knowledge, experience, intellect, and power to promote good in the world, then we are confronted with good in our life. Therefore, before we proceed to act, we must ask ourselves the question: Are we prepared to live with the consequences of our actions?

In the conscious and voluntary performance of our actions, the principle of 'what we sow is what we reap' holds true and constant. The universal operation of the aforementioned moral principle cannot be circumvented or denied. God's Justice is always served. Humanity is not at liberty to negate or refute this categorical fact. The purpose of human life is to seek union with God's Spirit. All other worldly endeavours are fruitless. All other worldly endeavours constitute vain attempts to appease the existence and function of our ego.

---

3   Milton, John. (Darbishire, Helen, Ed.) (1958). *The Poetical Works of John Milton*. London: Oxford University Press, p. 7.

As Lucifer's tragic rebellion against God confirms, misplaced pride, virtue, intelligence, beauty, wisdom, and ambition, only bring about one's inevitable disaster, demise, and downfall. Lucifer's ignorance, pride, and ego only served to reinforce his fall from grace. Lucifer's tragic banishment from the Kingdom of Heaven was a loss. A loss that forever altered this powerful angelic being's destiny.

Within the Holy Bible, in the Book of Isaiah, we are reminded of Lucifer's tragic fall from grace. The specific verses of scripture narrates the following discourse, 'How you are fallen from Heaven, O Day Star, Son of Dawn! How you are cut down to the ground, you who laid the Nations low! You said in your heart, 'I will ascend to Heaven; above the stars of God. I will set my throne on high. I will sit on the Mount of Assembly in the far reaches of the North. I will ascend above the heights of the clouds. I will make myself like the Most High.' But you are brought down to Sheol, to the far reaches of the pit.'[4]

With the unique attributes, traits, talents, abilities, expertise, knowledge, experience, skills, and wisdom that we have been provisioned by God, we must not misappropriate their employment. The temptation to transcend the Self, to become something or someone far greater is always present, however, we must prudently manage our aspirations and dreams. We must ensure that through our [misplaced] ambition, we do not [accidentally] effectuate our downfall.

---

4   The Holy Bible (ESV). (2016). The Book of Isaiah. Chapter 14, Verses 12–15.

'That durst dislike his reign, and me preferring. His utmost power with adverse power opposed in dubious battle on the plains of Heaven, and shook His Throne. What though the field be lost? All is not lost. The unconquerable will, and study of revenge, immortal hate, and courage, never to submit or yield: and what is else not to be overcome? That glory never shall his wrath or might extort from me. To bow and sue for grace with suppliant knee, and defy His Power, who from the terror of this arm so late doubted His Empire. That were low indeed. That were an ignominy and shame beneath this downfall. Since by fate, the Strength of God and this empyreal substance cannot fail.'[5]

The Devil has initiated disobedience, rebellion, and war in God's Kingdom of Heaven. This is a grand battle in which the Devil shall never claim a decisive victory. However, by the very corrupt and evil intention of the Devil, he seeks to undermine the performance of God's Sovereign Will on Earth. Having said that, God's Robe of Righteousness, Sceptre of Sovereignty, Journal of Justice, Scales of Sapphire, and Periscope of Prescience, none of these divine instruments are undermined. Satan is most certainly doomed to abject failure in his illegitimate quest to sabotage the peace, prosperity, perfection, and paradise found within God's Kingdom of Heaven. It is for this very reason that the Devil has committed his malevolent spirit to cause destruction, discord, disturbance, distress, depression, and death on Earth.

Simply put, the Devil seeks to corrupt humanity. The Devil's objective is to turn humanity away from God's Presence. The Devil leads humanity astray with the power of negative emotions, such as doubt, fear, anger, disappointment, confusion, agony,

---

5   Milton, John. (Darbishire, Helen, Ed.) (1958). *The Poetical Works of John Milton*. London: Oxford University Press, p. 8.

bitterness, despair, jealousy, embarrassment, envy, nervousness, regret, sadness, misery, and hate.

In the Holy Bible, within the First Letter of Peter, God's Eternal Word has forewarned us about the Devil. We are reminded, 'Be sober-minded. Be watchful. Your adversary the Devil prowls around like a roaring lion, seeking someone to devour.'[6] We must exercise vigilance, to ensure that we do not accept the logical fallacy of reasoning with the Devil. Eve made the honest mistake of entertaining a discourse with the Devil. Sincere Eve's innocent mistake in underestimating the Devil, ultimately led to sin, punishment, and death. The Devil is not in the moral enterprise to grant humanity any favours or blessings, but rather promote our expedient downfall and terminal destruction.

'Whether upheld by strength, or chance, or fate. Too well, I see and rue the dire event, that with sad overthrow and foul defeat, hath lost us Heaven, and all this mighty host in horrible destruction laid thus low. As far as God and Heavenly essence can perish. For the mind and spirit remains invincible, and vigour soon returns. Though, all our glory extinct, and happy state here swallowed up, in endless misery. But what if he, our conqueror, (whom I now of force believe almighty, since no less then such could have overpowered, such force as ours) have left us this, our spirit and strength? Entirely strong, to suffer and support our pains. That we may so, suffice his vengeful ire.'[7]

The cold hard truth is that we cannot rely solely upon our willpower, in order to overcome the obstacles, issues, problems, and challenges in our life. We must understand and align ourselves

---

6   The Holy Bible (ESV). (2016). The First Letter of Peter. Chapter 5, Verse 8.

7   Milton, John. (Darbishire, Helen, Ed.) (1958). *The Poetical Works of John Milton*. London: Oxford University Press, p. 9.

with God's Sovereign Will. If cultivated appropriately, the mind and spirit become indomitable. Whereas with the passage of time, the human body diminishes in its strength and vitality.

Suffering is an undeniable part and parcel of the human experience. Humanity cannot deny the incidence of suffering. Having said that, our suffering must not be in vain. We must adapt to our worldly reality. We must transcend our struggles, difficulties, and privations. We must run our race to the best of our ability. In the end, God is the Creator, Provider, and Sustainer of all life forms on Earth. In times of tribulation, God is the source of our remedy. God's Eternal Word is the respite, resolution, and relief for our troubled soul.

> *'Fallen Cherub. To be weak is miserable doing or suffering. But of this be sure. To do aught good never will be our task. But ever to do ill, our sole delight. As being the contrary to His High Will, whom we resist. If then His Providence out of our evil seek to bring forth good, our labour must be to pervert that end, and out of good still to find means of evil. Which oft times may succeed. So, as perhaps shall grieve Him. If I fail not, and disturb His inmost counsels from their destined aim.'*[8]

The desire for evil, the harbouring of a malevolent will, and the diabolical intentions of the Devil are an open secret. In all the Devil's detestable work on Earth, the Devil aims to promote death, destruction, disease, disillusion, disturbance, and depression upon human civilisation. It is the malevolent nature and maleficent purpose of the Devil to defy God's Perfect Vision of Creation. The battle between good and evil is comprised of sporadic and strategic spiritual battles. Too often, our life is consumed with the inconsequential battles of the flesh. These

---

8   Milton, John. (Darbishire, Helen, Ed.) (1958). *The Poetical Works of John Milton*. London: Oxford University Press, p. 9.

latter battles are dominated by pride, ego, fame, control, power, social status, private property, personal income, worldly glory, prestige, influence, and private wealth. However, these worldly battles are not our greatest battles.

In the Holy Bible, within the Book of Ephesians, we are reminded of the primacy of the spirit over the flesh. We must not misappropriate our finite energy, time, resources, and abilities in endless worldly battles, 'For we do not wrestle against the flesh and blood, but against the rulers, against the authorities, against the cosmic powers over the present darkness, against the spiritual forces of evil in the Heavenly places.'[9] Before we prematurely become engaged in a worldly battle, a battle that is consumed and defined by the flesh, we must ask ourselves the question: Does this battle further or hinder our destiny?

The Devil is constantly scheming to undermine the presence and proliferation of good in the world. In this ignoble quest, the Devil employs the age-old weapons of jealousy, loneliness, concupiscence, guilt, doubt, pride, envy, hate, anger, confusion, bitterness, shame, depression, insecurity, resentment, worry, hopelessness, indignity, intrusive thoughts, discouragement, procrastination, suicide, fear, uncertainty, revenge, temptation, self-harm, and failure.

Through God's Grace, if humanity remains attentive and conscious of the Devil's instruments of war, then such weapons are rendered ineffective. This objective is obtained with the proper and correct application of God's Spiritual Armour. The Devil has plans to ruin and destroy our life. The moral, ethical, and spiritual responsibility is upon us, that we do not permit the presence of temptation, evil, and sin, to define our brief tenure on Earth.

---

9   The Holy Bible (ESV). (2016). The Book of Ephesians. Chapter 6, Verse 12.

> *'The mind is its own place. In itself can make a Heaven of Hell. A Hell of Heaven. What matter where, if I be still the same? What I should be? All, but less than He.'*[10]

The mind is one of the most important components of the human constitution, along with the body, spirit, heart, and soul. Every day, our mind must be nourished with optimistic thoughts, the reinforcement of self-efficacy, a good value system, and positive beliefs about life, society, state, and the world. The mind possesses the unique capacity to torment the human experience, and make our life a living Hell on Earth.

On the other hand, and equally so, the mind can cause the human experience to be joyful and pleasant, wherein our life is considered Heaven on Earth. Our reality of being and the perception of our mind are interlinked. As much as we perceive the world in a coloured, distinct, and partial manner, this disparate perception taints our mind. Our experience of being in the world is not impartial, factual, and objective.

Just as we nourish our human body with the appropriate vitamins, minerals, hydration, and nutrients, we must nourish our mind with positive thoughts, wholesome beliefs, sensible ideas, moral doctrines, and good personal values. A life that is lived on the foundation of righteousness and moral principles is a good life. Therefore, it is incumbent upon us to periodically analyse the contents of our mind, so that we become better acquainted with how our thoughts, beliefs, doctrines, and principles subconsciously and consciously construct our life narrative. Through mindfulness and self-awareness, we live a rewarding and fulfilling life.

---

10 Milton, John. (Darbishire, Helen, Ed.) (1958). *The Poetical Works of John Milton.* London: Oxford University Press, p. 12.

'Here we may reign secure. And in my choice, to reign is worth ambition though in Hell. Better to reign in Hell. Than to serve in Heaven.'[11]

This assertion illustrates the shallow depth of the Devil's distorted reasoning. As long as we are existent in the flesh, our ego irrationally desires power, control, private wealth, private property, fame, social status, influence, prestige, and authority. However, the endless pursuit and irrational possession of such socially desirable traits and characteristics, only destroys our peace of mind and sabotages the equanimity of our spirit. All of Creation is a creative construct and exquisite expression of God's Majestic Power. Thus, we must remain conscious of our proper place in Creation. In all respects, we must know whom we serve and where we serve.

God's Divine Plans are superior to our ordinary plans concerning life. In a similar manner, God's Thoughts are superior to our rudimentary thoughts. It is through the fundamental and extreme expression of self-interest, that we find ourselves making inferior life choices. Thereafter, we are obliged to accept the long-term consequences of our free will in action. Our natural reason does not always make informed choices and the most suitable determinations. This is why errors of judgement and mistakes of fact are part and parcel of the human experience.

When we self-determine the most fundamental and consequential choices in our life, choices such as where to reside, what academic discipline of higher education to pursue, what profession to be employed in, whom to marry, whether to procreate, whether to donate our organs, whether to provide our medical doctor with an advanced care directive, or whether to execute an enduring or non-enduring power of attorney over

---

11   Milton, John. (Darbishire, Helen, Ed.) (1958). *The Poetical Works of John Milton*. London: Oxford University Press, p. 12.

our personal affairs, first we ought to carefully consider our intentions, values, ethics, beliefs, principles, and doctrines.

We need to ensure that the decisions we self-determine, we make them for the right reasons. At the best of times, human judgement is imperfect and it is deceived. Therefore, before we decide on the life-changing choices; choices that materially define our worldly existence, we must understand the rationale underlying our motives and intentions.

'*With dread of death, to flight or foul retreat? Nor wanting power to mitigate and swage. With solemn touches, troubled thoughts, and chase. Anguish and doubt and fear and sorrow and pain from mortal or immortal minds.*'[12]

The human condition consists of a diverse spectrum of emotions, inclinations, feelings, desires, passions, moods, instincts, sensations, attitudes, personalities, phenotypic variation, aptitudes, genetic variation, and regulated (or conditioned) behaviours. The advanced study of psychiatry and social psychology investigates the profundity of the human condition. This complexity and diversity of the human condition is only compounded, when we factor into our consideration the presence of environmental and social factors, such as culture, language, childhood experience, lived experience, sex, parentage, gender, religion, ethnicity, identity, education, race, social status, heritage, and national history.

This broad spectrum of the human condition ranges from chaotic and mad, all the way to bliss and joy. In the formation of our thoughts, this is where the embryonic development of our worldly reality begins. Within our thoughts, we have the remarkable opportunity to construct and define our life narrative. While we remain subject to the confinement of conventional

---

12 Milton, John. (Darbishire, Helen, Ed.) (1958). *The Poetical Works of John Milton*. London: Oxford University Press, p. 19.

reality and the human condition, we must exert personal agency and self-determination, to live the life that we truly desire. When we exercise mindfulness, we eradicate the negative emotions of doubt, fear, regret, hate, guilt, depression, frustration, envy, anguish, pity, shame, confusion, and sorrow. Practical wisdom is the enlightened realisation, that these inferior and negative emotions do not define our existence.

In all cases, the experience of an emotion does not define a person's identity. In accordance with the exercise of our sensibility, we ought to consciously identify and replace negative emotions with the presence of desirable and positive emotions, such as contentment, confidence, gratitude, faith, happiness, courage, joy, interest, love, belief, empathy, self-determination, hope, inspiration, serenity, authentic pride, and ambition.

It is the feelings, emotions, ideas, beliefs, principles, values, knowledge, and experiences that we consciously identify with, that define our state of being in the world. For example, consider whom we associate with. What we become acquainted with. Last but not least, if and when we accomplish the ideal endeavour of self-actualisation. All of these factors collectively construct our personal experience of being in the world.

Most importantly, each person is unique unto themselves. There are no two individuals that are alike in every respect. This conventional reality is affirmed in the Holy Bible, within the Parable of the Talents, 'For it will be like a man going on a journey, who called his servants and entrusted to them his property. To one he gave five talents, to another two, to another one. To each according to his ability. Then he went away. He who had received the five talents went at once and traded them, and he made five talents more. So also, he who had the two talents made two talents more. But he who had received the one talent went and dug in the ground and hid his master's money.'[13]

---

13   The Holy Bible (ESV). (2016). The Gospel of Matthew. Chapter 25, Verses 14–18.

This timeless parable affirms why the comparison of ourselves, our achievements, abilities, successes, and failures with a multitude of other individuals is harmful. Comparison is detrimental to our well-being and future development. Comparison is the incorrect method to ascertain our true progress along the remarkable journey of our life. Each person has an important race to run during their lifetime on Earth, and that is their individual race. We are not equipped with someone else's expertise, aptitude, traits, knowledge, talent, gifts, abilities, and skills. We ought to perform our very best, with the talents that we have been provisioned by God's Grace.

By the universal virtue of human dignity, we are all created equal, however, we are not all the same. God has distributed different gifts to different people. A material difference or significant distinction in individual talent does not render the universal principle of human dignity as void and inoperable. In the final analysis, we all have our unique talents, abilities, knowledge, expertise, and skill. It is incumbent upon us, to utilise our God-given gifts for the betterment of humanity. In the pursuit of this egalitarian ideal, we fulfil our inherent potential.

Often times, when we consciously compare our life to the significant people around us, we do not possess the complete and objective representation of all the facts. Even if we did possess all the relevant facts, the entire basis of our subjective comparison remains flawed and partial. This is due to fundamental and irreconcilable differences that are beyond our control. Despite this awareness, we yield to the irrational temptation to engage in surface-level comparisons with a plethora of people in the digital age. An age that is excessively defined by smartphones, smartwatches, and social media.

The indisputable reality is that cultural, lingual, racial, historical, biological, religious, psychological, economic, and political differences between individuals are responsible for our unique lived experience in the world. Therefore, this constant comparative approach to modern life positions us for inferior self-esteem, diminished self-confidence, and a reduced sense of self-worth. If we desire to improve our self-efficacy, then we must focus on ourselves. We must compare ourselves to ourselves. This is the true litmus test of self-improvement. We must ask ourselves: What have we accomplished or improved with the constant passage of time? Is our present self in a better place than our former self? What areas of our life are we prepared to change, so our next year self is better than our previous year self?

Due to the vast social, material, economic, genetic, and hereditary variations at birth, in addition to the distinctions and disparities along the continuum of life in modern society and the state, we cannot with any degree of equity and fairness, measure and compare progress on a linear scale against other people. But we can measure and compare progress against ourselves. Therefore, as stated above, the only valid comparison we ought to make is against ourselves. For example, consider the following questions: Where were we five years ago? Where are we today? How much progress have we achieved over the previous five years? What do we intend to accomplish in the next five years?

Ultimately, we are running our race, not the race of another person. Therefore, the authentic litmus test of progression and accomplishment is: Are we making real and substantial progress on ourselves with the constant passage of time? When we move the spotlight away from the significant and influential people in society, and onto ourselves, that is when we genuinely begin to concentrate on improving ourselves, on furthering our aims and objectives, to become the best version of ourselves. In all respects, passion drives purpose. If we figure out our passion, we have found our life purpose.

'In dim eclipse, disastrous twilight sheds on half the nations, and with fear of change perplexes monarchs. Darkened so. Yet shone above them all, the Archangel. But his face, deep scars of thunder had entrenched, and care sat on his faded cheek. But under brows of dauntless courage, and considerate pride waiting revenge. Cruel his eye, but cast signs of remorse and passion to behold.'[14]

While we remain subject to the human condition, the soul is tainted by light and darkness. While we remain subject to the confinement of the flesh, the soul is pushed and pulled into and out of metaphysical states of purity. In all that we do, we must be guided by the forces of faith, natural reason, rational deliberation, sensibility, and positive intentions. Over the finite tenure of our life, the cumulative merit and demerit of our actions determines our life trajectory. We must diminish the presence and function of evil in the world. We must strive to enhance the presence of love, charity, compassion, tolerance, community service, peace, mercy, benevolence, social justice, respect, harmony, dignity, and cooperation amongst humanity.

'O myriads of immortal spirits. O powers matchless. But with the Almighty, and that strife was not inglorious. Though the event was dire. As this place testifies, and this dire change hateful to utter. But what power of mind, foreseeing or presaging, from the depth of knowledge, past or present, could have feared.'[15]

Our capacity to fulfil our destiny resides within the power of our mind. We ought to concentrate and refine our ability to practice mindfulness in all our actions. Mindfulness makes us acutely

---

14 Milton, John. (Darbishire, Helen, Ed.) (1958). *The Poetical Works of John Milton*. London: Oxford University Press, pp. 20–21.

15 Milton, John. (Darbishire, Helen, Ed.) (1958). *The Poetical Works of John Milton*. London: Oxford University Press, p. 21.

conscious of the reality around us. Mindfulness enhances our accurate sensory perception and empirical observation of the natural world. Mindfulness brings the human experience ever closer to reality and nature. When we are mindful, not only are we observant of what is happening in our life, but we begin to examine the cognitive functions surrounding our psychological, emotional, spiritual, social, intellectual, and physical condition of being.

True wisdom is found in the proper understanding, that all material phenomena on Earth, including human life are finite, perishable, and exhaustible. Everything in and of this world is passing away. Only God is eternal and unchanging. Practical wisdom is living a good life. A life that is founded on moral principles and ethical values. Knowledge cannot secure us eternal peace. Knowledge cannot procure us with everlasting joy. Knowledge cannot satisfy the higher spiritual aspirations of the soul. Knowledge is only a means to an end in this world. Knowledge is not the end.

The American-English poet, playwright, and literary critic, T. S. Eliot (1888–1965) succinctly summarised our worldly knowledge and spiritual wisdom dilemma in his pageant play, *The Rock* (1934): 'Where is the wisdom we have lost in knowledge? Where is the knowledge we have lost in information? The cycles of Heaven in twenty centuries bring us farther from God and nearer to the dust.'

Indeed, much of transcendental reality is beyond our tangible experience of human life and empirical knowledge that is secured with the finite power of our intellect. Spiritual development is a lifelong endeavour, one that brings us ever closer to God. In the interim, to truly know oneself, to wholly master oneself, and to be completely at peace with oneself, these are the worthiest of all achievements.

The highest wisdom one can demonstrate is to position God at the core of one's life. God must be at the very centre of everything that a person does. This is an aspirational and lofty endeavour. When we come to trust in God, and place our faith in God, we secure greater confidence, clarity, and certainty in the significant decisions that we self-determine. With God's Counsel, we experience a greater satisfaction in our life. With God's Favour, we realise a greater purpose in the work that we do on Earth.

> *'Put forth at full, but still his strength concealed, which tempted our attempt, and wrought our fall. Henceforth, his might we know, and know our own. So as not either to provoke, or dread new war. Provoked. Our better part remains to work in close design, by fraud or guile, what force effected not. That he, no less at length from us may find, who overcomes by force, hath overcome but half his foe.'*[16]

Each person must select their battles carefully. The exercise of discretion, discernment, and prudence are important aspects of living a good life. Practical wisdom resides in the delicate process of selection and elimination. In all that we do, we must strive to live our life characterised by the higher principles of integrity, personal responsibility, confidentiality, trust, honesty, faith, generosity, gratitude, human dignity, forgiveness, mercy, forbearance, benevolence, community service, social justice, respect, and love.

The employment of force never overcomes an enemy. Force only serves to temporarily subdue an enemy. To truly win over the heart and mind of our opponents, we require the presence of unconditional love, mutual understanding, respect, sincere empathy, and tolerance for cultural, racial, sexual, ethnic, and

---

16 Milton, John. (Darbishire, Helen, Ed.) (1958). *The Poetical Works of John Milton*. London: Oxford University Press, pp. 21–22.

religious differences. The enduring presence of a pluralistic world cannot be denied. Having said that, the universal power of the oneness of humanity, far outweighs the many distinctions found within it.

CHAPTER 2

PARADISE LOST: BOOK TWO

'Great things resolved.
Which from the lowest deep.
Will once more lift us up.
In spite of fate.'

MILTON

BOOK TWO of *Paradise Lost* narrates the evil discourse between Satan and his legion of fallen Angels. The satanic spirits are vigorously debating whether or not to make a second attempt at securing the Kingdom of Heaven. In the end, Satan conscious of the real limitations on his angelic power, resolves to discover God's newest creation—humankind.

Satan determines to infiltrate the Garden of Eden with the presence of evil. Satan navigates his way through the Gates of Hell. Satan has embarked upon the ignoble journey for the search and destruction of Adam and Eve. The next battleground within the Devil's sight is the Garden of Eden. The ill-fated and forthcoming chain of events, involving Adam and Eve, conclude with the occurrence of Original Sin. The Fall of Man is now close at hand.

In the Kingdom of Heaven, God is conscious of the forthcoming events. God knows that the Devil shall produce his power against Adam and Eve. Yet, God does not interfere in the events that are about to unfold in the Garden of Eden. God has resolved not to interfere in Adam and Eve's ability to self-determine and seal their fate. In this respect, the duo's free will and moral conscience is wholly capable of affirming their righteousness in Paradise, or equally, promoting their fall from grace. Regardless of how Adam and Eve act, they only have themselves to hold accountable for their free willed actions.

'Satan exalted sat. By merit raised to that bad eminence; and from despair thus high. Uplifted beyond hope. Satan aspires beyond thus high. Insatiate to pursue vain war with Heaven, and by success untaught his proud imagination thus displayed.'[17]

The crestfallen story of Satan is one of terrible tragedy and dreadful disaster. Once a perfect Angel, Lucifer has fallen from God's Love, Favour, Blessing, and Presence. Vainglory was responsible for Lucifer's tragic fall from grace. Satan now employs his supernatural powers, remarkable abilities, and impressive capacities for the proliferation of evil and hate, as opposed to the universal promotion of community service, peace, and social justice. Satan is engrossed in destructive and violent thoughts. Satan serves to torment the human condition since the effectuation of Original Sin and the Fall of Man.

Unfortunately, the unsurpassable serenity that was once directly experienced by Adam and Eve in the Garden of Eden is now no more. Humanity must place its total trust and full faith in God's Goodness to overcome obstacles along our life journey. We must not become absorbed in self-conceit with our fleeting

---

17 Milton, John. (Darbishire, Helen, Ed.) (1958). *The Poetical Works of John Milton*. London: Oxford University Press, p. 26.

beauty, virtue, strength, courage, successes, accomplishments, honesty, knowledge, wisdom, intellect, integrity, endurance, or spirit. All of these favourable personal attributes constitute God's gift to humanity. As it pleases God, we are blessed to have God's Spirit dwell within us.

Lucifer made a terrible mistake. Lucifer forgot his Creator's sovereign place in the Universe. Regrettably, Lucifer became consumed with pride and arrogance. Lucifer ill-thought that it was his rightful and proper place to assume God's Throne in the Kingdom of Heaven. Lucifer became irrationally infatuated with the positive traits, power, beauty, wisdom, intelligence, and grace that God had bestowed upon him.

We too must learn the timeless lessons from the downfall of Lucifer. We are not immune from the dark desires of our ego, pride, envy, glory, fame, private wealth, beauty, wisdom, intelligence, and power. Even if we come close to the desired state of perfection, even if we live a good and decent life, we must remind ourselves that it is not by the sin living inside of us, that has made such a life possible. However, it is God's gift of grace, mercy, and blessing, which have allowed us to live our life defined by honour, integrity, and merit.

> *'Your bulwark, and condemns to greatest share of endless pain? Where there is then no good for which to strive. No strife can grow up there from faction. For none sure will claim in Hell precedence. None, whose portion is so small of present pain, that with ambitious mind will covet more!'*[18]

The Devil is constantly scheming novel and creative ways to corrupt humanity. Whilst we are in the flesh, temptation is ever present. After all, the path of righteousness is not a convenient

---

18 Milton, John. (Darbishire, Helen, Ed.) (1958). *The Poetical Works of John Milton*. London: Oxford University Press, p. 27.

endeavour. We are tested. We confront tribulations. We are subject to challenging times. However, the secret to our success in life includes conscientiousness, diligence, resilience, and perseverance. We must believe that all things are possible through God's Goodness, Mercy, Favour, and Grace.

To keep our life in perspective, an existence without travesty, privation, suffering, mistakes, injustice, grief, trauma, sorrow, heartache, guilt, and loss is not possible in this broken world. Nevertheless, a life of wholeness, goodness, love, productivity, belief, hope, community service, prayer, petition, intercession, mercy, faith, human dignity, and benevolence is always possible.

> *'To our destruction. If there be in Hell, fear to be worse destroyed. What can be worse, than to dwell here? Driven out from bliss. Condemned in this abhorred deep to utter woe. Where pain of unextinguishable fire must exercise us without hope of end.'*[19]

We must rationally discern the meaning of the narrative concerning Lucifer's disobedience and rebellion against God's Kingdom in Heaven, Sovereign Will, and Eternal Word. For our purposes herein, it is sufficient to infer that in the furtherance of evil thoughts and deeds, we experience considerable grief, pain, and suffering on Earth. Whereas in the furtherance of good thoughts and deeds, we experience considerable bliss, equanimity, and joy on Earth. This is not to infer the proposition, that those individuals who perform good actions, are not subject to suffering on Earth. God's Eternal Word reminds us that, 'it rains on the just and the unjust.'[20] There will be a mixed lot of blessings and burdens along every person's life journey.

---

19   Milton, John. (Darbishire, Helen, Ed.) (1958). *The Poetical Works of John Milton.* London: Oxford University Press, p. 28.
20   The Holy Bible (ESV). (2016). The Gospel of Matthew. Chapter 5, Verse 45.

There is injustice, poverty, discrimination, sexism, hatred, racism, inequality, and prejudice in this broken world. However, what is implied herein is that we are not free from the intended and unintended consequences that are attached to our free willed actions. Put another way, if we as moral agents perform evil, then we must consequentially harbour the expectation for evil to eventuate in our life. On the contrary, if we as moral agents perform good, then we must consequentially harbour the expectation for good to eventuate in our life. While God always has the infinite and unrestrained capacity to demonstrate undeserved mercy, humanity ought not to act in such an inconsiderate manner, that brings forth the condemnation and wrath of God. During our lifetime, we must not engage in actions that constrain God's Prerogative of Mercy towards us.

'Then miserable to have eternal being. Or if our substance be indeed divine, and cannot cease to be. We are at worst. On this side nothing; and by proof, we feel our power sufficient to disturb His Heaven, and with perpetual inroads to alarm. Though inaccessible, His Fatal Throne. Which if not victory, is yet revenge.'[21]

The vanity and irrationality of the Devil's flawed thinking is categorically self-evident. The Devil's power, before his tragic and troublesome fall from grace, was to preserve the peace, to uphold God's Eternal Word, and to bring glory and honour to the Living God. However, Lucifer freely and willingly determined rebellion against God. Satan shall never secure victory over God's Sovereign Kingdom in Heaven. Yet, this indisputable theological fact does not prevent the Devil from causing chaos and destruction during his reign on Earth.

---

21 Milton, John. (Darbishire, Helen, Ed.) (1958). *The Poetical Works of John Milton*. London: Oxford University Press, pp. 28–29.

The most convenient method for the Devil to seek revenge, is to disassociate humanity from God's Eternal Word. While we are in the flesh, we remain susceptible to the temptations and desires of the flesh. The Devil appeals to the demands of our flesh, so that the immense power of our spirit remains dormant. We must not fall into the trap of underestimating our true archenemy.

Satan deludes humanity through the sinful pleasures of the flesh, endless temptations, worldly desires, the pursuit of unbridled copulation, irrational impulses, extreme feelings, intrusive thoughts, powerful urges, self-sabotaging behaviours, destructive addictions, subconscious compulsions, psychological disorders, unsound beliefs of insanity, and finally, the act of suicide. A troubled soul is the Devil's prime target.

While we remain subject to the human condition, we ought to exercise greater inhibitory control, so that we are more conscious of our inherent weaknesses, limitations, and flaws. We must remain attentive to the fact that our understanding is imperfect. If we demonstrate not only an astute awareness, but also a keen appreciation of human fallibility, then we have the requisite opportunity to pause, think, and respond appropriately to our vulnerabilities and circumstances.

'A fairer person lost not Heaven. He seemed for dignity composed and high exploit. But all was false and hollow. Though his tongue dropped manna, and could make the worse appear the better reason. To perplex and dash maturest counsels. For his thoughts were low. To vice industrious, but to nobler deeds, timorous and slothful. Yet, he pleased the ear.'[22]

It is only by God's Grace that humanity is embodied with the especial gift of free will. It is our primary duty and personal

---

22   Milton, John. (Darbishire, Helen, Ed.) (1958). *The Poetical Works of John Milton*. London: Oxford University Press, p. 29.

responsibility to exercise self-restraint and discipline over our ideas, doctrines, thoughts, beliefs, speech, and conduct in the world. The Law of Manifestation is affirmed through our conscious ideas, doctrines, thoughts, beliefs, speech, and conduct. It is the case, that what we seek in our life, this is what defines our life. The majority of life is an experiential, edifying, educational, and experimental process. Our life will inevitability entail the unavoidability of mistakes and execution of errors in our imperfect judgement. This is the undeniable reality of human life. Peace be with you.

When we have the added benefit of hindsight, when we have the wisdom of a lifetime behind us, then we realise that human understanding incorporates much misunderstanding. The central issue under examination herein, is not the certainty with which our conduct gives rise to errors and mistakes throughout the course of our life. The fallacy of human judgement is all too self-evident. This is a valid and almost certain operating assumption. The crux of the issue here is, do we have the courage to confess our mistakes and assume responsibility for our errors? Put another way, will we assume personal responsibility for our failures and mistakes, by accepting them as our [unintentional] transgressions? Alternatively, shall we distance ourselves from our shortcomings and absolve ourselves from all fault?

The virtuous act of contrition facilitates the absolution of sin. Contrition develops our inherent sense of morality. Contrition enhances our conscience. Contrition improves our character. Most importantly, contrition ensures that we remain conscious of our inadequacies, limitations, weaknesses, and flaws. This pragmatic approach to life creates a firm awareness in our mind, that we are dependent upon God. In addition, contrition promotes our humility before God.

Contrition prevents us from constructing a [false] reality and [fictional] narrative of our life, upon the misguided directives of our ego. No person on Earth is perfect. Contrition helps us to recognise this reality, so that we live a genuine and authentic life. Now, it is by the actuality of human nature, that living a genuine and authentic life incorporates the acknowledgement of our [undeniable] weaknesses.

The art and science of sensibility takes a lifetime to master. Practical wisdom resides in the careful reflection and methodical introspection of our life's many experiences, both the good and the evil. In every case that we fall short, we ought to reflect, learn, and mature from what has transpired. The past is forever the past. We can never change what has transpired in our life. Having said that, we can change how we respond to what has transpired. That is to infer, we can change our perception of reality.

It is through mastering our reaction to what is outside of our control, that we exert control over our thought processes and life narrative. Thereby, we demonstrate greater awareness and appreciation of the flaws in our thinking and reasoning. In the future, when we are confronted with a very similar scenario, with comparable factual details, hopefully we are more likely than not to conduct ourselves in a manner that is fitting of a more mature response. Insight is relatively convenient to glean. The application of practical wisdom is the more challenging aspect of self-improvement. In the final analysis, there is no such thing as wasted years. Life is a lifelong learning process.

'Ages of hopeless end? This would be worse. War therefore, open or concealed. Alike, my voice dissuades. For what can force or guile with him, or who deceive his mind, whose eye views all things at one view? He from Heaven's height. All these, our motions vain, sees and derides. Not more almighty. To resist our might. Then wise to frustrate all our plots and wiles. Shall we then live thus vile? The race of Heaven thus trampled. Thus expelled. To suffer here chains and these torments? Better these. Than worse by my advice. Since fate inevitable subdues us, and omnipotent decree. The victor's will. To suffer, as to do. Our strength is equal; nor the law unjust.'[23]

We need to consciously observe our thoughts, motives, principles, doctrines, intentions, beliefs, and ideas. Unintentionally, our mind can construct a reality that is troubled with suffering and misery. Alternatively, our mind can construct a reality that is defined by the accomplishment of wholesome endeavours and the beneficial pursuit of positive ambitions. What we think, that is what we become in this world. The Law of Attraction is a simple, but deeply profound concept. In plain English, this universal law is enunciated as follows: Our conscious thoughts direct the outward expenditure of our energy, which creates the existential reality of our being. When we live our life absorbed in productive pursuits and constructive endeavours, then we sooner or later realise our inherent potential.

In life, the most important things are love, hope, expectancy, community service, positive mindset, respect, character, belief, confidence, human dignity, work, mercy, integrity, benevolence, social justice, peace, and faith. Our actions ought to contribute towards the furtherance of these things. When we consciously act and create our desired reality, is such a reality defined by

---

23   Milton, John. (Darbishire, Helen, Ed.) (1958). *The Poetical Works of John Milton*. London: Oxford University Press, p. 31.

these beneficial values and principles? Prior to the execution of our voluntary actions, our intentions define them. Subsequent to the execution of our voluntary actions, our consequences define them. Therefore, true wisdom entails factoring into our consideration, both the intentions and consequences of our free willed actions.

While we can be more conscious of our intentions, prior to the performance of our actions, we can never be certain of all the consequences of our free willed actions. For our free willed actions incorporate a degree of unintended consequences, of which we possessed no foreknowledge. That is why it is imperative and essential, that our voluntary actions are defined by love, hope, expectancy, community service, positive mindset, mercy, character, belief, confidence, human dignity, respect, work, integrity, benevolence, social justice, peace, and faith. For such actions will have unintended consequences, however, more likely positive than negative. In the instance our voluntary actions, defined by these beneficial values and principles have negative unintended consequences, we know that our intention was in the right place, when we performed them.

The brutality of war and conflict has been known to human civilisation since the advent of Adam and Eve. In war and conflict, the presence of the Devil is always a constant factor. Needless to say, the Truth is the first casualty of war. All too often, humanity repeats rather than learns from, the invaluable lessons of ancient and modern history. We must ensure that human nature is not consumed by desire, revenge, greed, corruption, vengeance, political power, authority, private wealth, private property, concupiscence, social status, influence, control, envy, and pride. But rather, we must focus on the elimination of these undesirable traits and destructive attributes found within the Self.

The aforementioned traits and attributes ought to be replaced with the noble attributes of wisdom, courage, love, compassion, mercy, moderation, justice, equality, generosity, benevolence, peace, and charity. At the end of our lifetime, we arrive at the undeniable realisation, that nothing in and of this world departs with us at the exact time of our death, but for our soul, and the permanent impression of our voluntary and conscious actions that have been tainted upon it. The vanity of this world, including unproductive human speech and frivolous conduct cannot be denied. Peace be with you.

'If we were wise, against so great a foe contending, and so doubtful what might fall. I laugh, when those, who at the spear are bold and venturous. If that fail them, shrink and fear what yet they know must follow. To endure exile, or ignominy, or bonds, or pain. The sentence of their conqueror. This is now our doom. Which if we can sustain and bear, our supreme foe in time may much remit his anger, and perhaps, thus far removed. Not mind us not offending. Satisfied with what is punished. Whence these raging fires will slacken, if his breath stir not their flames.'[24]

For all people on Earth, God's Righteous and Final Judgement is inevitable. The most precious commodity that we possess in this world is our finite time. Therefore, we ought to utilise our invaluable time to promote the common good and welfare of humanity. It is incumbent upon us to overcome the elusive presence of evil in the world. We have a non-delegable duty to reflect and effectuate into practice God's Eternal Word. The supreme responsibility is upon us, to be a morally righteous agent for positive change in the world. None of us are perfect, however, our work must earnestly strive to advance God's Sovereign Kingdom on Earth.

---

24 Milton, John. (Darbishire, Helen, Ed.) (1958). *The Poetical Works of John Milton*. London: Oxford University Press, p. 31.

The Devil is cunning and deceitful. To ensure that we remain entangled with life's inconsequential matters and to prevent us from the realisation of our God-given destiny, the Devil ensures that we remain preoccupied with trivial distractions, procrastination, apathy, indifference, addictions, indecisiveness, hesitation, confusion, envy, guilt, and uncertainty. In the final analysis, if the Devil fails to turn us towards a life of sin and evil, he can simply diminish our finite lifetime on Earth. In God's Eternal Word, we are foretold, 'if we had not delayed, we would now have returned twice.'[25] We must not reflect and reminisce on the past. We have a duty to direct our attention to the present moment, so that we attain our highest potential. Time lost is never regained.

A person's actions seal their fate, and so it was for the Angel, Lucifer. Let us not forget, that Lucifer had it all; beauty, intelligence, natural reason, wisdom, free will, divine power, God's Blessing, Favour, and Grace. Yet, Lucifer misappropriated God's unmatched gifts. Rather than serve, honour, and glorify God, Lucifer became obsessed with himself. In the vanity of Lucifer's self-perceived perfection, he rebelled against God and freely determined a state of being defined by sin. Lucifer was not free from the consequences of his immoral actions.

Ultimately, Lucifer was casted out of the Kingdom of Heaven. It was Lucifer's actions that transformed him into the Devil; a fallen angel suited to lead a miserable existence in the demonic depths of Hell. Now Satan directs his untiring efforts to cause conflict, destruction, confusion, envy, depression, suicide, and death on Earth. All the Devil has to do is fan the flames of our ego, pride, jealousy, insecurity, anger, or inflated sense of self-importance to wreak havoc in our life. Our downfall and ruin in society is considerably closer than we think.

---

25   The Holy Bible (ESV). (2016). The Book of Genesis. Chapter 43, Verse 10.

'We war, if war be best, or to regain our own right lost.
Him to unthrone. We then may hope. When everlasting
fate shall yield to fickle chance, and chaos judge the
strife. The former: vain to hope argues as vain. The latter:
for what place can be for us.'[26]

The Devil's depraved thinking exposes his logical fallacy. Acts of defiance, rebellion, and war cannot claim God's Sovereign Kingdom in Heaven. The human inclination for false hope in the irrational pursuit of unattainable ends is poisonous. No person can upend their destiny. Fate is the master of every person's destiny.

The Devil continues his ill-fated onslaught against God's Almighty Throne in the Kingdom of Heaven. In vain, the Devil continues to utilise his energy, talents, gifts, and power for destructive purposes. The Devil seeks to attain ends that are impermissible, namely the honour and glory that rightfully and exclusively belong to God. No matter the Devil's ill-intentioned plans, ideas, motivations, intentions, schemes, and thoughts for the proliferation of evil, the operation of God's Sovereign Will cannot be thwarted, transgressed, transcended, or trumped.

'Unacceptable. Though in Heaven, our state of splendid
vassalage. But rather seek our own good from ourselves,
and from our own. Live to ourselves. Though in this
vast recess, free, and to none accountable. Preferring
hard liberty, before the easy yoke of servile pomp.
Our greatness will appear.'[27]

Heaven is absolute perfection in every aspect and dimension. The fact that Lucifer found this most desirable state of being

---

26 Milton, John. (Darbishire, Helen, Ed.) (1958). *The Poetical Works of John Milton.* London: Oxford University Press, p. 32.

27 Milton, John. (Darbishire, Helen, Ed.) (1958). *The Poetical Works of John Milton.* London: Oxford University Press, p. 32.

unacceptable is a reflection of his haughty spirit. Despite Lucifer possessing everything a person could desire from God, including beauty, perfection, power, intelligence, love, wisdom, and grace; Lucifer lacked contentment, humility, and obedience.

We cannot seek our own good from ourselves, nor from our trivial works on Earth. Humanity is born through the act of sin, and therefore, humanity is plagued by sin. It is by the presence and function of God's Grace, that goodness dwells inside our spirit. God's Love perfects the human heart. All human actions are in vain to appease the body, mind, and spirit. In the end, the unfathomable height of the Peace of God, surpasses the finite depth of human understanding. To secure such a peace is the hallmark of a blessed life. If we live our life without ever losing our peace of mind, this a great blessing. After all, our sanity is our greatest treasure.

'O shame to men! Devil with Devil damned. Firm concord holds. Men only disagree of creatures rational. Though under hope of Heavenly grace. God proclaiming peace.'[28]

God has bestowed humanity with the especial gifts of personal agency, natural reason, moral conscience, wisdom, and free will. As moral agents, we possess the inherent capacity to reason, before we act. Therefore, we ought to methodically think through our actions, before we self-determine to act. We can reason, deliberate, and determine to live our life defined by the performance of good or evil actions. Men and women have the equal opportunity to define their life trajectory. We can live our life based on honourable deeds and productive endeavours. Alternatively, we can live our life based on evil deeds and destructive ambitions. Whichever path we consciously determine to traverse in our life, we are not absolved from its consequences.

---

28 Milton, John. (Darbishire, Helen, Ed.) (1958). *The Poetical Works of John Milton*. London: Oxford University Press, pp. 38–39.

While we are resident on Earth, we confront the endless struggle between the flesh and spirit. The flesh brings us down towards engrossment in worldly desires and temporal ambitions. On the contrary, the spirit brings us higher towards a life of tranquillity, happiness, gratitude, joy, faith, equanimity, compassion, love, benevolence, mercy, and hope. The spiritual battle between the flesh and spirit is a lifelong battle. We must not become so engrossed in our finite sense of being, that we no longer find our spiritual weakness imperceptible. From time to time, we ought to reflect upon our life, and ask ourselves the question: Are we provisioning greater attention to the flesh or the spirit?

> *'Thence more at ease. Their minds and somewhat raised by false presumptuous hope. The ranged powers disband, and wandering, each his several way pursues. As inclination, or sad choice leads him perplexed. Where he may likeliest find truce to his restless thoughts, and entertain the irksome hours. Till the great chief return.'*[29]

With an enduring consistency, if we possess an equipoise mind, embody a resilient spirit, and sustain equanimity within our heart, during both the highs and lows of our life, this is an invaluable positive attribute. Through the countless ebbs and flows of our life, we must keep our personal affairs in perspective. To varying degrees, our unique lived experience affirms that we inhabit a natural world that is often defined by grief, pain, suffering, privation, trouble, issues, loss, heartache, addictions, psychiatric disorders, non-communicable diseases, and social problems. In addition, we find our thoughts restless, however, our thoughts do not define our existence on Earth. Rather, we

---

29 Milton, John. (Darbishire, Helen, Ed.) (1958). *The Poetical Works of John Milton.* London: Oxford University Press, p. 39.

ought to self-determine which thoughts we associate with and permit influence upon our mind.

In the end, it is the ideas, concepts, principles, beliefs, subjects, theories, ideologies, and doctrines that we subscribe to, and thereby immerse our mind in, that impress upon and determine the very thoughts that shape our life trajectory. While we are subject to the human condition, we cannot circumvent, nor transcend the phenomenon of mortality. We are not on Earth for eternity. Successful people confront the inescapable facts of being. Successful people accept the cold hard truths of life. Successful people address their maladaptive behaviours. Successful people understand time is of the essence. Last but not least, successful people position their life into context.

'In thoughts, more elevate, and reasoned high of providence, foreknowledge, will, and fate, fixed fate, free will, foreknowledge absolute, and found no end. In wandering mazes lost. Of good and evil much they argued then. Of happiness and final misery. Passion and apathy. Glory and shame. Vain wisdom all. False philosophy.'[30]

The Holy Bible, in the Book of Isaiah, informs us that 'God's Ways are not our ways. God's Thoughts are not our thoughts.'[31] God's Divine Plans do not always resonate with our plans. This is where we have to affirm our faith in the Doctrine of God's Providence. In life, more often than not, we have to preserve our hope, trust, confidence, and belief that God has a superior plan for our life. We have to believe that God has a divine plan to prosper our endeavours. A divine plan to make us successful in our work. A divine plan to define and refine our character.

---

30 Milton, John. (Darbishire, Helen, Ed.) (1958). *The Poetical Works of John Milton.* London: Oxford University Press, p. 40.

31 The Holy Bible (ESV). (2016). The Book of Isaiah. Chapter 55, Verses 8–9.

A divine plan which ensures that we live a wholesome, rewarding, and fulfilling life.

The journey of our life does not always proceed as we had envisioned, however, at the end of our lifetime, what really matters is the final destination—God. In the interim, during our finite tenure on Earth, we ought to seek balance and harmony with the existential reality of our being.

To seek glory, private wealth, private property, social status, wisdom, honour, prestige, pleasure, knowledge, pecuniary gain, personal income, and political power, these are all fleeting and transitory pursuits. They are as temporary as the numbered days of our life. Even if we secured all these worldly ambitions, desires, aims, and objectives, we do so only for a short period of time, only to relinquish them all upon our death. Therefore, we ought to pursue what cannot be lost or diminished with the passage of time. We ought to pursue the eternal and everlasting Living God. The beauty of working towards the pursuit of God is that our progress in this endeavour brings us ever closer to our life purpose.

'In sweet forgetfulness and pain and woe. All in one moment, and so near the brink. But fate withstands, and to oppose the attempt.'[32]

The operation of fate in our life cannot be denied. High events have the ability to shape and define our life. Each and every person has a destiny, purpose, and mission to fulfil on Earth. Every day, we ought to utilise our talents, abilities, lived experience, wisdom, knowledge, learning, expertise, and endowments to pursue our productive and purposeful passion. We ought to make a positive impact in the world. The ability to achieve our highest potential is the intrinsic motivating force which propels our being into

---

32   Milton, John. (Darbishire, Helen, Ed.) (1958). *The Poetical Works of John Milton*. London: Oxford University Press, p. 41.

motion. The execution of constructive action is what defines an ambitious and productive life.

In all that we do, we do not start from the illogical premise, that we are certain of the outcome of our endeavours. It is by the undeserved Grace of God, that if and when we do succeed in our most noble endeavours, then we are assured that our pain, suffering, grief, heartache, trauma, and loss have not been in vain. In that pivotal moment of success, the endurance of our many privations and sacrifices become worthwhile.

Whatever be our fate, it is the real possibility that we can become, that we can achieve, and that we can attain, which makes the bold attempt at our lofty endeavours all the more worthwhile. In the end, it is better to have braved the attempt and lost, rather than not to have attempted at all. Life is short. Life is bittersweet. The wise person takes hold of every opportunity they receive to accomplish their dreams.

> *'Art thou that traitor Angel? Art thou he, who first broke peace in Heaven and faith? Till then unbroken, and in proud rebellious arms. Drew after him. The third part of Heaven's Sons conjured against the Highest. For which both thou and they, outcast from God, are here condemned to waste eternal days in woe and pain?'*[33]

The Devil made a conscious and deliberate determination to pursue evil over good. Therefore, the Devil must personally reap the consequences of such a free willed determination. It is true, troubles, temptations, tests, tragedies, tribulations, and trials also come our way. Humanity is not immune from the pervasive presence of evil.

Nonetheless, we must realise the vanity of all that the Devil tempts us with. The Devil employs the pleasures of the flesh,

---

33 Milton, John. (Darbishire, Helen, Ed.) (1958). *The Poetical Works of John Milton*. London: Oxford University Press, p. 43.

private wealth, the fame, riches, and glory of the world, prestige, political power, private property, the immense potential for pecuniary gain, and the endless desire for knowledge, all in the attempt to divert us from God's Eternal Word and Sovereign Kingdom in Heaven. Yet, we must take upon ourselves the Spiritual Armour of God, so that we withstand the falsehood of the Devil.

In the final analysis, to entertain evil only leads humanity further down the ill-fated path defined by pain, suffering, grief, guilt, sin, confusion, envy, condemnation, conflict, war, suicide, damnation, depression, and death. As moral agents, we must make our own informed choices, aided with the power of natural reason and deliberation. We must remember, that we are not free from the externalities, both the positive and negative, of our voluntary actions. With the power of personal agency, there comes the undeniable burden of personal responsibility.

In all his angelic greatness, power, wisdom, intelligence, and beauty, Lucifer was unable to escape the consequences of his transgression against God. We must not remain ill-informed that we can escape the universal law of 'what we sow is what we reap'. The formal application of logic in our thinking is a precondition, to effectuate sensible decisions and live the good life.

'Levied to side with warring winds, and poise their lighter wings. To whom these most adhere. He rules a moment. Chaos umpire sits, and by decision, more embroils the fray by which he reigns. Next him, high arbiter chance governs all. Into this wild abyss. The womb of nature and perhaps her grave, of neither sea, nor shore, nor air, nor fire, but all these in their pregnant causes mixed.'[34]

All of human life is marked and governed by the irresistible forces of nature. In our moment of victory, in the midst of us being at the highest accolade of our achievements, we feel invincible and immortal. Having said that, everything in and of this world withers and passes away. In all worldly things, the very existence of our life is uncertain. At best, our life is temporary and conditional. Therefore, we have an obligation to utilise our life to its fullest possible physical, spiritual, emotional, psychological, sporting, and intellectual capacities.

We must make the most of our temporal existence on Earth. For one day, our immediate existence, our present state of being, will be no more. The living of a full life is not concerned with supplanting the grim reaper. For this is an ideal that cannot be accomplished. Transcending the grim reaper is not a feasible human endeavour. Rather, a wholesome and productive life is tasked with accomplishing everything that we set our heart and mind to, within the limited and uncertain life span that we have on Earth.

---

34 Milton, John. (Darbishire, Helen, Ed.) (1958). *The Poetical Works of John Milton*. London: Oxford University Press, p. 49.

'So, he with difficulty and labour hard, moved on. With difficulty and labour, he; but he once passed. Soon after, when man fell. Strange alteration! Sin and death amain following his track. Such was the Will of Heaven. Paved after him a broad and beaten way over the dark abyss, whose boiling gulf tamely endured a bridge of wondrous length from Hell continued reaching the utmost orb of this frail world; by which the spirits perverse with easy intercourse pass to and from, to tempt or punish mortals. Except whom God and good Angels guard by special grace.'[35]

Since the advent of Creation, since the beginning of human civilisation, the unchanging reality is that man and woman are lost without God's Love, Spirit, Grace, Blessing, and Presence. We must self-determine to live our life in harmony with God's Divine Decree and Eternal Word. Too often, temptation, jealousy, envy, greed, and desire lead us down a delusional, dark, and destructive path. An immoral path defined by the definitive dead end of sin and death. We can self-determine to change the trajectory of our life, to follow God's Righteous Path, in the earnest hope that our spirit reaches the Kingdom of Heaven.

In the grand scheme of Creation, our lifetime on Earth is momentary. In the Holy Bible, within the Book of James, we are counselled of the unchanging and everlasting Truth, 'What is your life? For you are a mist that appears for a little time and then vanishes.'[36] Yet, the eternity that awaits us beyond this brief human life span, this is truly of indescribable consequence. Therefore, let us utilise this momentary lifetime as an unprecedented opportunity to define and refine our character, to strengthen our virtues, and to enhance our conscience.

---

35 Milton, John. (Darbishire, Helen, Ed.) (1958). *The Poetical Works of John Milton*. London: Oxford University Press, p. 52.

36 The Holy Bible (ESV). (2016). The Book of James. Chapter 4, Verse 14.

The divine presence and power of Angels as ministering spirits, function in our lives in mysterious and profound ways. Throughout the Holy Bible, we are constantly reminded of how Angels perfectly perform God's Sovereign Command in the Kingdom of Heaven and on Earth. God utilises Angels to provide divine messages of comfort and hope to all people. For example, consider when Paul the Apostle was experiencing distress during a violent storm while he was onboard a ship that was en route to Rome. During this challenging time, an Angel appeared to Paul and delivered the following message, 'Do not be afraid, Paul; you must stand before Caesar. And behold, God has granted you all those who sail with you.'[37] When Paul's life was in immediate danger, he placed his complete trust and confidence in God, to not only ensure his safety and survival, but also that his God-given destiny on Earth was accomplished.

Albeit in distinct personal circumstances to Saint Paul the Apostle, we too must confront our fair share of pain, suffering, heartache, loss, grief, trauma, and privation during our lifetime on Earth. During our make-or-break moments of tragedy, trouble, tribulation, and trial, we ought to not only persevere, but also strengthen our faith in God. It is within the Sovereign Power of God to ensure that we transcend any and all difficulties during our time on Earth. We must always remember, no matter the particular circumstances or the situation that we confront, when we earnestly believe, preserve our faith, and obey God's Sovereign Command, then a turnaround is possible.

God utilises Angels to relieve humanity of its suffering and provide for our many needs. For example, consider an Angel provisioned food for the journey of Prophet Elijah, 'But he himself went a day's journey into the wilderness and came and sat down under a broom tree. And he asked that he might die, saying, "It is enough; now, O LORD, take away my life, for I am

---

37   The Holy Bible (ESV). (2016). The Book of Acts. Chapter 27, Verse 24.

no better than my fathers." And he lay down and slept under a broom tree. And behold, an Angel touched him and said to him, "Arise and eat." And he looked, and behold, there was at his head a cake baked on hot stones and a jar of water. And he ate and drank and lay down again. And the Angel of the LORD came again a second time and touched him and said, "Arise and eat, for the journey is too great for you." And he arose and ate and drank, and went in the strength of that food forty days and forty nights to Horeb, the Mount of God.'[38]

In the final analysis, God's Grace cannot be explained, but its positive effects are experienced in our life. One of the many ways in which God's Blessings are delivered to humanity is through the presence and functon of Angels. In order for God's Grace to work in our life, we must have faith over mistrust. Trust over doubt. Belief over disbelief. Confidence over uncertainty. Last but not least, hope over despair. Through the presence and function of God's Grace, a turnaround in our personal affairs is always possible. Peace be with you.

---

38   The Holy Bible (ESV). (2016). The First Book of Kings. Chapter 19, Verses 4–8.

PARADISE LOST: BOOK THREE

'For should man finally be lost?
Should man thy creature late so loved,
thy youngest Son fall circumvented thus by fraud,
though joined with his own folly?
That be from thee far. That far be from thee.
Father, who art Judge of all things made.
Judgest only right.'

MILTON

BOOK THREE of *Paradise Lost* describes Satan's disturbing and evil scheme to tempt God's newest Creation—humankind. God has complete foreknowledge of Satan's evil plan. To begin with, the Devil intends to create chaos and disaster in the Garden of Eden. However, God has granted Adam and Eve the requisite free will and moral agency, to make their own decisions.

God has also proclaimed the Divine Commandment to Adam and Eve. That is, the duo is not to consume the Forbidden Fruit from the Tree of Knowledge of Good and Evil. This commandment has been categorically and explicitly made known to Adam and Eve. Therefore, neither of them can claim ignorance as a plausible defence to any transgression.

From a theological perspective, God's Grace is wholly sufficient for Adam and Eve to withstand the temptation of sin. Furthermore, God does not interfere with Adam and Eve's exercise of free will during their tenure in the Garden of Eden. As the unprecedented events unfold in the Garden of Eden, Adam and Eve eventually yield to the seductive temptation of sin. This is not of their own accord; however, they are masterfully deceived by the Devil, in the form of a serpent.

In this book, we directly witness the weakness and fallibility of the human condition. Indeed, despite humanity's earnest endeavours, human civilisation remains dependent upon God's Favour, Grace, Goodness, Blessing, and Mercy, to overcome the false temptation, fabricated allure, and empty promise of evil.

Interestingly, the Guardian Angels are not in a position to prevent the Devil's treachery and ill-fated scheme against Adam and Eve in the Garden of Eden. Nonetheless, God is in complete control of the narrative. God permits the Devil to put Adam and Eve's free will to the ultimate test. Unfortunately, Adam and Eve fall short in observing God's Sacred Commands. They both venture into the death-defying depths of sin. As a result, we witness the inevitable, the occurrence of Original Sin and the Fall of Man.

Adam and Eve's unreasoned actions have violated God's Divine Command. As a consequence, God's Justice must be served, where it is rightfully due. In spite of sin and evil, all hope is not lost. The Son of God intercedes, to save humankind from the devastating and everlasting consequences of sin. God accepts the Son's honourable sacrifice and deems it sufficient to restore humankind. The Son of God has demonstrated undeserved mercy to redeem humanity of its sinful conduct. The Son of God has paid the ultimate penalty for humankind's transgression against God's Eternal Word.

'May I express thee unblamed? Since God is light, and never but in unapproached light dwelt from eternity, dwelt then in thee.'[39]

God's Presence is always accessible to every person in the form of the spirit. In this context, the spirit and the light are synonymous concepts. Whilst we are in the flesh, through the spirit we seek communion and connection with God. It is not the case, that God is some distant, complex, incommunicable, and abstract theological phenomenon discovered through our clarification of obfuscated religious doctrines. Rather, the opposite is true. God's Love and Mercy are always close at hand. God's Love and Mercy are available to every person, by the sole virtue of human dignity. God's Love and Mercy are boundless.

For our part, we must perform conscious and reasoned actions to bring our spirit in union with God's Spirit. For example, consider actions of compassion towards other people. Forgiveness for transgression. Acts of charity. The noble act of prayer. Participating in community service. The performance of penance. Demonstrating the admirable quality of benevolence. Last but not least, sincere acts of confession, petition, intercession, and worship. In our finite lifetime, we must not ponder upon the illegitimate question: Is God waiting upon us, or are we waiting on God? The more pertinent question is: What actions are we performing to accommodate God in our life?

---

39   Milton, John. (Darbishire, Helen, Ed.) (1958). *The Poetical Works of John Milton*. London: Oxford University Press, p. 53.

'And man, there placed. With purpose to assay if him by force he can destroy, or worse, by some false guile pervert; and shall pervert. For man will hearken to his glozing eyes, and easily transgress the sole command. Sole pledge of his obedience. So will fall he and his faithless progeny. Whose fault? Whose, but his own? Ingrate, he had of me, all he could have. I made him, just and right. Sufficient to have stood, though free to fall.'[40]

The creation of humanity, including both man and woman, were made in God's Divine Image. Humanity, in God's Perfect Image, is graced with the unique gift of free will. God did not intend, and never has intended, to renege His Eternal Promise by interfering in the conscious choices and self-determined actions of man and woman. From the beginning, God's Sovereign Commands were categorically made known to Adam and Eve during their time in the Garden of Eden. Therefore, neither party can claim ignorance as a plausible defence for their conscious and voluntary actions.

However, in the Holy Bible, we witness the sheer arrogance of Adam, when he responds to God's question concerning his tragic fall from grace. For Adam responds, 'The woman whom you gave to be with me, she gave me fruit of the tree, and I ate.'[41] Herein we witness Adam transfer personal responsibility for his immoral actions to God and Eve. Unfortunately, Eve does no better. Eve also does not respond in a righteous manner when questioned by God. For Eve replies, 'The Serpent deceived me, and I ate.'[42] Eve assigns personal responsibility for her immoral actions onto the Serpent.

The aforementioned theological dialogue demonstrates our shortcoming. The crux of the matter is that we are reluctant

---

40 Milton, John. (Darbishire, Helen, Ed.) (1958). *The Poetical Works of John Milton*. London: Oxford University Press, pp. 55–56.
41 The Holy Bible (ESV). (2016). The Book of Genesis. Chapter 3, Verse 12.
42 The Holy Bible (ESV). (2016). The Book of Genesis. Chapter 3, Verse 13.

to assume personal responsibility. When it comes to humanity assuming personal responsibility for its sinful conduct, we are always eager to abrogate and absolve ourselves of all culpability. It is always more convenient for us to distance ourselves from the sense of personal responsibility for our immoral actions. This course of action is particularly tempting, when the consequences of our free willed actions are patently unfavourable. One [immoral] method for humanity to deal with [the guilt of] sin is denial.

The unchanging reality is that we must assume personal accountability for our conduct, including when the repercussions are negative. In summary, the practical resolution to the quandary of free will resides in assuming complete personal responsibility for our voluntary and conscious actions in the world. Our character, conscience, and credibility only matures, if and when we are prepared to assume personal responsibility for our conduct.

It is essential to acknowledge that the intentions, motivations, values, doctrines, principles, and rationale underlying our actions are not determined in confined parameters, nor according to the precise mathematical conventions of algebra. To varying degrees, we are all subject to the imposed and real limitations of unfavourable circumstances. Lack of personal experience. The presence of time and resource constraints. The inordinate influence of family, friends, and work colleagues. Limitations in human knowledge. Incomplete information. Errors in the exercise of our judgement. Last but not least, imperfect conditions that we confront in the employment of our personal agency.

In the final analysis, we are free to act. Having said that, the very parameters of our free actions are influenced by the aforementioned factors. In spite of such limitations upon our freely determined actions, we cannot absolve ourselves from personal responsibility for the consequences that arise from our voluntary and conscious actions. Personal responsibility is the foundation stone to living a good life.

> *'When will and reason (reason also is choice) useless and vain, of freedom both despoiled, made passive both, had served necessity, not me. They therefore as to right belonged, so were created, nor can justly accuse their Maker, or their making, or their fate. As if predestination overruled their will. Disposed by absolute decree or high foreknowledge. They themselves decreed, their own revolt, not I. If I foreknew, foreknowledge had no influence on their fault, which had no less proved certain unforeknown.'*[43]

It is true that God possesses complete foreknowledge of all events within Creation. God has predestined the trajectory of Creation, and this trajectory is only foreknown to God. However, God's foreknowledge does not function to render humanity's exercise of free will as inoperable. Humanity possesses the inherent capacity to act in accordance with its thoughts, ideas, assumptions, morals, doctrines, principles, and beliefs. The worldly reality of our conventional existence remains unimpeded. That is to infer, both free will and predestination co-exist within God's Creation. As the Creator, God has absolute foreknowledge of Creation. Yet, man and woman, through the conscious process of self-determination, make their own choices and decisions in life.

Thus, in all sensibility, humanity cannot blame God for its inadequacies, failures, compulsions, inclinations, errors, thoughts, instincts, passions, biases, prejudices, and desires. Instead, humanity needs to refine its virtues, such as courage, fairness, truthfulness, integrity, temperance, compassion, kindness, justice, forgiveness, gratitude, charity, patience,

---

43 Milton, John. (Darbishire, Helen, Ed.) (1958). *The Poetical Works of John Milton.* London: Oxford University Press, p. 56.

community service, and benevolence. In order to live a virtuous life, we ought to diminish the subjective value of the pleasures, aspirations, and satisfactions of the flesh. Rather, we must seek to associate and integrate with the indestructible spirit.

We must direct our thoughts away from the material desires of the world. Thereafter, we must concentrate our mind on God's Eternal Word. If we categorically transcend the trivialities of this temporal world, then we can concentrate our attention on the transcendental reality of God. This monumental endeavour is easier spoken than performed. For in part, this superior reality of our being revolves around God's Spirit. The construction and experience of this superior reality [of our being] requires us to overcome the instinctive, addictive, and compulsive behaviours of the flesh. In effect, we are confronted with transcending the ego of our being. In fact, the construction of such a superior reality requires the overcoming of our human nature. That is, to transcend the very core of our being in the flesh.

When we carefully reflect upon God's Eternal Word, we are reminded that the challenges of the flesh are not easily transcended. To seek harmony with the spirit and transcend the flesh is an onerous endeavour. A lofty endeavour that requires mindfulness, resilience, patience, and perseverance along our life journey. Indeed, the flesh presents us with a multitude of challenges, temptations, and distractions during our lifetime on Earth. Therefore, within the Holy Bible we are reminded, to 'watch and pray that you may not enter into temptation. The spirit indeed is willing, but the flesh is weak.'[44]

The collection of thoughts, ideas, doctrines, principles, and beliefs that we nourish and give attention to, these are the phenomena that transform and define the experiential reality of our being. If we devote our time, resources, and attention to the flesh, we live our life enraptured in the many pleasures of

---

44   The Holy Bible (ESV). (2016). The Gospel of Matthew. Chapter 26, Verse 41.

the flesh. On the contrary, if we devote our time, resources, and attention to the spirit, then it is the spirit which flourishes and prospers in our life. Peace be with you.

'They trespass. Authors to themselves in all. Both what they judge and what they choose. For so I formed them free, and free they must remain. Till they enthral themselves. I else must change their nature, and revoke the high decree. Unchangeable, eternal, which ordained their freedom. They themselves ordained their fall.'[45]

When God created Adam and Eve, God made them free to choose their path. God cannot refute a royal decree. For such an action amounts to God's transgression against God's Eternal Word. Thus, Adam and Eve self-determined with the exercise of their free will, to consciously disobey God's Sovereign Command. For this immoral action, they stand condemned in God's Presence and Righteous Judgement.

Concurrently, it is by God's Grace, Peace, Compassion, Love, and Mercy, that humanity genuinely redeems itself from the immeasurably deep chasm of sin, guilt, punishment, perdition, damnation, and death. God's Grace, Peace, Compassion, Love, and Mercy provisioned the unmerited opportunity for humanity's redemption and salvation. Despite our many inadequacies, mistakes, flaws, failures, weaknesses, and errors, God provisioned humanity with a perfect saviour.

We are the authors of our actions. Thereby, we come to live the life that we desire. Therefore, the practical imperative is upon us, not to act out of haste, fear, prejudice, emotion, feeling, insensibility, passion, bias, indignation, or irrationality. But rather, we must make our informed decisions with good judgement and adequate forethought for the known consequences

---

45   Milton, John. (Darbishire, Helen, Ed.) (1958). *The Poetical Works of John Milton.* London: Oxford University Press, p. 56.

of our personal conduct. Alongside our inherent capacity for free will, we have been gifted with the powers of discernment, intuition, intellect, reason, imagination, discretion, memory, understanding, and wisdom. Rather than rationalise our less than satisfactory conduct, we ought to realise our inherent ability to live our life to harness the fullness of our spirit and maximise human civilisation's potential.

In the final analysis, our freedom is a priceless gift from God. We ought not to misappropriate our freedom, but rather we must put it to productive and constructive endeavours. Endeavours that affirm human dignity, compassion, tolerance, love, forgiveness, respect, equality, security, peace, prosperity, mercy, benevolence, social justice, and progress for all people on Earth. The world is a reflection of our collective will in action. Therefore, human civilisation is collectively responsible for the present and immediate condition of the world.

The human-made presence of poverty, food insecurity, malnutrition, the incidence of curable diseases, the rapid rise of non-communicable diseases, water scarcity, forced migration, the proliferation of nuclear weapons, unemployment, public health inequities, deforestation, overpopulation, and illiteracy, all represent pressing twenty-first century global challenges that must be resolved. The challenge is now upon us, to create a more equitable and sustainable world for the succeeding generations to inhabit.

'As my eternal purpose hath decreed. Man shall not quite be lost, but saved who will. Yet not of will in him, but grace in me.'[46]

God concedes that man and woman have fallen short in this world. Even though God ordained Creation, and everything

---

46 Milton, John. (Darbishire, Helen, Ed.) (1958). *The Poetical Works of John Milton*. London: Oxford University Press, p. 57.

within it to absolute perfection, Adam and Eve misappropriated their free will in blatant contravention of God's Divine Commands. Following Adam and Eve's egregious conduct, humanity continues to indulge in sinful conduct. Humanity continues to act against God's Wishes. Humanity does not keep God's Eternal Word close to its heart. As a consequence, man and woman have lost their rightful way and ventured away from God's Eternal Presence.

However, in God's Greatness, Goodness, Love, Compassion, Benevolence, Grace, and Mercy, God has not withheld divine blessings from humanity. Through the undeserved gift of grace, God has saved humanity from the consequences of sinful conduct and the elusive power of evil. This especial and unmerited gift of salvation has not been earnt by humanity, but rather God has freely given this gift to us.

> *'I will place within them as a guide. My umpire conscience, whom if they will hear, light after light, well used they shall attain, and to the end persisting, safe arrive. This my long sufferance and my day of grace. They who neglect and scorn, shall never taste; but hard be hardened. Blind be blinded more. That they may stumble on, and deeper fall; and none but such from mercy I exclude.'*[47]

Humanity ought to utilise its natural reason in connection with its moral conscience. Our free willed actions ought to be righteous in both their outward form and internal substance. As opposed to the exclusive employment of our natural reason (or intellect), the instrument of moral conscience involves the exercise of our moral judgement.

For example, consider the following proposition: All human life is sacred. Now this assertion, by definition, necessarily

---

47   Milton, John. (Darbishire, Helen, Ed.) (1958). *The Poetical Works of John Milton*. London: Oxford University Press, p. 58.

involves an inherent value judgement concerning human life. Therefore, normative propositions are appropriately deliberated using both our natural reason and moral conscience. When we form a sound conclusion on how to resolve an ethical dilemma, therein the two dimensions of morality and rationality, cannot be separated and compartmentalised in our decision-making.

'The deadly forfeiture, and ransom set. And now without redemption, all humankind must have been lost. Adjudged to death and hell. By doom severe. Had not the Son of God, in whom the fullness dwells of love divine, his dearest mediation thus renewed.'[48]

If it was not for the Son of God, humanity would never have secured its undeserved salvation. The Son of God is the only intermediary that was in the righteous position to reconcile Creator and humanity. The Son of God, who sacrificed himself on the Cross, performed an act of unconditional love. This preordained act bridged the immense distance, the otherwise irreconcilable gulf between God and humanity. A gulf that was created by the presence of Original Sin and the Fall of Man. The *Messiah's* sacrifice was the ultimate, permanent, and complete sacrifice that forever constituted sufficient recompense for humanity's sinful conduct and fall from grace.

---

48   Milton, John. (Darbishire, Helen, Ed.) (1958). *The Poetical Works of John Milton.* London: Oxford University Press, p. 59.

'Because thou hast, though throned in highest bliss equal to God, and equally enjoying God-like fruition, quitted all to save. A world from utter loss, and hast been found by merit more than birth right, Son of God. Found worthiest to be so, by being good. Far more than great or high; because in thee love hath abounded more than glory abounds.'[49]

Even though the Son of God holds his esteemed place and eminent position of righteousness, it is not by the privilege of birth right that the Son of God is virtuous, but rather by the priceless value of merit. This distinction is important to acknowledge for every person on Earth. Milton's above-mentioned passage correctly informs us, that regardless of our race, ethnicity, gender, colour, private wealth, personal income, private property, vocation, age, sex, social status, or profession, we can perform positive actions to accrue merit and refine our character on Earth.

No person is excluded, or drawn closer or further from God's Presence, by the distinguishing attribute of birth right. Each person has God-given human dignity, which is the only prerequisite for union with God. The universality of human dignity cannot be denied, diluted, divested, or diminished. In the final analysis, love conquers all differences and distinctions across human civilisation.

---

49   Milton, John. (Darbishire, Helen, Ed.) (1958). *The Poetical Works of John Milton*. London: Oxford University Press, p. 61.

'Of all things, transitory and vain. When sin, with vanity had filled the works of men. Both all things vain, and all who in vain things built their fond hopes of glory or lasting fame, or happiness in this or the other life. All who have their reward on Earth. The fruits of painful superstition and blind zeal. Naught seeking, but the praise of men. Here find fit retribution. Empty as their deeds.'[50]

In a sombre manner, Milton reflects on the underlying universal reality of human life. Everything within our life is constantly passing us by, this includes our experiences, possessions, time, relationships, private wealth, assets, personal income, family, and private property. Whatever we earn, accumulate, possess, secure, and store within this world, all of this will surely diminish one day. In vain, individuals strive to secure the worthless praise and approval of distinguished, learned, and influential people. The most important aspect of living is the principles that we adhere to, the ideologies that we subscribe to, the doctrines that we put into practice, and the values that we demonstrate during our lifetime on Earth.

The inherent vanity of all human conquests, accomplishments, victories, and gains cannot be denied. In the end, even if we achieved all that we had desired in our lifetime, the heart cannot be replete with a permanent sense of satisfaction in this world. The uncontrolled will to live found within ourselves, combined with our unchecked ego, demonstrates a constant desire to secure ever-greater sensual pleasure, private wealth, personal income, glory, honour, empirical knowledge, and worldly fame. All things considered, it is our insatiable desires that obstruct our true happiness, joy, and contentment with our lot in life.

Practical wisdom resides in ceasing with the endless and irrational striving for ever-greater success, private property,

---

50   Milton, John. (Darbishire, Helen, Ed.) (1958). *The Poetical Works of John Milton*. London: Oxford University Press, p. 64.

pleasure, private wealth, empirical knowledge, pecuniary gain, personal income, prestige, and fame, but being content with what one has accomplished. Being content with who one is. Being content with our substance of being. Being at peace with ourselves. After all, contentment and peace are our most valuable possessions.

The unenlightened will in conjunction with the nescient ego, diminishes the happiness of man and woman. The will and the ego always position our attention squarely on what is missing from our life. What is absent. What is incomplete. In effect, what we do not have. Sensibility is found in being content with what one has attained, accomplished, and accumulated. Regardless of the exigent circumstances, or the sharp stroke of fate, contentment accommodates acceptance of what is in our possession and what is in our control. Contentment allows a person to live a blessed life of happiness within their means.

'Imagined, rather oft than elsewhere seen. That stone, or like to that which here below philosophers in vain so long have sought. In vain, though by their powerful art they bind.'[51]

All philosophy is human-made. Secular philosophy is subjective in its purpose, content, and context. Underlying every school of philosophy are theories, ideas, concepts, representations, principles, abstractions, paradigms, models, doctrines, and narratives. No philosophy is absolute. Rather, each person's philosophy is an expression of their unique perception of conventional reality. Philosophy represents only one incomplete and uncertain method, by which to express our finite human understanding of the natural world around us. Philosophy does

---

51 Milton, John. (Darbishire, Helen, Ed.) (1958). *The Poetical Works of John Milton*. London: Oxford University Press, p. 68.

enrich human understanding; however, philosophy will never resolve the long-standing mysteries of Creation and the Universe.

What is beyond the parameters of natural science, is a matter of faith. In saying this, one should not blindly adhere to any religious denomination, but seek to understand it. Religious dogma, or any secular dogma for that matter, is disadvantageous to the future progress of humankind. With any faith, one ought to learn and reflect upon its teachings, sacred scripture, profound doctrines, core ideas, significant parables, and major religious principles. After all, our engagement in critical thought is necessary for our intellectual development.

Now human learning and understanding naturally involves considerable questioning, analysis, debate, reflection, and even disagreement. Sometimes, our disagreements in matters of faith and scripture arise due to our limitations in human reasoning, lived experience, possession of knowledge, and inherent capacity for original thought. Not all matters of faith are explained empirically. Select matters of faith are for the spirit and not for the intellect. These matters require belief, where critical and reasoned explanation is inadequate. Most importantly, when our faith is tested, we need to know why we believe what we believe in. Why do we follow what we follow. Why do we subscribe to what we subscribe to. Blind faith always makes for weak faith.

'The Universal Maker, we may praise. Who justly hath driven out His rebel foes. To deepest Hell, and to repair that loss created this new happy race of humans. To serve God better. Wise are all of God's Ways.'[52]

Concerning all things within the realm of Creation, God has the Definitive and Final Judgement. The Eternal Kingdom of God is guarded by Angels who glorify and honour God's Presence. God's

---

52 Milton, John. (Darbishire, Helen, Ed.) (1958). *The Poetical Works of John Milton.* London: Oxford University Press, p. 70.

Angels ensure the immediate and unconditional performance of God's Sovereign Command in every respect. In the Kingdom of Heaven, God's Sovereign Will is always performed without qualification, exception, condition, or modification.[53] That is why there is no sin in the Kingdom of Heaven. The Kingdom of Heaven is perfect in every respect.

On Earth, each and every person has the unprecedented opportunity to work towards the improvement of their virtues, the proper application of their moral conscience, and the lifelong development of their character. Our limited and uncertain lifetime on Earth is the ultimate litmus test for our preparedness to enter the Kingdom of Heaven.

> *'For neither human, nor Angel can discern hypocrisy.*
> *The only evil that walks invisible, except to God alone.*
> *By God's Permissive Will, through Heaven and Earth:*
> *and oft though wisdom wake, suspicion sleeps.'*[54]

As the well-known saying goes, 'The Devil can quote scripture for his purpose.'[55] It is beyond the finite capacity of the human senses, which are limited to obtaining empirical evidence of the natural world, and also beyond the higher powers of the Angels, to accurately discern the presence of evil. God alone is Omnipotent, Omniscient, and Omnipresent. We must be vigilant to the pervasive presence of evil in the world. Our reliance and dependence must always remain upon God for our spiritual protection and salvation. It is with the application of God's Spiritual Armour, that we withstand the negative externalities of evil in the world.

---

53   The Holy Bible (ESV). (2016). The Gospel of Matthew. Chapter 6, Verse 10.
54   Milton, John. (Darbishire, Helen, Ed.) (1958). *The Poetical Works of John Milton.* London: Oxford University Press, p. 70.
55   Shakespeare, William. (1600). *The Merchant of Venice.* Act 1, Scene 3.

'Contented with report hear only in Heaven. For wonderful indeed are all His works. Pleasant to know, and worthiest to be all had in remembrance always with delight. But what created mind can comprehend their number, or the wisdom infinite?'[56]

God's Work of Creation, and everything that is within it, serves to express God's Power, Glory, Honour, and Majesty. Rationally speaking, we cannot perfectly reason and understand why everything in the natural world is the way it is. Natural science has its many limitations. Concepts such as infinity, immortality, timelessness, eternity, transcendence, God, void, absolute, mind, spirit, conscience, and soul, are beyond exact and accurate definition. Much less are such concepts able to be observed and quantified by humanity. Human imagination has the unfettered capacity to envision novel ideas, principles, doctrines, and theories pertaining to the Universe. Having said that, there is much beyond the scope of human imagination to fathom.

---

56 Milton, John. (Darbishire, Helen, Ed.) (1958). *The Poetical Works of John Milton*. London: Oxford University Press, p. 71.

CHAPTER 4

PARADISE LOST: BOOK FOUR

'My author and disposer.
What thou bidst, unargued I obey.
So, God ordains. God is thy Law.
Thou mine: To know no more.'

MILTON

BOOK FOUR of *Paradise Lost* is the tragic story of Satan setting his sights on destroying the happiness and peace found within the Garden of Eden. Satan is unrelenting in his demonic quest for the destruction of Adam and Eve in picture-perfect Paradise. Satan's malignant will desires to destroy the sinless and perfect reality of Adam and Eve in the Garden of Eden.

God's masterpiece creation—humankind—is subject to Satan's vehement and unrelenting assault. Satan is determined in his unyielding evil quest to usurp Paradise from Adam and Eve. At any cost, Satan is determined to realise the effectuation of Original Sin and achieve the Fall of Man. This book portrays the human condition troubled by doubt, regret, fear, faithlessness, temptation, anxiety, confusion, knowledge, desire, envy, and disobedience to God's Eternal Word.

Through manipulation, malice, and deception, Satan enters the Garden of Eden. Satan has now witnessed the peaceful and serene co-existence of Adam and Eve. Satan learns that God has strictly forbidden the duo from consuming the Forbidden Fruit of the Tree of Knowledge of Good and Evil. Thus, Satan fixes his evil mind to make the Forbidden Fruit of the Tree of Knowledge of Good and Evil as the foundation for Adam and Eve's ill-fated downfall. This book ends with Satan tragically tempting Eve in her dreams. Satan suggests that Eve transgress God's Sovereign Command.

Eve's mind is transfixed upon the Devil's ignoble idea to secure the undesirable knowledge of good and evil. An act that God has expressly forbidden to Adam and Eve. As a consequence, Eve is consumed with doubt, indecision, temptation, anxiety, confusion, envy, and fear. Regrettably, Eve probes the shallow depth of natural reason. Eve begins to rationalise if transgressing God's Eternal Word is not only permissible, but also beneficial. The Devil is seemingly conquering the psychological battle for Eve's mind. In this book, we witness how pondering on passion, thinking through temptation, or dwelling on desire, is a sure recipe for tragedy in our life.

'Now conscience wakes despair that slumbered. Wakes the bitter memory of what he was. What is, and what must be worse. Of worse deeds, worse sufferings must ensue.'[57]

The phenomenon of conscience, in one aspect is comparable to our higher faculties of memory, reason, awareness, logic, judgement, will, understanding, discernment, and rational deliberation. That one aspect being, our conscience must be repeatedly exercised, in order to be strengthened. If we do not

---

57 Milton, John. (Darbishire, Helen, Ed.) (1958). *The Poetical Works of John Milton.* London: Oxford University Press, p. 74.

exercise our conscience, its presence and capacity to inform our reasoning diminishes with the constant passage of time. Among our positive qualities and desirable attributes, it is conscience that makes humanity in God's Image. We have a moral duty to ensure our free willed actions are compliant with ethical values and normative principles of honourable conduct.

> *'O Sun! To tell thee how I hate thy beams that bring to my remembrance from what state I fell. How glorious once above thy sphere. Till pride, and worse ambition, threw me down.'*[58]

Inherently, the existence of personal agency and free will are positive attributes of humanity. This philosophical assertion is conditional upon the fact, that these God-given gifts are not misappropriated. Over the course of time, unchecked pride and limitless ambition transform into vices that threaten our downfall. Humanity must not blindly follow the unregulated desires of the ego. The unrestrained ego has the capacity to conveniently lead our life astray. The presence of humility, empathy, meekness, community service, charity, mercy, justice, benevolence, and compassion ensure the presence of equilibrium and harmony in our life.

Focusing on ourselves, in particular where it concerns our productive pursuits, educational endeavours, sporting aspirations, technological innovations, or constructive projects is a positive attribute. However, we must be consciously aware that we exist in an interconnected ecosystem of society, state, and the world, in which to be truly successful, one must also factor into consideration our obligations, duties, liabilities, privileges, responsibilities, and rights.

---

58 Milton, John. (Darbishire, Helen, Ed.) (1958). *The Poetical Works of John Milton*. London: Oxford University Press, p. 74.

We ought to remain conscious of our present state of mind and the contemporary state of our affairs, so that pride, honour, glory, fame, success, jealousy, and ambition do not bring about our unexpected downfall. We are only human, and therefore our fall from grace is always plausible, no matter how negligible the probability.

'The debt immense of endless gratitude. So burdensome. Still paying. Still to owe. Forgetful what from him I still received, and understood not that a grateful mind by owing owes not, but still pays. At once indebted and discharged. What burden then? O had his powerful destiny ordained.'[59]

The immaterial debt of gratitude is incredibly difficult to repay. We must be grateful to God for our blessings. In all cases, we must not forget that humanity is a resource. The one and only true source of all our blessings, including our sense of gratitude, joy, and contentment is God. Throughout our lifetime, we must not confuse this important distinction between worldly resource and the eternal source. Therefore, we have a higher duty to demonstrate our gratefulness to the eternal source of the unmerited blessings in our life—God.

Unmerited blessings include the privilege of birth right, favour, the abundance of private wealth, private school education, inheritance of intangible assets, affluent parentage, bequeathed private property, or the receipt of significant trust income. No matter our circumstances, it is always advisable to express our sincere gratitude towards God, with the power of prayer, acts of charity, the benevolence of volunteering, and through the demonstration of love.

---

59 Milton, John. (Darbishire, Helen, Ed.) (1958). *The Poetical Works of John Milton*. London: Oxford University Press, pp. 74–75.

We do not always secure what our heart desires. Sometimes, we are better served by counting our blessings and answered prayers. We must never discount the importance of being fortunate for what we do have in our life. From time to time, we ought to remind ourselves, there are countless people in the modern world, who go without the basic amenities to live a secure and decent life. From time to time, we ought to pause and reflect upon the humanitarian idea, that access to clean drinking water, essential medication, nutritious food, human dignity and security, a place to call home, good health, access to health care, adequate provision for our dental and mental health care, these are sufficient amenities for our immediate and personal needs. Amenities that a significant quantum of the human population do not have access to.

'But Heaven's free love dealt equally to all? Be then his love accursed. Since love or hate, to me alike, it deals eternal woe. Nay, cursed be thou. Since against his, thy will chose freely, what it now so justly rues. Me miserable! Which way shall I fly infinite wrath, and infinite despair? Which way I fly is Hell. Myself am Hell.'[60]

God has provisioned and honoured humanity with the especial gift of free will. Regardless of the presence and function of our free will, God's unconditional love for Creation and humanity does not waver. Often times we make questionable choices which result in destructive consequences. Our beliefs, thoughts, ideas, doctrines, principles, and actions have the equal capacity to create a living Hell, or a picture-perfect Heaven on Earth.

We must not let the Devil's malignant will and well-known instruments of temptation, anger, procrastination, confusion, loneliness, jealousy, resentment, guilt, fear, envy, failure, doubt,

---

60 Milton, John. (Darbishire, Helen, Ed.) (1958). *The Poetical Works of John Milton*. London: Oxford University Press, p. 75.

or discouragement to influence the trajectory of our thought, speech, or conduct.

> '*The lower still I fall. Only supreme in misery. Such joy ambition finds. But say I could repent and could obtain by act of grace my former state. How soon would height recall high thoughts? How soon unsay what feigned submission swore? Ease would recant vows made in pain, as violent and void.*'[61]

The trap of temptation and the seduction of sin guides countless men and women astray from the Path of Truth and Righteousness. Sometimes, we think we know what is best for our life. We must never forget that God's Ways are not our ways. God's Ways are superior to all of our ways. God has divine plans to prosper us and ensure that our lifetime on Earth is for our greater good. Following God's Counsel, we produce many good works that are a blessing to us and the people around us. There are a plethora of scripture verses that affirm and reaffirm this central message, that God has superior plans for our success, happiness, wealth, abundance, joy, and prosperity.

In the Holy Bible, consider the profound blessing for obedience narrated within the Book of Leviticus, 'If you walk in My statutes and observe My commandments and do them, then I will give you your rains in their season, and the land shall yield its increase, and the trees of the field shall yield their fruit. Your threshing shall last to the time of the grape harvest, and the grape harvest shall last to the time for sowing. And you shall eat your bread to the full and dwell in your land securely.'[62] The important moral principle we learn from this Biblical narrative, is that we reap the dividends of our conscious and voluntary actions.

---

61 Milton, John. (Darbishire, Helen, Ed.) (1958). *The Poetical Works of John Milton*. London: Oxford University Press, pp. 75–76.

62 The Holy Bible (ESV). (2016). The Book of Leviticus. Chapter 26, Verses 3–5.

Furthermore, in the Holy Bible we are reminded of God's Blessing in the Book of Deuteronomy, 'For the LORD your God has blessed you in all the work of your hands. He knows your going through this great wilderness. These forty years the LORD your God has been with you. You have lacked nothing.'[63]

Last but not least, within the Holy Bible, in the Book of Job we are advised, 'If they listen and serve Him, they complete their days in prosperity, and their years in pleasantness.'[64] In all these Biblical verses and many more, we witness the importance of positioning God in first place. It is our obedience to God's Eternal Word, which leads us to the reward of God's Blessing.

On the contrary, the monumental challenge with experiential learning, through the medium of trial and error, is that the approximate length of one lifetime is wholly inadequate. It is true, the accumulation of personal experience and the power of empirical knowledge progresses human civilisation forward. Yet, no person can profess to live their life in a manner that is greater than what God has determined to be beneficial and sagacious.

Once we have lived a full and whole life, once we have reached an advanced age nearing our death, when we reflect and deduce mature conclusions from our life journey, in hindsight we are more likely than not, to realise that we have made countless mistakes along our life journey. Indeed, practice refines our actions. However, practice entails the process of making several, if not a few injudicious errors of judgement.

A life that is lived in accordance with worldly principles, doctrines, trends, fashion, customs, ideas, values, ideologies, and popular culture is only meaningful in the superficial opinion and negligible worth of humanity. If we live our life based on God's Timeless Principles and Unsurpassable Counsel, we are assured that we have gained an immeasurable treasure. A treasure not of

---

63   The Holy Bible (ESV). (2016). The Book of Deuteronomy. Chapter 2, Verse 7.
64   The Holy Bible (ESV). (2016). The Book of Job. Chapter 36, Verse 11.

this world. A treasure that far surpasses the trivial approval and inconsequential validation of the billions of people of the world. In effect, we have gained God's acceptance. There is no prize higher than God's approval. All other worldly gifts and treasures are a mere consolation prize.

In our self-determination to live a Godly life, we must repent for our countless sins and seek God's Favour through acts of petition, penance, and prayer. God does not expect perfection from humanity, but rather that we demonstrate love, dedication, service, faith, integrity, charity, mercy, forgiveness, commitment, and perseverance in all that we do on Earth. God works in our life where there is belief, hope, confidence, trust, and faith.

Based on our actions, God is either proximate or distant to us. We must ask ourselves the following questions: How is our relationship with God? What do we want our relationship with God to look like? When are we going to make the requisite changes to transform our relationship with God? When are we going to position God at the centre of our life?

'For never can true reconcilement grow. Where wounds of deadly hate have pierced so deep. Which would, but lead me to a worse relapse.'[65]

For genuine reconciliation to be feasible, there must exist a meeting of the minds between the opposing parties. The defining events of history are harsh and cannot be undone. Having said that, the future remains to be written. We create and re-create the future. A future that is amenable to all parties in a conflict. For the present time always provides us with an opportunity to create a superior vision of the future.

In order to create a better and brighter future, the negative externalities of resentment, hate, animosity, sexism, racism,

---

65   Milton, John. (Darbishire, Helen, Ed.) (1958). *The Poetical Works of John Milton*. London: Oxford University Press, p. 76.

prejudice, jealousy, envy, regret, remorse, and anger must be eliminated. The wounds of the past can prevent real and tangible progress in the present moment. We have an obligation not to relive the past. While the past influences and informs our life trajectory, the past need not define our future.

'Dearer thyself than all. Needs must the power that made us, and for us this ample world be infinitely good, and of his good as liberal and free as infinite. That raised us from the dust and placed us here in all this happiness. Who at his hand have nothing merited. Nor can perform aught whereof he hath need. He who requires from us, no other service, than to keep this one. This easy charge. Of all the trees in Paradise, that bear delicious fruit so various, not to taste that only Tree of Knowledge, planted by the Tree of Life. So near grows death to life. Whatever death is. Some dreadful thing no doubt. For well thou knowest God hath pronounced it death to taste that tree. The only sign of our obedience left.'[66]

Transgression against God's Sovereign Command, always leads us into the dark realm of sin. It is due to the performance of sin that we experience guilt, hate, resentment, envy, denial, conflict, confusion, anger, and ultimately, spiritual death. There must be no doubt in our mind, that we are often tempted during our lifetime on Earth. Each person has their fair share of battles with temptation. However, God's Spirit and Eternal Word protects us from the disastrous pitfalls of worldly sin. The Devil has numerous stratagems to detach us from God's Service, the use of half-truths is just one of them. We must not be so naive as to underestimate the formidable power of the Devil.

---

66 Milton, John. (Darbishire, Helen, Ed.) (1958). *The Poetical Works of John Milton*. London: Oxford University Press, pp. 83–84.

Considerable wisdom is deduced from the Biblical story narrating the tragic downfall of Adam and Eve in the Garden of Eden. The Devil ensures that humanity remains devoid, detached, disobedient, disconnected, and distant to God's Eternal Word. The tell-tale method by which the Devil caused Original Sin and the Fall of Man was by instilling doubt in Eve's mind. That undesirable feeling of doubt took hold in Eve's mind. The presence of doubt eventually led Eve to irrationally question and transgress God's Eternal Word. This reality in turn, also led Adam to transgress God's Eternal Word. For Adam, by consuming the Forbidden Fruit, consciously joined Eve in both the thought of temptation and the ignoble act of sin. The moral of this Biblical story is the greater our disobedience to God's Eternal Word, the closer our life inches towards damnation, destruction, depression, denial, and death.

> *'One fatal tree there stands of knowledge called, forbidden for them to taste. Knowledge forbidden? Suspicious. Reasonless. Why should their LORD envy them that? Can it be sin to know? Can it be death? And do they only stand by ignorance. Is that their happy state? The proof of their obedience and their faith?'*[67]

At pivotal moments and inflection points in our life, we do not truly understand or wholly appreciate the rationale underlying God's Sovereign Commands. Nonetheless, we must believe. We must have faith. We must keep our conviction firmly grounded in God's Eternal Word. We must persevere in our quest to uphold the everlasting Truth.

There are inherent limitations with the exercise of our natural reason. For one, we cannot understand the entire cosmic scope of the Universe. Not to mention, nor can we truly and wholly

---

67 Milton, John. (Darbishire, Helen, Ed.) (1958). *The Poetical Works of John Milton*. London: Oxford University Press, p. 86.

comprehend God's demonstration of creative power in forming Creation. On the contrary, if we could fathom God's lofty thoughts, ideas, and actions, we would equal God. We would be God.

For our part, we have to appreciate that God has given us commands to prosper us, and to further our welfare on Earth. Faith cannot always be ascertained rationally, scientifically, and empirically. Faith is a lifelong litmus test of the endurance of our spirit. Our ability to keep that faith is the conclusive test, to ascertain our spirit's readiness to enter the Kingdom of Heaven.

Faith is believing when we do not perceive any signs of prosperity or genuine progress in our life. Faith is holding on to hope. Faith is having an unrelenting expectation in God to deliver us from our challenges. Faith is boldness and courage in our personal confrontation with uncertainty, privation, loss, grief, heartache, trauma, and suffering along our life journey. Faith is the belief, that no matter what comes our way, God's Eternal Word and Promises remain indissoluble. Even at the irreplaceable expense of our life, the proper and righteous place of our faith always takes precedence.

Within the Holy Bible, in the Book of Daniel, we are told a remarkable story of faith concerning Shadrach, Meshach, and Abednego. These three young gentlemen refused to follow the royal decree of King Nebuchadnezzar. The trio were given an ultimatum: either submit or face certain death. This Biblical story narrates the following exchange, 'Shadrach, Meshach, and Abednego answered and said to the King, "O Nebuchadnezzar, we have no need to answer you in this matter. If this be so, our God whom we serve is able to deliver us from the burning fiery furnace, and he will deliver us out of your hand, O King. But if not, be it known to you. O King, that we will not serve your Gods or worship the golden image that you have set up."'[68]

---

68   The Holy Bible (ESV). (2016). The Book of Daniel. Chapter 3, Verses 16–18.

As the aforementioned scripture verse informs us, during this most unwelcome ordeal with King Nebuchadnezzar, the three young gentlemen; Shadrach, Meshach, and Abednego consciously determined to affirm their faith in God, without a shred of doubt, or a second thought for their own welfare. These three brave gentlemen openly defied the King's edict. Such a provocative response by the trio produced anger and outrage in His Majesty King Nebuchadnezzar.

The above scripture verse continues, informing us, 'Then Nebuchadnezzar was filled with fury, and the expression of his face was changed against Shadrach, Meshach, and Abednego. He ordered the furnace heated seven times more than it was usually heated. And he ordered some of the mighty men of his army to bind Shadrach, Meshach, and Abednego, and to cast them into the burning fiery furnace. Then these men were bound in their cloaks, their tunics, their hats, and their other garments, and they were thrown into the burning fiery furnace. Because the King's order was urgent and the furnace overheated, the flame of the fire killed those men who took up Shadrach, Meshach, and Abednego. And these three men, Shadrach, Meshach, and Abednego, fell bound into the burning fiery furnace.'[69]

In the midst of tragedy, terror, and trouble, God's Grace provided for the immediate need of Shadrach, Meshach, and Abednego, 'Then King Nebuchadnezzar was astonished and rose up in haste. He declared to his counsellors, "Did we not cast three men bound into the fire?" They answered and said to the King, "True, O King." He answered and said, "But I see four men unbound, walking in the midst of the fire, and they are not hurt; and the appearance of the fourth is like a Son of the Gods."'[70] The moral principle of this Biblical story is that faith is the formidable power of the spirit to guide us forward. The spirit

---

69   The Holy Bible (ESV). (2016). The Book of Daniel. Chapter 3, Verses 19–23.
70   The Holy Bible (ESV). (2016). The Book of Daniel. Chapter 3, Verses 24–25.

guides us through our challenges, issues, and problems during our lifetime.

> '*As when thou stoodst in Heaven upright and pure. That glory then, when thou no more waste good. Departed from thee, and thou resemble now thy sin and place of doom obscure and foul. But come, for thou, be sure, shall give account to Him who sent us. Whose charge is to keep this place inviolable, and these from harm.*'[71]

Ultimately, each and every person is answerable to God for their conscious and self-determined actions. Therefore, the Kantian Categorical Imperative is upon us, that we do not misappropriate our free will. Our lifetime on Earth is the litmus test for the perfection of our character. At the end of our lifetime, our actions have either drawn us closer, or made us distant to God's Spirit. We must not be deceived into thinking that God's Justice is escapable. We are all responsible for our voluntary actions, and we are certainly not free from their consequences, both the intended and unintended.

71　Milton, John. (Darbishire, Helen, Ed.) (1958). *The Poetical Works of John Milton*. London: Oxford University Press, p. 94.

'Satan, I know thy strength, and thou knowest mine. Neither our own, but given. What folly then, to boast what arms can do. Since thine no more than Heaven permits. Nor mine. Though doubled now to trample thee as mire. For proof look up, and read thy lot in yon celestial sign. Where thou art weighed, and shown how light, how weak, if thou resist. The fiend looked up and knew his mounted scale aloft, nor more, but fled. Murmuring, and with him fled the shades of night.'[72]

The Devil operates in an erratic, elusive, evil, egocentric, and evasive manner. The Devil seeks to manipulate humanity. The Devil always twists the Truth to achieve the downfall of man and woman. The Devil's game is deception. We need to understand that the Devil cannot stand in the presence of God's Sovereign Kingdom. The sooner we correctly discern good from evil, virtue from sin, spiritual wisdom from worldly ignorance, reason from folly, and wholesome thoughts from unwholesome thoughts, the sooner the Devil's ability to wage war against our mind is rendered ineffective.

The Devil always seeks to gain a foothold in our mind by focusing our attention away from the undeserved blessings and favours that God has freely given to us. Rather, the Devil employs his malignant will and malevolent spirit to turn our attention towards what is absent in our life. What is deficient in our life. What is void in our life. The Devil intends for us to ruminate upon what we most desire in our life. What we desire, but is currently not in our possession.

Through the ignoble practice of treachery, the Devil misleads us into worldly temptation. The Devil plays foul on the strings of our unchecked desires, and rather than give us our heart's content, the Devil only seeks to destroy our life. Therefore, it is

---

72   Milton, John. (Darbishire, Helen, Ed.) (1958). *The Poetical Works of John Milton*. London: Oxford University Press, pp. 98–99.

an essential imperative, that we do not give our attention to the fallacy of the Devil's diabolical ideas. Diabolical ideas which promise a great deal in return for our cooperation, however, only bring about our disastrous downfall.

CHAPTER 5

PARADISE LOST: BOOK FIVE

'To be both will and deed created free.
Yet, that we never shall forget to love our Maker, and
obey Him. Whose command single, is yet so just.
My constant thoughts assured me, and still assure.
Though what thou tellest hath past in Heaven,
some doubt within me moves.'

MILTON

BOOK FIVE of *Paradise Lost* is the story of Eve informing Adam of her harrowing dream. In response, Adam loves and comforts distressed Eve. God dispatches the Archangel Raphael to forewarn Adam of humanity's potential transgression against God's Eternal Word. The central thesis of this book concerns Adam and Raphael's theological dialogue. These two characters engage in a reflective and thoughtful discourse on Satan.

During this time, Satan is in the vicinity of Paradise. Adam methodically and relentlessly questions Raphael. Adam intends to better understand God's Divine Message. Raphael patiently and faithfully answers Adam's thought-provoking inquiries. Once God's Divine Command has been faithfully performed, the Archangel Raphael departs Paradise.

In this book, Raphael does not directly confront Satan. Instead, the powerful Archangel Raphael personifies the role of a trusted confidant to Adam. Raphael does not intervene in Adam and Eve's destiny. In accordance with God's Sovereign Will, Raphael leaves Adam and Eve's free will unimpeded. However, Raphael imparts considerable wise counsel to Adam.

Following this preordained conversation, Adam cannot claim willful ignorance of Satan's casting out of Heaven. Adam now possesses a comprehensive understanding of the historical events pertaining to the Fall of Lucifer. In addition, Adam is well informed of the Devil's malevolent will. Therefore, Adam and Eve must assume personal responsibility for their forthcoming sinful conduct, and its catastrophic consequences.

> *'Created pure. But know that in the soul are many lesser faculties that serve reason as chief. Among these fancy next her office holds. Of all external things, which the five watchful senses represent. She forms imaginations. Aery shapes, which reason joining or disjoining, frames all what we affirm or what we deny, and call our knowledge or opinion. Then retires into her private cell, when nature rests.'*[73]

An introspection into the fathomless depth of the soul is a mystical and spiritual experience. The human condition is profound and complex. The vast expanse of our being does not only encompass the physical dimension, but also the metaphysical dimension. The human condition is not only defined by the presence of reason, but it also incorporates the presence of passion, emotion, sensation, feeling, rationality, understanding, inclination, thought, experiential learning, lived experience,

---

73 Milton, John. (Darbishire, Helen, Ed.) (1958). *The Poetical Works of John Milton*. London: Oxford University Press, pp. 102–103.

memory, free will, instinct, intuition, imagination, and cognitive perception.

The existential reality of our being, which is attuned to the input of the five senses (i.e., sight, sound, smell, taste, and touch) only constitutes the beginning of our human experience. The informative insights obtained through our five senses provide us with an accurate perception of the natural world; however, the metaphysical and spiritual reality of our being is experienced through the faculty of our mind.

The superior faculties of our being (i.e., imagination, intuition, perception, reason, will, moral conscience, and memory), serve to enhance our logical and rational analysis of life. On the contrary, the inferior faculties of our being (i.e., reproductive capacity, sensual desire, natural and primal instincts, pleasure-seeking behaviour, unregulated appetites, uncontrollable urges, and unchecked passions), these only serve to diminish our spiritual and intellectual capacities.

Therefore, to live a good life we must consciously recalibrate the hierarchy of our faculties of being. This reasoned recalibration must be performed in such a manner, that the constructive and beneficial faculties, that is to say the superior faculties are strengthened. For the superior faculties must become the guiding force of our life.

Equally, the inferior faculties ought to be strictly regulated. These inferior faculties are an inalienable part of our human condition. Therefore, it is inappropriate to infer in the ideal sense, that these inferior faculties be eliminated from our experience of being. This assertion is simply not feasible in reality, nor is it possible in fact. It is for this reason, that prudence resides in our ability to exercise self-control, and through self-control, regulate the influence of these inferior faculties upon our life. Whatever we cultivate in our life develops. Therefore, it is essential that we cultivate the higher faculties of our being, while provisioning adequate and regulated expression of the inferior faculties. This pragmatic approach assists us to live a good life.

> *'Evil, into the mind of God or man, may come and go. So unapproved, and leave no spot or blame behind. Which gives me hope. That what in sleep thou didst abhor to dream. Waking thou, never will consent to do.'*[74]

Our subliminal thoughts become productive and constructive, when we entertain wholesome ideas, principles, practices, beliefs, values, and doctrines. Alternatively, our unconscious thoughts can also become irrational and catastrophic. We must always remember that our thoughts, in their embryonic form, are simply conceptual and abstract ideas. Ideas that originate from within our mind. Our subconscious and conscious thoughts only transform into our conventional reality, that is our living reality, if and when we act upon their impressions.

Thus, we always have a conscious choice. We can self-determine through the exercise of our personal agency, which thoughts we give effect to vis-à-vis the performance of our free and voluntary actions. We can create our desired reality, if we consciously select which thoughts we self-determine to associate with, and which thoughts we disassociate ourselves from. If we exercise power over our mind, then we create the reality that we desire for ourselves. It is by the persistent application of mindfulness and self-control that we exercise such profound power over our mind.

Through action in the pursuit of wholesome and productive endeavours, and inaction concerning unwholesome and destructive endeavours, we construct our life narrative in the direction that we desire. The two forces of action and inaction are incredibly powerful instruments. If these two instruments are

---

74 Milton, John. (Darbishire, Helen, Ed.) (1958). *The Poetical Works of John Milton*. London: Oxford University Press, p. 103.

truly mastered, the application (or inapplication) of them assist us to consciously manifest our ideal life. A person who truly understands the immense power of both action and inaction, has the destiny of their life in their hands.

Practical wisdom resides in not being pushed and pulled by the many social, economic, political, historical, and legal forces into acting without proper foresight, reason, judgement, and understanding. If we are honest with ourselves, then we accept that we do not always determine to act or not to act, after careful consideration of all the empirical information and objective knowledge pertaining to the matter at hand. We are not perfect, but we can be better.

'Raphael, said he, thou hearest what stir on Earth. Satan from Hell escaped through the darksome gulf hath raised in Paradise, and how disturbed this night the human pair. How he designs in them at once. To ruin all humankind.'[75]

We cannot claim complete ignorance of the Devil's intentions and plans, chief among them to destroy the peace, justice, love, joy, and harmony amongst humanity. The Devil does not cease in his relentless assaults on humanity. For our part, the Spiritual Armour of God is our grand strategy, to overcome the presence of evil with the power of good.[76] In this protracted spiritual battle between good and evil, we cannot rest on our laurels. In the world, we self-determine to traverse the path of obedience or rebellion to God's Eternal Word.

In the grand battle of spiritual warfare, the Devil employs every method, instrument, and temptation at his disposal. This includes phenomena that is known and unknown to humankind. The Devil intends to exploit our will, so that we act in the pursuit

---

75   Milton, John. (Darbishire, Helen, Ed.) (1958). *The Poetical Works of John Milton*. London: Oxford University Press, p. 106.

76   The Holy Bible (ESV). (2016). The Book of Ephesians. Chapter 6, Verses 10–20.

of vengeance, war, conflict, retribution, evil, hate, prejudice, discrimination, and disobedience to God. We must resist the Devil's targeted onslaught. We must preserve our righteous principles and cherished values. We must fight the good fight of faith.

We must strive, suffer, and struggle for the sake of goodness and Truth in the world. We must transcend the ignoble baseness of the human condition. To experience a lifetime that is wholly absorbed in the pursuit of the flesh, is to live our life less than its inherent potential. We must not live our life consumed and defined by unchecked pleasure, the presence of sin, and unwholesome desires.

It is only through the Spiritual Armour of God, which consists of the Helmet of Salvation,[77] the Breastplate of Righteousness,[78] the Sword of the Spirit,[79] the Shield of Faith,[80] the Belt of Truth,[81] and the Shoes of Peace,[82] that we secure a decisive victory for the Glory of God. In such a formidable spiritual battle between the forces of good and evil, we must remain circumspect and vigilant. Peace be with you.

---

77   The Holy Bible (ESV). (2016). The Book of Ephesians. Chapter 6, Verse 17.
78   The Holy Bible (ESV). (2016). The Book of Ephesians. Chapter 6, Verse 14.
79   The Holy Bible (ESV). (2016). The Book of Ephesians. Chapter 6, Verse 17.
80   The Holy Bible (ESV). (2016). The Book of Ephesians. Chapter 6, Verse 16.
81   The Holy Bible (ESV). (2016). The Book of Ephesians. Chapter 6, Verse 14.
82   The Holy Bible (ESV). (2016). The Book of Ephesians. Chapter 6, Verse 15.

'Happiness, in his power, left free to will. Left to his own free will. His will though free, yet mutable. Whence warn him to beware he swerve not too secure. Tell him, withal his danger, and from whom. What enemy late fallen himself from Heaven is plotting now. The fall of others from like state of bliss. By violence? No. For that shall be withstood. But by deceit and lies. This let him know. Lest, wilfully transgressing, he pretend. Surprisal, unadmonished, and unforewarned.'[83]

Sometimes we perceive our life trajectory is being determined by forces that are beyond our immediate control. For example, consider the onset of economic crises. Unsustainable financial commitments. Major international events that have global ramifications. Material changes in state government policy. The operation of federal legislation. The potency of dire circumstances. The diagnosis of a serious medical condition. The unfolding of unexpected personal events or situations. The untimely death of a loved one. Dealing with the fallout of a divorce. Loss of a respected friendship. Endless contractual commitments. Changes in our employment status. Last but not least, the uncertainty of legal proceedings.

In all the aforementioned cases and many more, to affirm a state of contentment is always a conscious choice that is open to us. Despite all the water under the bridge, we always have a choice to determine the present state of our mind, in response to the events and the environment that we find ourselves situated in. Yes, we can still self-determine how to respond. In fact, at this present moment in time, we can self-determine to be content, in spite of what our circumstances and reality dictate. This is not to infer, that we ought to become ambivalent in our thoughts, and not demonstrate an astute awareness of our surrounding

---

83   Milton, John. (Darbishire, Helen, Ed.) (1958). *The Poetical Works of John Milton.* London: Oxford University Press, p. 106.

environment and personal struggles, but rather that we ought not to let our struggles define our life.

Through the application of mindfulness, we self-determine not to be defined by our struggles, privations, hardships, and challenges. This positive perception of life starts within the nucleus of our thoughts. The higher faculties of our mind are strengthened and reinforced with the application of logic and the employment of natural reason. The internal perception of our mind manifests into our external reality.

When we confront our difficulties in the world, we must remember that nothing lasts forever. We shall transcend the testing, tragic, and turbulent times to create a newfound reality. In the final analysis, we must not let our reality define us. Rather, we must define our reality. We must write our life story, not have one imposed, impressed, or insinuated upon us.

'O Adam, one Almighty is, from whom all things proceed, and up to Him return. If not depraved from good. Created all such to perfection. One first matter all. Endued with various forms. Various degrees of substance, and in things that live, of life. But more refined. More spiritous and pure. As nearer to Him placed, or nearer tending each in their several active spheres assigned.'[84]

God is the Creator of all life forms in the Universe. The origin and final destination of our spirit is God. Human life on Earth presents an unparalleled opportunity for humanity to further God's Sovereign Kingdom on Earth. We are not perfect. From time to time, we all fall short in the grand pursuit of our crucial endeavours; however, we must strive and persevere to effectuate God's Calling in all that we do on Earth. During our lifetime on Earth, we must perform God's Sovereign Will. We were created

---

84 Milton, John. (Darbishire, Helen, Ed.) (1958). *The Poetical Works of John Milton*. London: Oxford University Press, p. 112.

for God's Divine Purpose. We were created to bring God glory, prestige, and honour. The pursuit of God's Sovereign Will is the epitome of a truly rewarding, wholesome, and fulfilling life.

On the other hand, if we live solely for our sake, for the furtherance of our accumulation of private wealth, endless entertainment of pleasures, pursuit of private property, accumulation of excessive pecuniary gain, and our irrational attachment with luxurious material goods, our mind is not appeased. Not to mention, our spirit remains restless. In the pursuit of self-interest, we do not attain lasting satisfaction or fulfilment with our life.

The vanity of much human thought, speech, and conduct is difficult to deny. It is only by living beyond the superficial confines of self-interest, that we realise life is not all about us. When we place God, compassion, community service, charity, peace, love, forgiveness, respect, human dignity, benevolence, tolerance, hope, and prayer at the centre of our life, then we live a rewarding, wholesome, and fulfilling life.

'To intellectual. Give both life and sense. Fancy and understanding. Whence the soul, reason receives, and reason is her being. Discursive or intuitive. Discourse is oftest yours. The latter most is ours. Differing, but in degree. Of kind, the same. Wonder not then, what God for you saw good. If I refuse not, but convert, as you, to proper substance. Time may come when men with Angels may participate, and find no inconvenient diet. Not too light fare: and from these corporal nutriments perhaps your bodies may at last turn all to spirit. Improved by tract of time, and winged, ascend ethereal, as we; or may at choice, here or in Heavenly Paradise dwell. If you be found obedient, and retain unalterably firm His love entire. Whose progeny you are.'[85]

We must never forget, that we are all Sons and Daughters of the Most High God. The human intellect is finite in its capacity to comprehend the Universe. Even with the scientific progress of the New World over the former 500 years, our total dependence upon God has not altered or diminished in the slightest. Despite the technological, scientific, medical, and industrial advances of the modern world, the human condition remains the same. The human condition is defined by conception, fertilisation, human embryogenesis, fetal development, birth, infancy, childhood, adolescence, adulthood, old age, palliative care, and death.

Only by God's Favour, Grace, and Mercy, do we run our race from start to finish. During our race, as we fight the good fight of faith, we must overcome the powerful forces of evil. Throughout the course of our life, we must always remember our identity. Who we are. Who we belong to. Who we serve. In the end, to unconditionally love God is the greatest action that we perform during our lifetime on Earth.

---

85 Milton, John. (Darbishire, Helen, Ed.) (1958). *The Poetical Works of John Milton*. London: Oxford University Press, pp. 112–113.

'By steps we may ascend to God. But say, what meant that caution joined, if you be found obedient? Can we want obedience then to Him, or possibly His love desert who formed us from the dust, and placed us here, full to the utmost measure of what bliss human desires can seek or apprehend?'[86]

The cumulative effect of the everyday decisions and choices that we resolve, along the continuum of our life, collectively determine if we progressively move towards or further away from God. We possess the requisite free will, to either obey or disobey God's Divine Command. God created humanity with the admirable attribute of free will. Our free will ensures that we obey and love God from our own heart, not from a mechanised, thoughtless, and robotic perspective, that serves to subconsciously ritualise our obedience to God. God has left humanity at liberty, to obey or disobey God's Sovereign Command. When we consciously perform actions to position God's Eternal Word and Command at the very centre of everything that we do, then we create a superior world. A world that is defined and immersed in God's Divine Vision.

The material dimension of our being on Earth is temporary. From Earthly substance we were fashioned. To dust we return. It is the spiritual dimension of our being that defines our eternal reality. Long after our human body disintegrates, the phenomenon of our spirit survives. Only the soul endures for eternity. The soul has the capacity to transcend the limitations and inferior condition of the human body. During our limited time on Earth, the human body is subject to all types of desires, temptations, sensations, pleasures, inclinations, emotions, feelings, and passions, however, this ecstatic bliss that the human

---

86   Milton, John. (Darbishire, Helen, Ed.) (1958). *The Poetical Works of John Milton*. London: Oxford University Press, p. 113.

body experiences through the five senses is temporary, fleeting, and transient.

It is the unchanging reality of our being, that the pursuits, promises, passions, and pleasures of the flesh always leave our mind unsatisfied. No matter how many times we partake in the seductive pleasures of the flesh, we never secure an enduring state of contentment. It is only by the Grace of God, that a person experiences the highest bliss on Earth. A profound bliss which is experienced with the union of our spirit with God's Uncreated, Eternal, and Infinite Spirit.

> *'God made thee perfect. Not immutable; and good He made thee. But to persevere, He left it in thy power. Ordained thy will, by nature free. Not over-ruled by fate, inextricable, or strict necessity. Our voluntary service, He requires, not our necessitated. Such with Him, finds no acceptance. Nor can find. For how can hearts, not free, be tried, whether they serve, willing or no, who will but what they must. By destiny, and can no other choose?'*[87]

Humanity is created in God's Divine Image. God has ordained humanity with unique gifts. Among God's many magnificent gifts, we have the ability to experience a wide range of emotions. To reason. To love. To feel. To understand. To be understood. To act with personal agency. To engage in original thought. To imagine. To create new human life. Last but not least, to employ our moral conscience. In addition, we possess the capacity to self-determine our thoughts and actively engage in the construction of our worldly reality. We also possess invaluable spiritual gifts, these include: the fear of God, leadership, understanding, discernment, fortitude, temperance, knowledge, faith, giving, mercy, counsel,

---

87 Milton, John. (Darbishire, Helen, Ed.) (1958). *The Poetical Works of John Milton*. London: Oxford University Press, p. 113.

wisdom, and piety. Underlying each of these unique gifts is the supreme power of free will.

The phenomenon of free will provides humanity with the requisite personal agency to live our life upon the principles, doctrines, ideas, and beliefs that we self-determine to subscribe to and abide by. By virtue of the existence of free will, the operation of fate and the doctrine of determinism cannot hold true and constant. Nevertheless, God as the Creator still possesses complete foreknowledge of our destiny.

The doctrine of predestination holds true and constant alongside our free will. For God is Omnipotent, Omniscient, and Omnipresent. It is the case, that God knows how we will act, before we effectuate our self-determined actions in the world. This is not to imply, that God intervenes or interferes with the exercise of our personal agency. God's Foreknowledge does not negate or impede the operation of our free will. Rather this theological assertion affirms that God is all-knowing. The Creator knows the created. On the contrary, what the Creator knows is forever inaccessible to humanity. No person shall ever know God's Secrets.

'Hold, as you yours. While our obedience holds; on other surety none. Freely we serve, because we freely love. As in our will, to love or not. In this we stand or fall: and some are fallen, to disobedience fallen, and so from Heaven to deepest Hell. O fall, from what high state of bliss into what woe!'[88]

In the world, we become what we think and how we act. The world is a reflection of our beliefs, thoughts, doctrines, ideas, and actions. To a considerable degree and a certain extent, it is possible that we self-determine our destiny by our thoughts, ideas,

---

88 Milton, John. (Darbishire, Helen, Ed.) (1958). *The Poetical Works of John Milton*. London: Oxford University Press, pp. 113–114.

beliefs, principles, doctrines, and actions. While our thoughts, ideas, beliefs, principles, doctrines, and actions are ours, we are not absolved from their consequences, both the good and evil. If we self-determine to traverse the path of good, then our obedience to God must be from a place of love, authenticity, and sincerity. We must self-determine, whether we live our life in rebellion or obedience to God's Eternal Word.

In accordance with our free will, we have a choice; to serve, obey, and love God. God does not necessitate the imposition of our service, worship, penance, prayer, obedience, or love. The deliberate performance of an intentional act of community service, worship, penance, prayer, or love, that is to say an act that is effectuated from a sense of obligation, law, duty, force, or compulsion of the will, such an act is not freely rendered from the heart of that person.

When God examines our service, worship, penance, prayer, obedience, or love, God is searching for the underlying intention that informs the deliberate performance of our actions. Were our actions performed from a place of sincerity? For community service, worship, penance, prayer, obedience, or love to be invaluable, they must be freely given, with a heart of gratitude, hope, faith, benevolence, peace, and contentment. The joy of receiving is described. The joy of giving is indescribable. Giving always enriches the person who gives. Giving always nourishes the soul.

'*Yet, by experience taught we know how good, and of our good, and of our dignity how provident He is. How far from thought. To make us less, bent rather to exalt our happy state. Under one head more near united.*'[89]

Even with the subjective lessons of lived experience and the

---

89 Milton, John. (Darbishire, Helen, Ed.) (1958). *The Poetical Works of John Milton*. London: Oxford University Press, p. 121.

scientific proof of empirical knowledge, we ought to position our trust in God. To trust in God is the hallmark of a life lived by faith. Faith is believing in God, when we are not in a position to perceive, foresee, or possess foreknowledge of the future outcome of our present actions.[90] Faith is having an unyielding conviction that God has plans to prosper us.[91] Faith is placing our complete confidence in God. Faith is trusting God, to grant us success in our endeavours.

Often in hindsight, with an invaluable lifetime of experience making our own decisions, choices, and living life according to our personal values, principles, doctrines, and ideologies, our life narrative affirms that God had more beneficial and superior plans for our life. Magnificent plans that we were incapable of imagining, self-determining, and accomplishing with the finite power of our personal understanding. In all major life decisions, we must not rely exclusively upon our personal understanding, but rather supplement our understanding with God's Unsurpassable Counsel. This approach advances us forward in life. Forward with the benefit of better decisions and more favourable outcomes.

'Doctrine which we would know whence learnt. Who saw when this Creation was? Rememberest thou thy making, while the Maker gave thee being? We know no time, when we were not as now.'[92]

God's Eternal Secrets are forever inaccessible to humanity. What we do know is that God has created the world and everything that is contained within it. The divine act of Creation is an expression of God's Majestic Glory and Creative Power. Within Creation, God has provisioned humanity with the especial gifts of life,

---

90   The Holy Bible (ESV). (2016). The Book of Hebrews. Chapter 11, Verse 1.
91   The Holy Bible (ESV). (2016). The Book of Jeremiah. Chapter 29, Verse 11.
92   Milton, John. (Darbishire, Helen, Ed.) (1958). *The Poetical Works of John Milton.* London: Oxford University Press, p. 121.

imagination, reason, memory, intuition, personal agency, will, and intelligence.

All aspects of being human, including to see, hear, smell, taste, touch, feel, empathise, discern, cognise, reminisce, worship, reflect, act, love, pray, and create new life, these are all God's invaluable gifts to humanity. It is beyond our brief experience of human life, to comprehend of an existential reality that transcends the human condition.

CHAPTER 6

PARADISE LOST: BOOK SIX

'Servant of God. Well done.
Well hast thou fought the better fight, who single hast
maintained against revolted multitudes the Cause of Truth.
In word mightier than they in arms.
And for the Testimony of Truth,
hast born universal reproach.'

MILTON

BOOK SIX of *Paradise Lost* depicts the good fight of faith. Initially, the two powerful Angels, Gabriel and Michael proceed into a fierce battle against their archenemy, Satan. However, in an extraordinary turn of events, God sends his Beloved Son to convincingly defeat Satan. God has preordained victory for His Beloved Son in this grand battle of good and evil. The *Messiah* conquers the enemy. God secures the glory of Satan's tragic demise. Satan and his legion of fallen Angels are overwhelmed with ignorance, conceit, ego, evil, anger, hate, resentment, falsehood, jealousy, confusion, and pride. Given Satan has transgressed God's Sovereign Will, he is banished far away from the Kingdom of Heaven.

Book Six demonstrates the inherent futility of transgressing God's Eternal Word. Herein we witness how the Devil has succumbed to the powerful force of temptation, and caused chaos and disaster in the Kingdom of Heaven. We must not think that we are immune from the allure of temptation. We must not permit our ego and pride to make us oblivious to our surrounding reality.

Book Six presents the reader with a pressing and important question to reflect upon: As servants of God, are we doing everything within our power to advance the Cause of Truth? Temptation is a formidable foe. Temptation keeps us tied and bound to a life of servitude to the flesh. It is within the inherent capacity of our spirit, to advance the just and noble Cause of Truth.

'To stand approved in sight of God, though worlds judged thee perverse. The easier conquest now remains thee. Aided by this host of friends. Back on thy foes, more glorious to return.'[93]

God's approval and vindication is our greatest victory, accomplishment, and success. In all that we do during our lifetime on Earth, we must act with care and concern, that we are righteous, noble, and honourable in our thoughts, speech, and conduct. Our Final Judgement is before God. We cannot conceal our thoughts, ideas, representations, doctrines, principles, motivations, intentions, actions, and speech from God. God is the Searcher of Hearts and Keeper of Souls. Therefore, we must earnestly strive to conquer the Self. We must strive to create the best version of ourselves, in order that at the fulfilment of our lifetime, we secure the only approval that truly mattered—God's just and righteous approval.

---

93 Milton, John. (Darbishire, Helen, Ed.) (1958). *The Poetical Works of John Milton*. London: Oxford University Press, p. 125.

'Right reason for their law, and for their King Messiah, who by right of merit reigns. Go Michael of celestial army's prince, and thou in military prowess next Gabriel. Lead forth to battle these my Sons, invincible. Lead forth my armed Saints. By thousands and by millions ranged for fight. Equal in number to that Godless crew rebellious. Them with fire and hostile arms, fearless assault, and to the brow of Heaven pursuing, drive them out from God and bliss. Into their place of punishment, the Gulf of Tartarus, which ready opens wide. His fiery chaos to receive their fall.'[94]

It is important to underscore that King *Messiah* rules by the virtue of merit, and not by the attributes of birth right, nobility, privilege, education, social status, royalty, private property, private wealth, parentage, social class, education, gender, colour, sex, race, heritage, ethnicity, creed, or any other distinguishing factor. This is an invaluable point to appreciate. One that cannot be overemphasised for the immediate purposes of our investigation.

For we too have the unprecedented opportunity to gain merit in our lifetime. We too can accrue merit through our actions, speech, thoughts, and remembrance of God. This protracted battle between good and evil is constantly in motion in the Universe. But the end result is certain. The victory belongs to the *Messiah*. The glory and honour of this epic battle between good and evil belongs to God. No matter the struggle, privation, grief, heartache, trauma, suffering, pain, and loss that we endure along our life journey, the end result of the triumph of good over evil is certain.

---

94 Milton, John. (Darbishire, Helen, Ed.) (1958). *The Poetical Works of John Milton*. London: Oxford University Press, p. 125.

'O Heaven! That such resemblance of the Highest should yet remain, where faith and reality remain not. Wherefore should not strength and might there fail where virtue fails, or weakest prove, where boldest: though to sight unconquerable? His puissance, trusting in the Almighty's aid, I mean to try, whose reason I have tried, unsound and false; nor is it aught but just.'[95]

Humanity only accomplishes so much by the application of will-power, exertion of personal effort, employment of initiative, application of intellect, accumulation of personal experience, and formal learning of empirical knowledge. In all things, God is Supreme, Sovereign, and Sagacious. Our faith in God is the foundation stone of our life. In addition to the centrality of faith, we must supplement our life narrative with our willpower, personal effort, initiative, natural reason, lived experience, and empirical knowledge.

The case in point is that God must always be at the core of our life. No matter the life stage, exigent situation, or perilous circumstance that we find ourselves in, God always comes first. Our individual attributes and personal qualities are positioned at the periphery of our identity and lived experience. Our reason fails us, but our faith succeeds.

---

95 Milton, John. (Darbishire, Helen, Ed.) (1958). *The Poetical Works of John Milton*. London: Oxford University Press, p. 127.

'To whom in brief thus Abdiel stern replied. Apostate! Still, thou errest. Nor end will find of erring. From the Path of Truth remote. Unjustly thou depravest it with the name of servitude to serve whom God ordains, or nature. God and nature bid the same. When he who rules is worthiest, and excels them whom he governs. This is servitude.'[96]

Attempt as we may to discern, divide, delineate, depict, dissect, deduce, and define the Path of Truth as distinct from God, this secular endeavour is not feasible. God is inextricably linked to Truth. The positive correlation between God and Truth is certain. Truth is God. God is Truth. It is a blessing of a lifetime to serve and advance God's Kingdom on Earth, regardless of our social status, vocation, or personal contribution.

In the fullness of time, we shall witness the LORD's Prayer come to fruition on Earth, 'Our Father in Heaven, hallowed be Your Name. Your Kingdom come, Your Will be done, on Earth as it is in Heaven.'[97] It is a great blessing to further the just and noble cause of advancing God's Sovereign Kingdom on Earth.

---

96 Milton, John. (Darbishire, Helen, Ed.) (1958). *The Poetical Works of John Milton*. London: Oxford University Press, p. 128.

97 The Holy Bible (ESV). (2016). The Gospel of Matthew. Chapter 6, Verses 9–10.

'As each divided legion might have seemed a numerous host. In strength each armed hand a legion led in fight. Yet, leader seemed each warrior single as in chief. Expert when to advance, or stand, or turn the sway of battle, open when, and when to close the ridges of grim war. No thought of flight. None of retreat. No unbecoming deed that argued fear. Each on himself relied. As only in his arm the moment lay of victory. Deeds of eternal fame.'[98]

During our momentary lifetime, as we run our race, we confront significant adversities, tests, challenges, obstacles, issues, and problems. This is an inevitable fact of life. We cannot live our life without the presence of opposition, setback, loss, grief, pain, suffering, trauma, heartache, and resistance. The key to our success is to fight the good fight of faith. We have a monumental decision to determine: Which side of the grand battle of good and evil do we fight on? In following our moral conscience and exercising our morality, we must ensure that the major battles in our life are for the advancement of good.

Our voluntary and conscious actions must transcend the temptation to pursue evil. Our conquests are only heroic and noble, if our deeds are performed for the betterment of humanity. When we overcome evil with good, there the Spirit of God dwells within us. Thereafter, we secure our final refuge in the Eternal House of the LORD. Therefore, we must not diminish this precious opportunity of a lifetime, by ignorantly partaking in the many sinful and trivial pleasures of the flesh. Inadequate pleasures of the flesh, which only endure for as long as we remain among the living.

God's Eternal Word reminds us of the fleeting nature of the countless pleasures of the flesh. Pleasures that on the surface, appear sublime and enticing to our present condition of being in

---

98 Milton, John. (Darbishire, Helen, Ed.) (1958). *The Poetical Works of John Milton*. London: Oxford University Press, p. 130.

the world. Within the Holy Bible, in the Book of Ecclesiastes, we are reminded of the vanity of sin, 'I said in my heart, "Come now, I will test you with pleasure; enjoy yourself." But behold, this was also vanity. I said of laughter, "It is mad," and of pleasure, "What use is it?" I searched with my heart how to cheer my body with wine—my heart still guiding me with wisdom—and how to lay hold on folly, till I might see what was good for the children of man to do under Heaven during the few days of their life. I made great works. I built houses and planted vineyards for myself. I made myself gardens and parks, and planted in them all kinds of fruit trees. I made myself pools from which to water the forest of growing trees.'[99]

The aforementioned Biblical narrative continues, further narrating the shallow depth of desire. These verses of scripture inform us of the inability of pleasure to grant us lasting peace, joy, and happiness, 'I bought male and female slaves, and had slaves who were born in my house. I had also great possessions of herds and flocks, more than any who had been before me in Jerusalem. I also gathered for myself silver and gold and the treasure of kings and provinces. I got singers, both men and women, and many concubines, the delight of the sons of man. So, I became great and surpassed all who were before me in Jerusalem. Also, my wisdom remained with me. And whatever my eyes desired I did not keep from them. I kept my heart from no pleasure, for my heart found pleasure in all my toil, and this was my reward for all my toil. Then I considered all that my hands had done and the toil I had expended in doing it, and behold, all was vanity and a striving after wind, and there was nothing to be gained under the Sun.'[100]

The aforementioned Biblical text is a remarkably profound passage of scripture. If understood correctly, we ascertain the

---

99 The Holy Bible (ESV). (2016). The Book of Ecclesiastes. Chapter 2, Verses 1–6.
100 The Holy Bible (ESV). (2016). The Book of Ecclesiastes. Chapter 2, Verses 7–11.

vanity of all our striving on Earth. In the end, no matter how far we traverse the Earth, how much personal experience or empirical knowledge we accumulate, how much pleasure we indulge our five senses in, how much private wealth we secure, how much profit we have amassed, or how much real property we secure a legal or equitable interest in, all these transitory phenomena only provision us with short-term gratification. Such phenomena never grant us a lasting and immovable peace. The satisfaction of desire is never sufficient, period.

No matter the monetary value of our financial capital, there remains the ambition, determination, and desire to secure evermore private wealth, private property, and profit. The shallowness of our pursuit of pleasure, prestige, political power, private property, profit, private wealth, and pecuniary gain is revealed to all of us, at the exact time of our death. In the world, the things that seem desirable to obtain, only serve to obstruct our spiritual progress.

'Liken on Earth conspicuous, that may lift human imagination to such height of God-like power. For likest Gods they seemed. Stood they or moved, in stature, motion, arms fit to decide the Empire of Great Heaven. Now waved their fiery swords, and in the air made horrid circles.'[101]

Human imagination is truly endless. More importantly, the true source of human imagination is God's Creative Nature. In fact, all human power, skill, positive attributes, understanding, knowledge, natural reason, ability, and talent are received by God's dispensation of grace. Thus, we have an obligation to utilise God's immeasurable gifts to advance God's Sovereign Kingdom on Earth. We ought to employ our skills, abilities, expertise,

---

101 Milton, John. (Darbishire, Helen, Ed.) (1958). *The Poetical Works of John Milton.* London: Oxford University Press, pp. 131–132.

knowledge, experience, and talents to defeat the presence of evil in all regions across the world.

The epic battle between good and evil is no convenient endeavour. This is a protracted and enduring battle. A formidable contest, in which to secure a lasting victory we are required to perform acts of courage, perseverance, integrity, love, worship, petition, intercession, cooperation, compassion, tolerance, community service, mercy, prayer, sincerity, commitment, temperance, forgiveness, and social justice.

The Biblical narrative of Paul the Apostle in the New Testament is a remarkable story of the good fight of faith. Paul was a learned gentleman of faith. Paul was also a Roman citizen. Paul confronted unfounded accusations, trials, shipwrecks, imprisonment, inhuman punishment, solitary confinement, and torture on his remarkable journey of Discipleship throughout the Roman World. Above all, Paul's conscience was sincere and his heart was pure. For Paul's Conversion on the Road to Damascus transformed him into a beloved Disciple of God. Until the very last moment of Paul's life, he remained steadfast in his belief in God. Paul's exemplary service, as a servant of the Most High God, to bring God honour and glory, secured him the 'Crown of Righteousness' for all time.[102]

---

102 The Holy Bible (ESV). (2016). Book of Second Timothy. Chapter 4, Verse 8.

'In might or swift prevention; but the sword of Michael from the Armour of God was given him tempered so. That neither keen, nor solid might resist that edge. It met the sword of Satan with steep force to smite. Descending, and in half cut sheer, nor stayed, but with swift wheel reverse, deep entering sheared, all his right side. Then Satan first knew pain.'[103]

The spiritual war between good and evil is fought between Angels and Demons. As a result, human casualties of this time immemorial war are inevitable. Most importantly, Satan does not escape the consequences of his despicable record of countless evil deeds. Indeed, Satan experiences trauma, pain, suffering, harm, misery, grief, tragedy, and loss, for the evil that he has brought into the world.

Satan continues to wreak havoc upon God's newest Creation. No person escapes the operation of the universal moral law, 'you reap what you sow.' Clearly, in this epic spiritual battle between the supreme forces of good and evil, Saint Michael has the moral high ground. Whereas, Satan ignorantly continues unabated, in his evil quest to promote destruction, disaster, depression, and death on Earth.

Satan relinquished the priceless Blessing of God, in exchange to receive an inferior place in the demonic dungeon of Hell. The Kingdom of Heaven lost and eternal damnation gained. By any standard of measurement, a most meritless exchange. During our evanescent lifetime on Earth, we are tempted by the presence of sin, pleasure, and evil. No doubt, the presence of sin, pleasure, and evil, promise us much, however, we must not forget they are full of empty promises.

The strong allure of sin, pleasure, and evil is only found upon their surface. It is the superficial and outward appeal of sin,

---

103 Milton, John. (Darbishire, Helen, Ed.) (1958). *The Poetical Works of John Milton.* London: Oxford University Press, p. 132.

pleasure, and evil, that captivates our flesh. The enlightened mind perceives through all the seductive forms of temptation, in order to ascertain the true substance of sin. In all cases, the pursuit of sin is an inferior exchange, an exchange that costs us our priceless soul.

'Eternise here on Earth; but those elect Angels contented with their fame in Heaven seek not the praise of men. The other sort, in might though wondrous and in acts of war. Nor of renown less eager. Yet by doom cancelled from Heaven and sacred memory. Nameless in dark oblivion let them dwell. For strength from Truth divided and from just, illaudable, naught merits but dispraise and ignominy. Yet to glory aspires vain glorious, and through infamy seeks fame.'[104]

The praise of humanity is superficial, fleeting, transitory, and inconsequential. The actions that we perform in our life, we must not perform them with the underlying motive and primary intention to secure the fame, love, approval, validation, glory, admiration, and respect of the countless people of the world. Rather, we ought to perform our deeds with the intention that our conduct secures God's approval and validation in the eternal and timeless Kingdom of Heaven. For if we are proven righteous in God's Sovereign Court, we have truly secured a victory that is beyond this world. A victory that is beyond all time, space, matter, energy, and force. A victory that is of lasting significance and indescribable consequence.

---

104 Milton, John. (Darbishire, Helen, Ed.) (1958). *The Poetical Works of John Milton*. London: Oxford University Press, p. 133.

'Then first with fear surprised and sense of pain fled ignominious. To such evil brought by sin of disobedience. Till that hour not liable to fear, or flight, or pain. Far otherwise, the inviolable Saints.'[105]

As long as we remain in the flesh, there is the incidence of loss, grief, pain, remorse, trauma, heartache, and suffering. Beyond doubt this is a broken world. A world that is marred by sin, guilt, punishment, pain, suffering, damnation, depression, suicide, and death. We must not live our lives in ignorance. We ought to dispel the darkness in the world with the unchanging Truth of God's Eternal Word. In formulating our thoughts, beliefs, ideas, values, doctrines, and principles, we must look to the remarkable lives of the Saints of Old that have established the true precedent on how to live an honourable and noble life in the world. For example, consider Saint John of the Cross, Saint Teresa of Ávila, Saint Thomas Aquinas, Saint Catherine of Siena, Saint Augustine of Hippo, and Saint Thérèse of Lisieux.

The phenomenon of fear is a major hindrance to living a productive, ambitious, wholesome, and good life. The unwelcome presence of fear prevents us from reaching our inherent potential. We must be conscious of fear and its ability to paralyse our life. We must not permit fear refuge in our mind. If we examine our conscious mind very carefully, we realise that often it is the fear of failure, as opposed to failure itself, that prevents us from achieving substantial progress in our life. But herein resides the paradox. If we fear to fail, then we have already failed in our endeavour, as we have not braved the attempt.

Failure in and of itself is not a cause for concern. The [undesirable] outcome of failure is [undeniably] part and parcel of human life. The outcome of failure creates the opportunity

---

105 Milton, John. (Darbishire, Helen, Ed.) (1958). *The Poetical Works of John Milton*. London: Oxford University Press, p. 134.

for learning, reflection, and iteration. When we fail in our endeavours, we must focus on the process and not the outcome.

On the contrary, the fear of failure is true failure. For the fear of failure equates to total surrender in our attempt to accomplish what we desire and set our mind to. Thus, where there is the fear of failure, there we find the certainty of our defeat. In the final analysis, failure is part of the process characterised by learning and iteration. On the condition that we learn from our mistakes, and we do not make the same mistakes again, we are assured that we have made real progress. No quantum of progress is inconsequential.

Over the constant passage of time, progress accumulates to the inflection point, where the probability of success becomes more likely than the outcome of failure. In all things, it is the combination of persistence, discipline, patience, belief, confidence, hope, love, dedication, commitment, faith, and consistency that result in a turnaround in our endeavours.

'Of mightiest, sense of pleasure we may well. Spare out of life perhaps, and not repine, but live content, which is the calmest life. But pain is perfect misery, the worst of evils, and excessive, overturns all patience.'[106]

Our five senses seek the endless pleasures and limitless comforts of this transient world. Even if we secure pleasure, private wealth, private property, empirical knowledge, and the material comforts of this world, it is difficult to live a content life. Content with who one is. Content with what one has achieved. Content with one's material possessions, private property, personal income, intangible assets, and private wealth. Content with one's spouse. Content with one's children. Content with one's education.

---

106 Milton, John. (Darbishire, Helen, Ed.) (1958). *The Poetical Works of John Milton*. London: Oxford University Press, p. 135.

Content with one's illustrious career. Ultimately, content with what life has to offer us.

The state of contentment grants us a profound equanimity of mind. Yet, what is so desirable, is also incredibly challenging to secure. We cannot secure everything that our heart desires in the world. There are the well-known constraints of financial capital, time, energy, the finite human lifespan, empirical knowledge, formal education, physical health, soundness of mind, and the limitation of our lived experience. Not to mention, the incidence of arbitrary factors in our life, such as the twists and turns of fortune, the operation of fate, the master stroke of destiny, and the unpredictable force of luck. It is a valid proposition to assert, that such determinants perform an inordinate role in our life.

In every person's lifetime, significant choices, monumental decisions, consequential trade-offs, and important selections have to be made along the journey. It is a sign of maturity, when a person makes their own significant life decisions. We do not always determine the best decisions, however, the opposite scenario, indecisiveness is a major obstacle to navigating the defining moments and difficult conversations that life presents us with. While the journey of life cannot be traversed without pain, pain is overcome by the instruments of faith, prayer, love, petition, intercession, belief, and hope.

In all cases, indecision is the worst possible course of action. Indecision denies us the opportunity to live and experience the fullness of life. Indecision destroys human potential. If understood correctly, there is an immense opportunity cost associated with inaction. From time to time, we self-determine unfavourable decisions and inferior choices, but it was our inherent ability to have made that very decision or choice, which affirmed our exercise of personal agency, to have lived our life on our terms. Without the exercise of personal agency, no matter how inexact and fraught with errors, there is no true experience of human life.

*'Two days are therefore past. The third is thine. For thee,
I have ordained it, and thus far have suffered, that the glory
may be thine of ending this Great War. Since none but
thou can end it. Into thee such virtue and grace immense
I have transfused. That all may know in Heaven and Hell,
thy power above compare, and this perverse commotion
governed thus, to manifest thee worthiest to be heir of
all things. To be heir and to be king by sacred unction.
Thy deserved right.'*[107]

The Son of God secured the decisive victory in the grand spiritual battle between good and evil. This defining moment in world history was possible because God ordained the terminal result of this epic conflict. It was concordant with God's Sovereign Will, that the *Messiah* defeat and conquer Satan. By God's Grace, Favour, Blessing, and Mercy, we defeat evil with good. The Son of God has established a distinguished and matchless example of how to live an honourable life. A life that is characterised by faith, integrity, mercy, social justice, benevolence, compassion, work, forgiveness, love, family, charity, equality, and respect.

Every person has a moral duty and obligation to follow their conscience, to exercise their natural morality, and to live a virtuous life on Earth. For in the performance of righteous and proper actions, our character is defined and refined. Thereafter, our soul reaps an immense reward, as the rightful beneficiary of our deeds. A reward that does not diminish in its value with the passage of time, but rather its true value, in the fullness of time, is affirmed to us in God's Sovereign Kingdom of Heaven.

---

107 Milton, John. (Darbishire, Helen, Ed.) (1958). *The Poetical Works of John Milton*. London: Oxford University Press, pp. 141–142.

CHAPTER 7

PARADISE LOST: BOOK SEVEN

*'Divine interpreter. By favour sent down from the Empyrean
to forewarn us timely of what might else have been our loss.
Unknown, which human knowledge could not reach.
For which to the infinitely good, we owe immortal thanks.
His admonishment receive with solemn purpose to observe
immutably His Sovereign Will. The end of what we are.'*

MILTON

BOOK SEVEN of *Paradise Lost* details Adam requesting Raphael
to inform him of how and why God created the world. Raphael
informs Adam of the Angel, Lucifer's repulsive rebellion against
God's Sovereign Will. Through Raphael and Adam's dialogue,
humanity understands how Lucifer was expelled from God's
Kingdom of Heaven. Furthermore, Adam learns that it was God's
Good Pleasure to create a new world with man and woman.
God's Unfathomable Work of Creation was done to manifest
God's Creative Power and express God's Glory.

Due to the Devil's malevolent actions, Adam and Eve were
tempted to transgress God's Eternal Word. Both of them fell short
and succumbed to the allure of temptation and the performance
of sin. As a consequence, humanity became corrupted by sin,

guilt, damnation, and death. To redeem the world of sin, God sends forth His Beloved Son. The *Messiah*, in his infinite mercy, compassion, love, benevolence, and humility, submits himself to God's Sovereign Will. To ensure the deliverance of God's Righteous Justice, the *Messiah* takes upon himself the divine punishment for humanity's redemption from Original Sin. In effect, the *Messiah* atones for the Fall of Man.

The Angels are in attendance to God's Eternal Word and Sovereign Command. The Angels sing lovely and beautiful hymns to honour, praise, and glorify God. The Angels also diligently attend to the Beloved Son's every request. The perfection of the Angels service in the Kingdom of Heaven gives us a glimpse of the beauty, splendour, bliss, elegance, and peace found within God's Heavenly Kingdom. We are resigned to conclude, that our present human condition requires considerable refinement and iteration, to prepare our soul for Heaven.

'Of things so high and strange. Things to their thought. So unimaginable as hate in Heaven, and war so near the Peace of God in bliss with such confusion. But the evil soon driven back, redounded as a flood on those from whom it sprung. Impossible to mix with blessedness. Whence Adam soon repealed the doubts that in his heart arose and now led on. Yet sinless, with desire to know.'[108]

The human condition is such, that from time to time our thoughts become chaotic, ambivalent, disorderly, and convoluted. During the times of distress, we ought to concentrate our mind on God's Presence, Word, Grace, Mercy, and Love. This divine thought, coupled with the righteous action of prayer never fails us.

As long as we are confined to the human condition, we are betwixt the spiritual forces of good and evil. The Devil always

---

108 Milton, John. (Darbishire, Helen, Ed.) (1958). *The Poetical Works of John Milton*. London: Oxford University Press, p. 149.

deceives humanity with sadness, frustration, envy, doubt, worry, anxiety, fear, apprehension, confusion, despair, anger, denial, jealousy, guilt, shame, depression, suicide, and death. The obligation is upon humanity to decide between a life of obedience or rebellion to God. The closer we bring ourselves to God, the lesser the opportunity for the Devil to infiltrate our thoughts and mislead our life.

'What words or tongue of Seraph can suffice, or heart of man suffice to comprehend? Yet what thou canst attain, which best may serve to glorify the Maker, and infer thee also happier, shall not be withheld thy hearing. Such commission from above I have received. To answer thy desire of knowledge within bounds. Beyond, abstain to ask. Nor let thine own inventions hope things not revealed, which the invisible King, only omniscient, hath suppressed in night. To none communicable in Earth or Heaven.'[109]

There are certain phenomena in the Universe, which are far beyond the capacity of our five senses to perceive. Not all of reality is communicated, experienced, perceived, or understood through empirical evidence obtained from our observation of the natural world. Nonetheless, we are certain of one thing, and that is: God created the Universe as an expression of God's Creative Power, Majestic Glory, and Absolute Sovereignty.

For our part, our actions ought to further God's Sovereign Kingdom on Earth. By doing so, we glorify the Maker, the Provider, and the Sustainer. In performing God's Work on Earth, we create a superior world. A world that is defined by compassion, love, mercy, charity, honesty, equality, integrity,

---

109 Milton, John. (Darbishire, Helen, Ed.) (1958). *The Poetical Works of John Milton.* London: Oxford University Press, p. 151.

community service, joy, benevolence, human dignity, tolerance, respect, social justice, forgiveness, and generosity.

In the final analysis, the endless and irrational pursuit of empirical knowledge, pleasure, private wealth, personal income, and private property cannot resolve all the difficulties pertaining to human life. Nor do these worldly pursuits embody the inherent capacity to grant us an everlasting peace of mind, endless joy, enduring equanimity, or lifelong contentment. There must be the acknowledgement that God has the Final Judgement, where knowledge, pleasure, wealth, and property cannot venture, nor forever stay.

No matter our vocation, education, knowledge, or lived experience, our life is defined by what we desire, what we seek, and what we value. When we have absolute clarity on our desires, objectives, and values, we are less likely to be distracted and unfocused. The ideal vision of a good life cannot be lived without clarity of purpose, adherence to moral principles, and awareness of one's personal values.

The greatest blessings and treasures in life are joy, peace, faith, love, friendship, wisdom, and hope. It is interesting, but not surprising to acknowledge, that all of these phenomena share one common attribute—they are non-material in nature. This is important to appreciate for an array of reasons. First, we too can secure our happiness, even if we have little in valuable material possessions, private property, private wealth, prestige, personal income, or fame. Second, these invaluable blessings and treasures of joy, peace, faith, love, friendship, wisdom, and hope, are available to every person, regardless of an individual's gender, race, sex, colour, occupation, nationality, age, education, vocation, marital status, religious denomination, or any other distinguishing factor.

'But knowledge is as food, and needs no less her temperance over appetite. To know in measure what the mind may well contain, oppresses else with surfeit, and soon turns wisdom to folly. As nourishment to wind.'[110]

The pursuit of learning and knowledge is a good ambition. Knowledge assists humanity to enhance its understanding of the natural world. The acquisition of knowledge is also a fundamental process concerning the proper development of the individual within civil society and the nation-state. Nevertheless, we must appreciate that empirical knowledge is only secured within and through the capacity of our five senses. Knowledge serves practical and theoretical purposes. Any attempt to utilise knowledge to understand matters of faith, or to affirm our belief in God's Existence is of no utility whatsoever. True wisdom resides in our conscious awareness of the real limitations associated with empirical knowledge.

Worldly knowledge has the powerful capacity to resolve many of our immediate and pressing problems. For example, consider the following global problems: Improve public health outcomes. Enhance the physical and psychological well-being of the individual. The elimination of child labour. The protection of civilians during armed conflict. Universal school education for children. Affordable housing. Stable employment. Challenges confronting Indigenous peoples. Food security. Eradication of poverty. Water scarcity. Deforestation. Economic inequality. Last but not least, improved life expectancy.

Notwithstanding the benefits of knowledge, our possession of knowledge cannot solve the inward spiritual poverty of humankind. Not to mention, knowledge cannot grant us peace for a single day on Earth. In the final analysis, the security we have found in knowledge, does not position us for an existential

---

110 Milton, John. (Darbishire, Helen, Ed.) (1958). *The Poetical Works of John Milton.* London: Oxford University Press, p. 151.

reality without mortality on Earth. However, with the proper application of knowledge, we define our lived experience as pleasant, peaceful, prosperous, and productive.

> *'Boundless the deep, because I am who fill infinitude, nor vacuous the space. Though I uncircumscribed myself, retire, and put not forth my goodness. Which is free to act or not. Necessity and chance approach not me, and what I will is fate. So spoke the Almighty, and to what He spoke, His Word, the Filial Godhead, gave effect. Immediate are the Acts of God, more swift than time or motion. But to human ears, cannot without process of speech be told.'*[111]

Humanity attempts to reason or understand God's Thoughts, Ideas, Endeavours, and Actions, however, this supreme endeavour is in vain. God is the unrivalled and unequalled Creator. God embodies an indescribable and inexplicable appreciation of Creation. God possesses an awareness of all phenomena within Creation. God's Sovereign Act of Creation cannot be fathomed by the finite knowledge and research methods of reasoning found within clinical science, theology, philosophy, law, medicine, mathematics, history, natural science, and psychology. Human knowledge is incapable of observing, learning, and examining the Creator.

We must accept that there are certain phenomena in the world, which we cannot change or comprehend. We may ask why countless times, but metaphysical questions such as: Is there life after death? Do we embody a soul? Does God exist? Did we exist before we were born? The subjective answer to these perennial questions and many more like them, is merely bound up in our beliefs, traditions, lived experience, heritage, language, customs, religion, and ideologies. Based on one's partial perspective of

---

111 Milton, John. (Darbishire, Helen, Ed.) (1958). *The Poetical Works of John Milton*. London: Oxford University Press, p. 152.

reality, this either constitutes a blessing or curse of the common fate of human civilisation. In the final analysis, to know what we shall never know, this is impossible.

> *'And worship God supreme, who made Him chief of all His works. Therefore, the Omnipotent Eternal Father (For where is not He present?), thus, to His Son audibly spoke. Let us make now man in our image. Man in our similitude, and let them rule over the fish and fowl of sea and air, beast of the field, and over all the Earth, and every creeping thing that creeps the ground. This said, He formed thee, Adam, thee, O man, dust of the ground, and in thy nostrils breathed the breath of life. In His own image, He created thee. In the Image of God, express, and thou became a living soul.'*[112]

During our lifetime on Earth, we can express our love, gratitude, commitment, and devotion to God in numerous ways. For example, consider the act of worship, confession, fellowship, community service, charity, petition, intercession, prayer, and thanksgiving. God has given humanity dominion over the Earth to further God's Eternal Kingdom. Ultimately, everything in and of the world belongs to God.

On Earth, we do not own anything in perpetuity. We merely have temporal possession of all material phenomena that we consider our personal and real property. We are only temporary stewards on Earth. Human civilisation is entrusted with God's resources for a brief period of time. As stewards of God's resources, we have an obligation to ensure that we effectively utilise what God has given to us. How we utilise our God-given gifts, including our talents, resources, intelligence, expertise, inheritance, knowledge, private wealth, assets, personal income,

---

112 Milton, John. (Darbishire, Helen, Ed.) (1958). *The Poetical Works of John Milton.* London: Oxford University Press, p. 161.

status, position, education, influence, political power, and abilities determines our destiny.

> *'This garden, planted with the trees of God. Delectable both to behold and taste; and freely all their pleasant fruit for food gave thee. All sorts are here that all the Earth yields. Variety without end. But of the Tree, which tasted works of knowledge of good and evil, thou mayest not. In the day thou eatest, thou diest. Death is the penalty imposed. Beware, and govern well thy appetite. Least sin surprise thee, and her black attendant—death.'*[113]

God gave Adam and Eve explicit sovereign commands on how to live a good and honourable life in the Garden of Eden. Literally, Adam and Eve had it all in Paradise. In the Garden of Eden, life could not have been improved, enhanced, or refined. Human life in Paradise was perfect. In the quintessential Garden of Eden, God left intact the free will of Adam and Eve, to act as they determined and wished. This God-given gift of free will, includes the unrestrained ability to freely transgress God's Sovereign Command. For otherwise, free will is not wholly and truly free. For our love and obedience to hold any real value or merit, it must be voluntarily given to God.

Unfortunately, Adam and Eve yielded to the power of temptation and engaged in sinful conduct. Adam and Eve self-determined to venture down the immoral path of sin. They knowingly and willingly transgressed God's Sovereign Command. We can all deduce a moral lesson from this all-too-human experience of Adam and Eve in the Garden of Eden. Often times, we think that we know better. We perceive that we know what is best for our life, even though our finite capacity for natural reason unequivocally contradicts God's Sovereign

---

113 Milton, John. (Darbishire, Helen, Ed.) (1958). *The Poetical Works of John Milton*. London: Oxford University Press, pp. 161–162.

Command. We prematurely exercise our personal agency, in a manner that appears thoughtful and righteous to us, however, ultimately results in our fall from grace.

Sometimes, it is only with the formative power of hindsight, that we perceive the dreaded realisation, that our exercise of natural reason was misplaced. That is to say, the employment of our personal agency was misappropriated. That our initial assessment of a situation, event, or circumstance, turned out to be an incomplete representation of fact. The longer we live life, the more personal experiences we encounter. Therefore, logically it follows, the greater is our accumulation of experiential learning and secular knowledge. In the end, having learnt, realised, and experienced the fullness of life, we come to the [inevitable] realisation of the frailty associated with human judgement and understanding.

Despite our best intentions, it is an unfortunate fact of our being, an undeniable reality of our existence, that from time to time we do not always make the best decisions in our life. No person surpasses the Almighty Creator in thought, speech, and conduct. In all cases, proper understanding and practical insight into God's Eternal Word supports our judgement.

In times of uncertainty, doubt, or confusion, we must always rely upon God's Eternal Word for wise counsel. God always forewarns us how to act, and equally, how not to act. Therefore, it logically and rationally follows, that where God's Eternal Word has been violated, then the undesirable consequences of our immoral actions are unavoidable, as they are undeniable.

'Great are thy works, Jehovah! Infinite thy power! What thought can measure thee, or tongue relate thee! Greater now, in thy return than from the giant Angels. Thee that day, thy thunders magnified. But to create is greater than created to destroy. Who can impair thee, Mighty King, or bound thy empire? Easily the proud attempt of spirits apostate, and their counsels vain. Thou hast repelled. While impiously they thought thee to diminish, and from thee withdraw, the number of thy worshippers. Who seeks to lessen thee, against his purpose serves to manifest the more thy might. His evil thou usest, and from thence createst more good.'[114]

God's Superior Thoughts, Incomparable Deeds, Unexplainable Miracles, Unmatched Power, Creative Works, and Majestic Vision cannot be understood by the finite intelligence of humanity. After all, how can the created understand the Creator? God's Divine Acts are far greater than the finite capacity of human reason to logically express, mathematically calculate, or scientifically explain them.

Regardless, God's Divine Acts be communicated or expressed in any language, medium, or format, we are not able to wholly and truly decipher their profound meaning. In order for God's Providence to function in our life, we must demonstrate belief, trust, hope, confidence, and love. We cannot doubt God's Eternal Word, and concurrently expect the fruits of God's Plan to materialise in our life. The litmus test of our faith is to believe, when we do not witness any results.

For our part, we ought to concentrate our time, energy, endeavours, and resources to further the cause of good in the world. We can all be a positive force for global change. A force that reforms and transforms the world into a social, political,

---

114 Milton, John. (Darbishire, Helen, Ed.) (1958). *The Poetical Works of John Milton*. London: Oxford University Press, p. 163.

legal, and economic construct that is superior than its present condition. Our lifetime on Earth is not without end. Therefore, we must act now, in order to create the desired future of our tomorrow.

It is through the unrivalled power of initiative and action, that the immeasurable value of our life is always won or lost in the present moment. The past and future are non-existent states. Reality is what is existent in the here and now. The reality of our life always commences with the reality of our being. Through making the most of the present time, we focus on creating our desired reality of becoming. So that one day, we become all that we were destined to be.

CHAPTER 8

PARADISE LOST: BOOK EIGHT

'Thy words. Creator bounteous and benign.
Giver of all things fair. But fairest this of all thy gifts,
nor enviest. I now see bone of my bone.
Flesh of my flesh. My self before me. Woman is her name,
of man extracted. For this cause, he shall forgo father
and mother, and to his wife adhere.
They shall be one flesh. One heart. One soul.'

MILTON

BOOK EIGHT of *Paradise Lost* narrates Adam's prolonged discourse with Raphael. Adam constantly seeks to further the boundaries of human knowledge. Adam desires to learn more about the Universe, God's Creation, and the Celestial Motions. Raphael counsels Adam to inquire of knowledge that concerns phenomena which is pertinent and tangible to human life.

In spite of Raphael's good advice, Adam continues with his thoughtful inquiries, many of which concern the difficult questions of existentialism. Raphael and Adam continue to engage in their profound theological and philosophical discourse. Among other things, these two influential figures discuss God's Work concerning Creation and the Garden of Eden. Adam also inquires as to whether the individual is best placed to live a solitary life, or integrate in the midst of society.

> *'To ask or search, I blame thee not. For Heaven is as the Book of God before thee set. Wherein, to read His wondrous works, and learn His seasons, hours, or days, or months, or years. This to attain, whether Heaven move or Earth, imports not. If thou reckon right; the rest from man or Angel the Great Architect did wisely to conceal, and not divulge His secrets. To be scanned by them who ought rather to admire.'*[115]

It is within the inherent disposition of human nature, to desire the attainment of ever greater worldly knowledge. Human intelligence seeks not only to observe, but also to understand the functions and processes of the natural world around us. We seek to learn about life. We seek to mature from our many personal experiences. Yet, above all, we seek wisdom.

Having said that, we must appreciate that there are select metaphysical questions surrounding reality, that are forever beyond the finite capacity of the human intellect to resolve with the finite instrument of natural reason. For example, consider we cannot come to know God's Secrets, Doctrines, Concepts, and Divine Plans. We can estimate, and we can approximate God's Providence, but we cannot foreknow it. Therefore, we must concentrate our talents, gifts, abilities, expertise, imagination, intuition, and curiosity on resolving the countless challenges and pressing problems of the modern world.

In the twenty-first century, there is present an urgency to address international challenges across the globe. Some of these worldwide challenges include: poverty, food and water insecurity,

---

115 Milton, John. (Darbishire, Helen, Ed.) (1958). *The Poetical Works of John Milton.* London: Oxford University Press, pp. 166–167.

nuclear proliferation, deforestation, terrorism, civil war, ethnic conflicts, the economic development of third world countries, rising sea levels, the melting of glaciers, the spread of infectious diseases, child asylum seekers, and preventing the increased incidence of non-communicable diseases.

In order to successfully resolve the aforementioned global issues, humanity needs to transcend the artificial barriers of division that prevent international cooperation. Barriers such as race, religion, private wealth, nationality, indigeneity, poverty, economic inequality, education, and national debt. When we realise that without an inhabitable planet Earth, none of us will exist, our trivial tribal identities shall give way to the oneness of humanity.

Equally, at the domestic level, within the sovereign nation-state, there are a multitude of problems confronting civil society. For example, consider the well-known issues of domestic violence, alcohol and drug abuse, illicit substance abuse, political corruption, the over-representation of Indigenous people in the criminal justice system, cyberbullying, suicide, obesity, income inequality, housing affordability, crime, unemployment, homelessness, self-medication, access to justice, poverty, and socio-economic disadvantage.

In all the things that we do, we must act with a sense of righteousness, purpose, and duty towards our fellow citizens. A better society starts with how we treat each other. A better society starts with love, dignity, understanding, compassion, empathy, and respect. If every person treats another person, as they would like to be treated, then many of the political, social, medical, economic, moral, and legal problems of modern society are resolved.

'To the terrestrial moon, be as a star, enlightening her by day, as she by night. This Earth? Reciprocal, if land be there. Fields and inhabitants. Her spots thou seest as clouds, and clouds may rain, and rain produce fruits in her softened soil. For some to eat allotted there; and other suns perhaps. With their attendant moons, thou will descry, communicating male and female light. Which two great sexes animate the world.'[116]

We must live our life to further the honourable and noble cause of peace, security, love, prosperity, happiness, joy, social justice, mercy, forgiveness, benevolence, respect, human dignity, and harmony on Earth. Man and woman ought to live in union with each other. God created the two sexes—male and female. God created man and woman to equally complement one another. The power of two is always greater than the power of one. With man and woman coming together, through the sacred institution of marriage, humanity progresses considerably further than the individual capacity of either sex.

We must overcome the ever-present temptation to concentrate on the imperfections of the male and female sex. We must look to harness the unique abilities, expertise, knowledge, life experience, talents, education, and skills of every person, regardless of their sex. Often times, practical wisdom resides in setting aside the points of difference and promoting cooperation in areas of mutual agreement. Such an approach to our relationships fosters mutual trust, love, respect, and confidence.

In our relationships, we must expand common ground and compartmentalise issues that constitute a sticking point. The instruments of active listening, respect, tolerance, compassion, unconditional love, understanding, and empathy work wonders to foster trust, intimacy, affection, and confidence. These

---

116 Milton, John. (Darbishire, Helen, Ed.) (1958). *The Poetical Works of John Milton.* London: Oxford University Press, pp. 168–169.

instruments assist us to create healthy, harmonious, and happy relationships. Wherever possible, the two sexes must build bridges to form social connections over the minor differences that separate us. When it comes to the art of nurturing good relationships, pragmatism is the philosophy of choice.

'Solicit not thy thoughts with matters hid. Leave them to God above. Him serve and fear. Of other creatures, as Him pleases best, wherever placed, let Him dispose. Joy thou in what He gives to thee. This Paradise and thy fair Eve. Heaven is for thee, too high to know, what passes there. Be lowly wise. Think only what concerns thee and thy being. Dream not of other worlds. What creatures there live. In what state, condition, or degree. Contented, that thus far hath been revealed.'[117]

The human condition is such, that we constantly desire to know. We desire to inquire. We desire to learn. Our desire for knowledge is without end. Such is the unfathomable power of the human imagination, curiosity, mind, and spirit. Nonetheless, God's Thoughts are inaccessible to humanity. We cannot venture where we have no authority.

In any case, we have sufficient pressing social, moral, political, ethical, and economic problems to contend with during our lifetime on Earth. It is a more constructive and productive use of our time, to address the more immediate and pressing matters found within civil society and the nation-state. Matters that are within our personal agency and intellectual capacity to resolve. To concern ourselves with metaphysical questions, that are forever beyond our knowledge and experience is an unproductive endeavour.

---

117 Milton, John. (Darbishire, Helen, Ed.) (1958). *The Poetical Works of John Milton.* London: Oxford University Press, p. 169.

'To whom thus Adam, cleared of doubt, replied. How fully hast thou satisfied me. Pure intelligence of Heaven. Angel serene, and freed from intricacies. Taught to live the easiest way. Nor with perplexing thoughts to interrupt the sweet of life. From which God hath bid dwell far off all anxious cares, and not molest us. Unless we ourselves, seek them with wandering thoughts, and notions vain. But apt the mind or fancy is to rove unchecked, and of her roving is no end. Till warned, or by experience taught. She learns, that not to know at large of things remote from use, obscure and subtle. But to know, that which before us lies in daily life, this is the prime wisdom. What is more, is fume, or emptiness, or fond impertinence, and renders us in things that more concern unpracticed, unprepared, and still to seek. Therefore, from this high pitch let us descend. A lower flight, and speak of things at hand.'[118]

All philosophy is inherently subjective in its content and subject matter. Each person's philosophy is influenced by the forces of language, lived experience, knowledge, thought, culture, politics, history, geography, identity, sex, gender, parentage, childhood, ethnicity, race, heritage, nationhood, and religion. Philosophy is a social construct. In the final analysis, we cannot claim to have made any real or substantial progress on the timeless metaphysical questions through the study of philosophy.

The solution to living a good life is the application of practical wisdom. We ought to direct our mind towards addressing the cares, challenges, and concerns that are present in our life. The power of our mind ought to be employed for real and practical endeavours, rather than purely speculative and theoretical endeavours. If each and every person in the world concerns their

---

118 Milton, John. (Darbishire, Helen, Ed.) (1958). *The Poetical Works of John Milton.* London: Oxford University Press, pp. 169–170.

life with resolving the challenges and problems confronting society and state, then we re-create the Garden of Eden on Earth.

> *'But who I was, or where, or from what cause, I knew not. To speak, I tried, and forthwith spoke. My tongue obeyed and readily could name whatever I saw. Thou Sun, said I, fair light, and thou enlightened Earth. So fresh and gay. Ye hills and dales. Ye rivers. Woods. Plains, and ye that live and move, fair creatures. Tell, tell, if ye saw. How came I thus, how here? Not of myself; by some Great Maker then, in goodness and in power pre-eminent. Tell me, how may I know Him, how adore, from whom I have that thus I move and live, and feel that I am happier than I know.'*[119]

Within our spirit, there is a deep-seated natural inclination and moral sentiment that desires to learn more about God. Sometimes we perceive that understanding God, along with the formal study of theology, is an abstract and conceptual inquiry. An inquiry that is concerned with complicated doctrines, convoluted principles, and perplexing parables. The reality is that God is accessible to each and every person in the world.

God's Love is not contingent on our ability to understand God. It is an act of faith to believe in God. Through acts of prayer, worship, petition, intercession, community service, and charity, we experience God's Presence, Grace, Love, and Compassion in our life. Almost all of faith is anecdotal evidence. God works in unique ways in each person's life. Just as no two people are identical in every respect, thus, the operation of faith is not identical in any two person's lives.

---

119 Milton, John. (Darbishire, Helen, Ed.) (1958). *The Poetical Works of John Milton*. London: Oxford University Press, p. 172.

'Author of all this thou seest above, or round about thee or beneath. This Paradise I give thee. Count it thine. To till and keep, and of the fruit to eat. Of every tree that in the garden grows eat freely with glad heart. Fear here no dearth. But of the tree whose operation brings knowledge of good and evil, which I have set the pledge of thy obedience and thy faith, amid the garden by the Tree of Life. Remember, what I warn thee. Shun to taste, and shun the bitter consequence. For know, that day thou eatest thereof, My sole command transgressed. Inevitably, thou shall die. From that day mortal, and this happy state shall lose. Expelled from hence into a world of woe and sorrow.'[120]

Adam and Eve's immoral actions have undoubtedly given rise to a broken world. An inferior world that is marred by conflict, destruction, death, guilt, shame, confusion, hate, damnation, anger, denial, punishment, envy, depression, suicide, and sin. Adam and Eve freely determined to consume the Forbidden Fruit from the Tree of the Knowledge of Good and Evil. Their conscious and free willed actions have consequently created a broken world. A world that is defined by the presence of Original Sin. While we cannot change the past, nor can we assume personal responsibility for the actions of preceding generations, we have an obligation, a duty, a moral responsibility, to observe God's Sovereign Command, to the very best of our ability.

The *Messiah* has established a distinguished example of how to live a good, honourable, noble, and morally righteous life on Earth. We ought to look to such a lofty example, in our unending quest for self-improvement. Too often, we find ourselves evading personal responsibility for our self-determined actions. We attempt to assign personal responsibility for our

---

120 Milton, John. (Darbishire, Helen, Ed.) (1958). *The Poetical Works of John Milton.* London: Oxford University Press, p. 173.

inadequacies, failures, and questionable judgement onto the change of circumstance, the exigent demand of necessity, the operation of fate, the power of chance, the inordinate influence of luck, or the unwarranted conduct of a third party, however, all this achieves is our denial of reality.

The major problem with this all-too-convenient approach to life, is that we deny ourselves the opportunity to confront our weaknesses. To learn and mature from our personal challenges. To improve our character. But, above and beyond all this, we deny ourselves the opportunity to affirm that we are only human. Only human, complete with our flaws, failings, and frailties. Sometimes in life, it is our short-sighted response to sin, that is of far greater consequence, rather than the guilt of sinful conduct.

'With blandishment, each bird stooped on his wing. I named them, as they passed, and understood their nature. With such knowledge, God endued my sudden apprehension. But in these, I found not what me thought I wanted still; and to the Heavenly vision thus presumed. O, by what name, for thou above all these. Above humankind, or aught than humankind higher. Surpassest far my naming. How may I adore thee? Author of the Universe, and all this good to man. For whose well being so amply, and with hands so liberal, thou hast provided all things. But with me, I see not who partakes. In solitude what happiness, who can enjoy alone, or all enjoying, what contentment find?' [121]

All too often, we fail to realise that God's Grace is the underlying instrument that is responsible for all the blessings that we have received in the course of our lifetime. Our secular and empirical knowledge is insufficient to comprehend the vast expanse of the

---

121 Milton, John. (Darbishire, Helen, Ed.) (1958). *The Poetical Works of John Milton*. London: Oxford University Press, p. 174.

Universe. Our finite capacity for intelligent and rational thought cannot comprehend the infinite expression of God's Grace. Our life is an iterative process of coming into agreement with God's Sovereign Will.

Our happiness ultimately resides in living our life in complete agreement with God's Sovereign Command. While it is difficult to secure a lasting sense of contentment with everything that we have accomplished in our life, we must focus our heart and mind towards spiritual union with God. When the ebbs and flows of our life are unfavourable, we must never forget, that the power of patience secures all that our heart desires.

'To attain the height and depth of Thy Eternal Ways, all human thoughts come short. Supreme of things! Thou in thyself art perfect, and in thee is no deficiency found. Not so is man, but in degree, the cause of his desire by conversation with his like to help, or solace his defects. No need that thou shouldst propagate, already infinite, and through all numbers absolute. Though one, but man by number is to manifest his single imperfection, and beget like of his like. His image multiplied. In unity defective. Which requires collateral love, and dearest amity.' [122]

God is perfect in every dimension. God has no superior or equal. It is beyond the intellectual capacity of humanity's rational thought to comprehend God's Ways. Humanity is on Earth to further God's Divine Purpose, Sovereign Will, and Eternal Kingdom. All other purposes that we self-create are superficial, fictitious, and artificial.

In the illusion of human-made ideologies, such as fascism, materialism, capitalism, nationalism, communism, liberalism, feudalism, democratism, socialism, anarchism, colonialism,

---

122 Milton, John. (Darbishire, Helen, Ed.) (1958). *The Poetical Works of John Milton*. London: Oxford University Press, p. 175.

conservatism, individualism, and totalitarianism, humanity constantly organises and reorganises the nation-state along secular principles and newfound doctrines. The inherent problem with organising society and state along a secular constitution is that there are endless political disagreements, deadlocks, and divisions amongst the populace.

The majority of humanity demonstrates an insatiable desire for political power, control, fame, private wealth, gold, financial capital, pecuniary gain, influence, prestige, knowledge, social status, private property, personal income, and valuable possessions. Yet, in all of these material phenomena, there is an inherent sense of intrinsic emptiness. The only certain method to resolve the spiritual void of our soul, the one and only true means to transcend the enduring poverty of our human condition, is by the union of our spirit with God's Eternal and Everlasting Spirit. We can lack all the desirable and material phenomena of the world, however, if we have found God, we have secured our everlasting refuge.

In earnest, we hope and strive to live our life defined by good, wholesome, productive, honest, authentic, just, and honourable actions. However, in all that we do on Earth, the central pillar of our life must be God. The closer we are to God, the more exemplary we become in our thought, speech, and conduct. The closer we are to God, the more forgiving, tolerant, generous, loving, understanding, and compassionate we become of each other. So long as we are conscious of our own imperfections and flaws, we are better able to appreciate the imperfections and flaws in other individuals. In so far as it concerns our human condition, perfection is an ideal, whereas imperfection is real.

'My image, not imparted to the brute. Whose fellowship therefore unmet for thee. Good reason was thou freely shouldst dislike, and be so minded still. I, ere thou spakest. Knew it not good for man to be alone, and no such company as then thou sawest intended thee. For trial only brought, to see how thou couldest judge of fit and meet. What next, I bring, shall please thee. Be assured. Thy likeness. Thy fit help. Thy other self. Thy wish. Exactly to thy heart's desire.'[123]

Humanity, the male and female sex alike, were created in God's Divine Image. Man and woman were formed to provide lasting companionship to one another through the sacred institution of marriage. Each sex complements the opposite sex. Marriage is not about one sex having dominion or exercising control over the opposite sex. A lasting and faithful marriage is established on the timeless principles of equality, respect, human dignity, benevolence, unconditional love, compassion, trust, honesty, acceptance, selflessness, integrity, and faithfulness. For marriage to endure the test of a lifetime, it must be founded upon the partnership of equals.

All other relationships outside of the sacred union of marriage are fellowships. There is a diverse spectrum of fellowships that exist in our society. For example, consider brothers, sisters, mothers, fathers, friendships, professional associations, romantic partnerships, platonic relationships, and civil partnerships. The type and status of non-marital fellowships change according to the prevailing value system, morals, ideologies, customs, laws, fashion, and popular culture of contemporary society.

On the other hand, marriage is not founded upon, nor is it dependent upon, the popularity of secular values, the operation of in-force legislation, or the acceptance of novel ideas of any

---

123 Milton, John. (Darbishire, Helen, Ed.) (1958). *The Poetical Works of John Milton.* London: Oxford University Press, p. 176.

particular period of time in the history of the human civilisation. Marriage is a divine union between man and woman. Marriage is the coming together of male and female. As ordained by God's Sovereign Will, the intention of marriage is to create an Earthly bond between husband and wife.

The Holy Bible has many profound scripture verses that speak to the importance of marriage in human life. Among these, the Gospel of Matthew highlights the natural stages of growth within the human life cycle, where a man and woman leave their parents, to come together, to create a new union. A union of marriage, that is sanctified by God and ordained in God's Image, 'Have you not read that He who created them from the beginning made them male and female, and said, 'Therefore a man shall leave his father and his mother and hold fast to his wife, and the two shall become one flesh?' So, they are no longer two but one flesh. What God has joined together, let not man separate.'[124]

In addition, marriage provides a lasting and fulfilling relationship that fosters strong social, economic, emotional, physical, spiritual, practical, and informational support between the spouses. The Book of Ecclesiastes reminds us that, 'Two are better than one, because they have a good reward for their toil. For if they fall, one will lift up his fellow. But woe to him who is alone when he falls and has not another to lift him up!'[125] In the final analysis, marriage is an important relationship in the moral, social, and ethical construct of our civil society. The institution of marriage must be strengthened and supported, but also nourished and nurtured. Without the institution of marriage, the social order of civil society ruptures.

---

124 The Holy Bible (ESV). (2016). The Gospel of Matthew. Chapter 19, Verses 4–6.
125 The Holy Bible (ESV). (2016). The Book of Ecclesiastes. Chapter 4, Verses 9–10.

'Her loss, and other pleasures all abjure. When out of hope, behold her. Not far off, such as I saw her in my dream. Adorned with what all Earth or Heaven could bestow to make her amiable. On she came, led by her Heavenly Maker. Though unseen, and guided by His voice, nor uninformed of nuptial sanctity and marriage rites. Grace was in all her steps. Heaven in her eye. In every gesture, dignity and love.' [126]

The unseen, unrivalled, and unequalled Creator has formed the male and female sex. Through the sacred institution of marriage, the two become one. Both the male and female characteristics and attributes complement the opposite sex. This makes co-existence between the two sexes amiable and desirable in the world. It is by God's Gift of Grace that the female sex has an array of attributes which make women talented, beautiful, intelligent, accomplished, wise, generous, courageous, knowledgeable, kind, and conscientious. In marriage, both parties, man and woman alike, can make an original, meaningful, personal, and profound contribution to the life of their spouse. The exclusive intimacy of marriage is to be cherished.

Marriage makes life worth living. Among other things, marriage provisions the husband and wife with emotional, psychological, physical, tangible, informational, and esteem support, to navigate the countless ebbs and flows of life. When man and woman are joined in union, the journey of life becomes more bearable. When man and woman are united in marriage, the countless sufferings, privations, difficulties, losses, setbacks, and challenges of life are transcended. When man and woman come together, through the bond of marriage, they become a single entity, unified in thought, ideas, beliefs, principles, doctrines, values, and practices. For marriage to endure the test

---

126 Milton, John. (Darbishire, Helen, Ed.) (1958). *The Poetical Works of John Milton.* London: Oxford University Press, p. 177.

of a lifetime, there must be hope, love, faith, joy, forgiveness, and happiness.

> *'My story, to the sum of Earthly bliss, which I enjoy, and must confess to find in all things else delight indeed. But such as used or not, works in the mind no change. Nor vehement desire. These delicacies, I mean of taste, sight, smell, herbs, fruits, and flowers. Walks and the melody of birds. But here far otherwise, transported I behold. Transported touch. Here passion first I felt. Commotion strange. In all enjoyments else superior and unmoved. Here only weak, against the charm of beauty's powerful glance.'*[127]

Each person is on a unique journey in their life. We must place our faith, hope, and trust in God, to commence, endure, and finish our life journey. We must keep our life in perspective and context. That is to say, no person's life journey is perfect. There are highs and lows. There are met and missed expectations. There are good days and bad days. There is satisfaction and disappointment. There is joy and despair. There is happiness and sadness. There is gain and loss. There is pleasure and pain. There is love and indifference. There is favour and animosity. At the end of our race, the lived experience of our lifetime is all that we have genuinely accomplished.

In the swift course of our lifetime, the seemingly endless energy dedicated to the pursuit of our passions, the prodigious power of our insatiable desires, the exhilarating experience of our emotions, the potent expression of our hormones, the immense gravitational force of our feelings, and the heightened awareness of our five senses, all of them dull and fade away.

---

127 Milton, John. (Darbishire, Helen, Ed.) (1958). *The Poetical Works of John Milton*. London: Oxford University Press, p. 178.

In the final analysis, nature is wholly indifferent to the pain and suffering of the individual. Nature is only concerned with the survival of the human species. To rightfully infer that beauty, romance, love, sexual attraction, natural chemistry, and charm serve the dominant purpose of nature, is to make the observation that sexual reproduction—the survival of our genetic material through our biological children—is our fundamental purpose on Earth.

'Therein enjoyed were worthy to subdue the soul of man, or passion in him move. What higher in her society thou findest attractive, human, rational, love still. In loving thou dost well. In passion not, wherein true love consists not. Love refines the thoughts, and heart enlarges, hath his seat in reason, and is judicious, is the scale by which to Heavenly love thou mayest ascend. Not sunk in carnal pleasure, for which cause among the beasts, no mate for thee was found.'[128]

Love and passion are not the same phenomenon. Love is gentle. Love is pure. Love flows from the heart. Love is generous. Love is forgiving. Love is natural. Love is unconditional. Love is gracious. Love is honourable. Love is noble. Love is life. On the contrary, passion is chaotic. Passion is irrational. Passion is extreme. Passion is selfish. Passion is narcissistic. Passion is vanity. Passion is harmful. Passion has the power to destroy our life. Passion is uncontrolled desire. Passion is deadly. In all respects, we must live our life in a balanced and reasoned manner. Our love must be tempered and restrained. Otherwise, we risk the very love that we express towards someone or something, transforming into unbridled passion.

---

128 Milton, John. (Darbishire, Helen, Ed.) (1958). *The Poetical Works of John Milton*. London: Oxford University Press, pp. 179–180.

In harmony with nature, we ought to practice moderation in our desires, ambitions, endeavours, urges, appetites, inclinations, emotions, feelings, and drives. We cannot completely eliminate the multitude of our desires, ambitions, endeavours, urges, appetites, inclinations, emotions, feelings, and drives from our life. Such an approach to life is not feasible, nor is it in alignment with our human condition.

Through the employment of our natural reason, we ought to regulate the superior and inferior faculties of our being. For it is in and through moderation, that we live a harmonious life. It is through the practice of moderation, that we accomplish the greatest fulfilment from our lifetime of work, action, faith, love, prayer, hope, community service, and charity. Practical wisdom is not found in abstinence, but rather it resides in a modest application of self-restraint.

'Let it suffice thee, that thou knowest us happy, and without love no happiness. Whatever pure thou in the body enjoyest (and pure thou wert created) we enjoy in eminence, and obstacle find none.'[129]

We were created to live a happy, love-filled, blessed, productive, prosperous, and purposeful life. Without love, there is no joy, peace, faith, hope, and happiness on Earth. Love is the enduring and eternal substance that binds humanity together. Love crosses boundaries. Love builds bridges. Love unites humanity like no other force on Earth. It is through the power of love, that humanity transcends the multitude of superficial distinctions of race, gender, sex, colour, faith, private property, private wealth, personal income, religion, nationality, and education.

Most importantly, in all that we do on Earth, we must never forget to love God. To love the Creator is to acknowledge, that all

---

129 Milton, John. (Darbishire, Helen, Ed.) (1958). *The Poetical Works of John Milton*. London: Oxford University Press, p. 180.

the blessings that we have been bestowed in our lifetime, including the paramount gift of human life itself, have all originated from God. It is because God loves us, that we are able to love God and each other.

Within the Holy Bible, there are numerous passages of scripture that give voice to the theme of love. For example, consider the Book of Colossians which gives credence to the power of love, 'Put on then, as God's chosen ones, holy and beloved, compassionate hearts, kindness, humility, meekness, and patience, bearing with one another and, if one has a complaint against another, forgiving each other; as the LORD has forgiven you, so you also must forgive. And above all these put on love, which binds everything together in perfect harmony.'[130] Love has the power to understand, forgive, and reconcile. Love fosters trust, confidence, belief, mercy, and faith. Love brings peace on Earth. It is in and through love, that all things are possible.

> *'Be strong. Live happy. Love. But first of all, Him, whom to love is to obey, and keep His Great Command. Take heed, least passion sway thy judgement to do aught. Which else, free will would not admit; thine, and of all thy sons, the weal or woe in thee is placed. Beware! I in thy preserving shall rejoice, and all the blest. Stand fast. To stand or fall. Free in thine own arbitrement it lies. Perfect within. No outward aid require; and all temptation to transgress repel.'*[131]

Humanity was formed in God's Divine Image. Our highest purpose is to love our Creator. We have a duty and obligation to obey God's Eternal Word, an act which is inherently for our

---

130 The Holy Bible (ESV). (2016). The Book of Colossians. Chapter 3, Verses 12–14.

131 Milton, John. (Darbishire, Helen, Ed.) (1958). *The Poetical Works of John Milton*. London: Oxford University Press, p. 181.

greater good. God has graced humanity with free will; however, we must employ this powerful instrument for a productive and constructive purpose. There are enticing temptations and dark desires that we confront along our life journey, however, with God's Providence we overcome them. In all respects, we ought to pray to God for the requisite materials that we need to succeed in the major challenges that are before us.

In the Holy Bible, within the Book of Nehemiah, we witness God's Providence in action. A cupbearer named Nehemiah asks King Artaxerxes for a favour to attend to his personal affairs, 'I said to the King, "Let the King live forever! Why should not my face be sad, when the city, the place of my fathers' graves, lies in ruins, and its gates have been destroyed by fire?" Then the King said to me, "What are you requesting?" So I prayed to the God of Heaven. And I said to the King, "If it pleases the King, and if your servant has found favour in your sight, that you send me to Judah, to the city of my fathers' graves, that I may rebuild it." And the King said to me (the Queen sitting beside him), "How long will you be gone, and when will you return?" So it pleased the King to send me when I had given him a time.'[132]

The discourse between Nehemiah and King Artaxerxes continues, 'And I said to the King, "If it pleases the King, let letters be given me to the Governors of the province beyond the river, that they may let me pass through until I come to Judah, and a letter to Asaph, the keeper of the King's Forest, that he may give me timber to make beams for the gates of the fortress of the temple, and for the wall of the city, and for the house that I shall occupy." And the King granted me what I asked, for the good hand of my God was upon me.'[133] This Biblical story is incontrovertible proof and irrefutable testimony, to the fact that

---

132 The Holy Bible (ESV). (2016). The Book of Nehemiah. Chapter 2, Verses 2–6.
133 The Holy Bible (ESV). (2016). The Book of Nehemiah. Chapter 2, Verses 7–8.

a servant named Nehemiah, through his unwavering faith, belief, and trust in God, secured the necessary means to accomplish his desired endeavour.

To overcome evil with good is a noble test of our character. We are always free to self-determine which path we select. Having said that, our voluntary and conscious actions are influenced by forces and circumstances beyond our immediate control. Nonetheless, we remain free to act in the pursuit of good or evil on Earth. We must always remember, that it is the content of our character which is defined by our actions.

If we engage in a methodical introspection into our state of being, we come to the inevitable realisation, that we have the capacity for self-control. We have the instrument of willpower. We have the gift of discernment. The more we exercise self-control, willpower, and discernment in our life, the greater our sense of morality, philanthropic responsibility, duty to our fellow citizens, compassion, social justice, benevolence, forgiveness, mercy, and love. Over time, we begin to self-determine prudent choices and judicious decisions that accord with the ideas, doctrines, and principles of natural law.

When and where we fall short, we must not be unforgiving unto ourselves. Instead, we ought to embrace the sensible, compassionate, and pragmatic approach to life. We must dispassionately analyse the rationalisation underlying our psychology and behaviour. What were the determinative motives, drives, feelings, intentions, ideas, emotions, impulses, sensations, thoughts, beliefs, inclinations, and values that informed our free willed actions?

When we carefully reflect upon and understand our thought processes, then we have an important opportunity to effectuate informed and judicious decisions in the future. That is to say, we become more conscious of the errors, fallacies, mistakes, prejudices, and biases in our thinking. We all have a plethora of weaknesses. Emotional intelligence is not about perfect self-control over our feelings, inclinations, sensations, instincts, thoughts, ideas, and emotions. In fact, emotional intelligence is being sufficiently self-aware of our weaknesses, to the extent that we are less susceptible to mishap, myopia, and mayhem.

CHAPTER 9

PARADISE LOST: BOOK NINE

'I now must change these notes to tragic.
Foul distrust and breach. Disloyal on the part of man,
revolt, and disobedience. On the part of Heaven,
now alienated, distance, and distaste.
Anger and just rebuke, and judgement given.
That brought into this world, a world of woe.
Sin, and her shadow, death and misery.'

MILTON

BOOK NINE of *Paradise Lost* is the harrowing account of how Satan, in the form of a serpent, stealthily enters the Garden of Eden. Satan has one primary aim—the downfall of Adam and Eve. In accomplishing this evil quest, Satan relentlessly promotes his evil influence upon Eve's innocent mind. Misappropriating the powers of persuasion, rhetoric, flattery, and charm, Satan attempts his level best to convince Eve, that she too can acquire worldly knowledge of good and evil. An immoral endeavour in direct violation of God's Sovereign Command. In effect, the Serpent proposes that Eve trust him, over God's Eternal Word. In the fulfilment of this illegitimate quest, the Serpent employs adulation and praise, to tempt Eve to consume the Forbidden Fruit of the Tree of Knowledge of Good and Evil.

At first, Eve is hesitant to trust the Serpent's unfounded claims. However, the Serpent is emboldened with a false sense of pride, glory, honour, and ego. In the proliferation of much falsehood, the Serpent is boastful of the benefits that he has personally reaped, from the possession of the knowledge of good and evil. The Serpent dispels Eve's doubts, that she would be worse off for consuming the Forbidden Fruit. Rather, the Serpent orates a false narrative, that Eve shall obtain the advantage of the knowledge of good and evil. Needless to say, the Serpent does not cease in his evil quest to achieve Adam and Eve's tragic fall from grace.

Finally, the Serpent is successful in convincing Eve to consume the Forbidden Fruit. In achieving this wicked aim, the Serpent masterfully manipulates Eve. Once Eve has consumed the Forbidden Fruit, she immediately narrates her regrettable experience to Adam. Adam finds Eve's speech and conduct to be distorted from reality.

Once Adam acknowledges the facts, then denial is no longer plausible. Eve finally convinces Adam to also consume the Forbidden Fruit. In a sincere act of love, faithfulness, and devotion, Adam accepts his destiny to be bound by fate to his beloved wife, Eve. Now Adam and Eve have ventured into uncharted territory. The satanic evil of Original Sin has been effectuated in the Garden of Eden. The tragic and ill-fated Fall of Man is complete.

'But what will not ambition and revenge descend to? Who aspires must down as low, as high he soared. Obnoxious, first or last, to basest things. Revenge, at first though sweet, bitter ere long back on itself recoils. Let it; I reck not. So, it light well aimed. Since higher I fall short, on him who next provokes my envy. This new favourite of Heaven. This man of clay. Son of despite. Whom us the more to spite His Maker raised, from dust. Spite then, with spite is best repaid.'[134]

The combination of axiomatic ambition, potent pride, destructive desire, powerful passion, relentless revenge, abnormal anger, and guilt-ridden greed, ultimately lead to a person's tragic ruin and disastrous downfall. These cardinal sins destroy a person's character, morality, natural reason, moral conscience, serenity, presence of peace, equanimity of mind, and integrity. On the other hand, to demonstrate lofty aspirations can be characterised as either good or evil. The correct answer concerning towering human aspirations is a relative one. That is to infer, the answer is contingent, it is always dependent upon what we aspire to achieve in our life.

Herein we apply the aforementioned moral proposition to real-world scenarios. For example, consider if we aspire to create a future world that eliminates the incidence of curable diseases. Provision food and clean drinking water to the world's human population. Reduce preventable infant mortality towards zero. Last but not least, eradicate illiteracy. These represent positive aspirations. On the contrary, if we aspire to promote acts of terror, this is an example of an evil aspiration. Before we engage in conscious acts that have far-reaching ramifications, we must ask ourselves the question: What do we aspire to become in life?

---

134 Milton, John. (Darbishire, Helen, Ed.) (1958). *The Poetical Works of John Milton.* London: Oxford University Press, pp. 186–187.

For our aspirations define our physical and psychological state of being in the world.

From the perspective of human psychology, personal aspirations are a crucial element of intrinsic motivation in our life. However, we need to self-regulate our aspirations, to ensure that they are righteous and just in their nature. For example, consider the aspiration to advance God's Sovereign Kingdom on Earth. This is a superior and transcendental ideal. One that is a most worthy cause to pursue. On the contrary, if we aspire to promote anarchy and hate crime in civil society, this is undeniably a reprehensible aspiration. No matter the towering heights that we scale, or how far we venture, we must always remember that our fall from grace is close at hand.

'His fraud is then thy fear. Which plain infers thy equal fear that my firm faith and love can by his fraud be shaken or seduced. Thoughts, which how found they harbour in thy breast. Adam, misthought of her, to thee so dear?'[135]

The Devil achieves his evil objectives by the immoral means of deception, jealousy, anger, guilt, confusion, prejudice, shame, temptation, rage, treachery, envy, hate, and manipulation. The Devil is exceedingly skilled in the utilisation of half-truths to mislead humanity. The Devil knows no end, in his attempt to turn our heart and mind towards all that is evil in nature. In all respects, we must depend upon God's Eternal Word to guide our life journey on Earth.

The multitude of our thoughts, ideas, doctrines, actions, values, principles, beliefs, and ideologies that do not concur with God's Eternal Word, these we must confidently discard from our mind. We must never underestimate, nor attempt to accurately assess the Devil's formidable power. Remember, the Devil can

---

135 Milton, John. (Darbishire, Helen, Ed.) (1958). *The Poetical Works of John Milton*. London: Oxford University Press, p. 189.

also quote scripture to fulfil his illegitimate purpose on Earth. In all our thoughts, speech, and actions, we must be vigilant and attentive. A person is unlikely to be faulted for being circumspect in their thought, speech, and conduct.

> *'Daughter of God and man, immortal Eve! For such thou art, from sin, and blame entire. Not different of thee do I dissuade thy absence from my sight, but to avoid, the attempt itself. Intended by our foe. For he who tempts, though in vain, at least asperses, the tempted with dishonour foul. Supposed not incorruptible of faith. Not proof against temptation. Thou thyself with scorn.'*[136]

We are all sons and daughters of God. We must learn from the monumental experience of Adam and Eve in the Garden of Eden. We ought to carefully reflect upon both the good and the not so good aspects of Adam and Eve's time in the Garden of Eden. One lesson that we deduce from Adam and Eve's fall from grace is that our actions have profound and lasting consequences.

We cannot escape, nor can we diminish personal responsibility for our free willed actions. Regardless of the circumstances or situations in which we self-determine to act, the penalty for our unconscionable conduct must be paid. The presence of mitigating factors does not function to absolve us from personal responsibility for our free and voluntary conduct. In all cases, God's Justice is unequivocally served. Therefore, the moral imperative is upon us, that we self-regulate our emotions, ideas, feelings, instincts, thoughts, doctrines, principles, ideologies, inclinations, passions, behaviours, and sensations, to resist the pervasive influence of evil in the world.

No person is immune from the pervasive influence of temptation and sin. We can all harbour good intentions, however,

---

136 Milton, John. (Darbishire, Helen, Ed.) (1958). *The Poetical Works of John Milton*. London: Oxford University Press, pp. 189–190.

from time to time, we all fall short in our ability to live up to them. The fixed and unchanging reality is that the human condition is defined by both the flesh and the spirit. Life is a remarkable contest between the will of the flesh and the will of the spirit. If we sincerely and honestly reflect upon our life, we bear witness to the fact, that in this protracted, rather in this lifelong contest, the flesh always possesses the advantage.

It is exclusively by God's Grace, that our spirit is strengthened, nourished, and cultivated. God's Providence directs the trajectory of our spirit. God's Providence defines our Earthly existence in a positive and beneficial manner. The strength of God's Spirit is obtained through the power of prayer, petition, and penance. These acts of faith strengthen our spirit and guide our life in a righteous direction. It is incumbent upon us, to live in accordance with the spirit, as opposed to living an inferior life. We must rise above the mediocre life that is characterised by entertaining the endless caprices and whims of the flesh.

The towering figure of the Christian faith, Saint Paul the Apostle, reminds us of just how difficult it is to constantly do good in the world. Even though our heart and mind embodies every desire to make the world a better place, the true path of righteousness is not a convenient endeavour. From time to time, we all struggle to perform righteous actions, 'For we know that the law is spiritual, but I am of the flesh, sold under sin. For I do not understand my own actions. For I do not do what I want, but I do the very thing I hate. Now if I do what I do not want, I agree with the law, that it is good. So now it is no longer I who do it, but sin that dwells within me. For I know that nothing good dwells in me, that is, in my flesh. For I have the desire to do what is right, but not the ability to carry it out. For I do not do the good I want, but the evil I do not want is what I keep doing.'[137]

---

137 The Holy Bible (ESV). (2016). The Book of Romans. Chapter 7, Verses 14–19.

Saint Paul the Apostle continues in his profound spiritual reflections, 'Now if I do what I do not want, it is no longer I who do it, but sin that dwells within me. So, I find it to be a law that when I want to do right, evil lies close at hand. For I delight in the Law of God, in my inner being, but I see in my members another law waging war against the law of my mind and making me captive to the law of sin that dwells in my members. Wretched man that I am! Who will deliver me from this body of death? Thanks be to God through Jesus Christ our Lord! So then, I myself serve the Law of God with my mind, but with my flesh I serve the law of sin.'[138] It is exclusively by God's Grace, that we transcend our sinful and corrupt nature. Purified from our sins, we perform righteous deeds in the world.

In the final analysis, our spirit is prepared to endure the protracted struggle for the advancement of good, however, so long as we embody the flesh, we must always remain vigilant of the frailties, infirmities, and pitfalls associated with the human condition. At any time, the flesh may yield to the ever-present power of passion, temptation, and desire. Indeed, within the Holy Bible, we are reminded of the infirmities of the flesh, which only serve to hinder and obstruct the cultivation of our spirit, for 'the Spirit is indeed willing, but the flesh is weak.'[139] Therefore, we must keep periodic observation over our heart and mind, so that our state of being resists the evil desires of the flesh. In this noble endeavour, we must secure the support of God through our prayer, penance, and petition.

The presence of God's Grace in our life is pivotal. God's Grace ensures that we possess the ability to live a wholesome, productive, prosperous, and righteous life. We do not have our affairs perfectly organised. Even at the best of times, life is a complicated affair. Understandably, we do not have it altogether

---

138 The Holy Bible (ESV). (2016). The Book of Romans. Chapter 7, Verses 20–25.
139 The Holy Bible (ESV). (2016). The Gospel of Matthew. Chapter 26, Verse 41.

in our life, however, so long as we have God's Grace, Favour, and Blessing, we proceed forward on our life journey with confidence, conviction, and certainty.

In the Holy Bible, within the New Testament, we are made privy to the many challenges and privations that Saint Paul the Apostle endured during his lifetime on Earth. However, Paul the Apostle had total faith in God's Grace to complete his journey, 'But He said to me, "My grace is sufficient for you, for My power is made perfect in weakness."'[140] Throughout the highs and lows of our life, we must know what and where our treasure is. For we may suffer the loss of everything that we have in this life, however, God's Grace assures our unmerited salvation.

> '*How are we happy, still in fear of harm? But harm precedes not sin. Only our foe tempting affronts us with his foul esteem of our integrity. His foul esteem, sticks no dishonour on our front. But, turns foul on himself. Then, wherefore, shunned or feared by us? Who rather double honour gain from his surmise proved false. Find peace within. Favour from Heaven. Our witness from the event. And what is faith, love, virtue, unassayed alone, without exterior help sustained?*'[141]

In our human condition, the divergent emotions of happiness and fear cannot co-exist. These are mutually exclusive emotions. When we express the desirable emotion of happiness, we are content with our life. We are full of joy. We are ecstatic. We are truly and wholly brimming with life. On the contrary, when we express the undesirable emotion of fear, we are inhibited in our thoughts. We are full of worry and anxiety in our actions.

---

140 The Holy Bible (ESV). (2016). Second Epistle to the Corinthians. Chapter 12, Verse 9.
141 Milton, John. (Darbishire, Helen, Ed.) (1958). *The Poetical Works of John Milton*. London: Oxford University Press, p. 190.

We become overly concerned with the challenges, problems, and issues that confront our life.

We must not permit the Devil to tempt us into experiencing deceptive, destructive, and delusional thoughts. We must not become ambivalent in our thinking. Even if we entertain a blessed and happy life, there is no need for our pride or ego to take centre stage. We must always remember that the source of all our virtues is God. For the sin that resides within us cannot be defeated by our willpower. However, it is by God's Grace, that we transcend our sinful nature and live a virtuous and content life.

'O woman, best are all things as the Will of God ordained them. His creating hand, nothing imperfect or deficient left. Of all that He created. Much less man, or aught that might his happy state secure. Secure from outward force. Within himself the danger lies. Yet, lies within his power. Against his will, he can receive no harm. But God left free the will. For what obeys reason is free, and reason, He made right.' [142]

God created man and woman righteous, perfect, and just. God has ordained humanity with free will. God never reneges an eternal promise. Therefore, the personal responsibility is upon humanity, to utilise its free will in a resourceful, beneficial, and sensible manner. Through the instruments of natural reason, discernment, and moral conscience, we employ our free will to live a harmonious and good life on Earth. Alternatively, we misappropriate our free will to partake in the endless, egotistic, and empty sinful pleasures of the flesh. In the vain pursuit of satisfying our ego, we seek trivial worldly treasures and live our life characterised by avarice, envy, self-interest, pride, profit, pecuniary gain, and self-love.

---

142 Milton, John. (Darbishire, Helen, Ed.) (1958). *The Poetical Works of John Milton*. London: Oxford University Press, p. 191.

The endless and excessive pursuit of private wealth, never produced fine character in man or woman. The power of natural reason, if applied correctly, assists us to make sensible decisions that benefit our life, create a more harmonious civil society, and advance the sovereign nation-state. Through the application of natural reason, we ensure that our life makes a significant difference and positive contribution to the world. It is by the virtue of natural reason, that when we effectuate well-informed actions, we leave the world in a considerably better place than we found it.

'Since reason not impossibly may meet. Some specious object by the foe suborned, and fall into deception unaware. Not keeping strictest watch. As she was warned. Seek not temptation then, which to avoid were better, and most likely if from me.'[143]

We must be acutely aware of the infirmity of our natural reason. Human understanding is not always lucid. Furthermore, we must never attempt to reason our way through the profound depth of temptation. This is an irrational utilisation of the finite power of our natural reason. If we seek and entertain the very thought of temptation in our mind, we are more likely than not to succumb to it. When we become consciously aware of the real limitations in our willpower to resist temptation, then we must modify our approach to confronting it. In effect, we ought to adopt a more plausible, pragmatic, and practical approach to addressing temptation.

When we confront the presence of any temptation in our life, we must be circumspect in our thinking. The pursuit of pleasure need not inform and determine our understanding. We must adequately consider the entirety of positive and negative

---

143 Milton, John. (Darbishire, Helen, Ed.) (1958). *The Poetical Works of John Milton*. London: Oxford University Press, p. 191.

externalities associated with following a select course of action. It is essential that we do not accept fallacies in our reasoning. A false premise is more likely than not to lead to an erroneous conclusion. Somethings in life are better avoided altogether.

To practically demonstrate the aforementioned assertion, let us consider the following scenario. Simply because a phenomenon organically exists in the natural world, this does not necessarily infer that it is beneficial to our well-being. There are a multitude of natural substances, plants, compounds, asphyxiants (i.e., toxic gases), and chemical elements in the natural world that are poisonous or hazardous to human health. For example, consider the presence of mercury, arsenic, ricin, mentha pulegium, lead, hydrogen sulfide, formaldehyde, sulfur dioxide, hydrogen cyanide, and urushiol. A significant quantum of inhalation or digestion of the aforementioned natural phenomena, causes serious injury or death to humans.

'But of this tree, we may not taste, nor touch. God so commanded, and left that command sole daughter of His voice. The rest, we live. Law to ourselves. Our reason is our law. To whom the tempter guilefully replied. Indeed? Hath God then said that of the fruit of all these garden trees ye shall not eat? Yet, Lords declared of all in Earth or air? To whom thus Eve yet sinless. Of the fruit of each tree in the Garden we may eat. But of the fruit of this fair tree amidst the garden, God hath said: You shall not eat. Thereof, nor shall you touch it. Lest you die.'[144]

We must not reason our way through temptation or transgression against God's Sovereign Command. The Devil is exceedingly skilled in the art of rhetoric, persuasion, adulation, charm, flattery, and praise; however, the Devil misappropriates these

---

144 Milton, John. (Darbishire, Helen, Ed.) (1958). *The Poetical Works of John Milton*. London: Oxford University Press, pp. 198–199.

desirable traits for evil purposes. God's Sovereign Command is eternal, absolute, and final. In the aforementioned passage, we witness Eve engage in discourse with the Serpent. This innocent approach, concerning Eve's engagement with the Serpent, was a certain formula for her spectacular downfall. As soon as Eve had entertained the unwelcome presence and misconstrued speech of the Devil, she had inevitably permitted doubt, uncertainty, confusion, fear, hesitation, and temptation to enter her mind.

Following this dark dialogue between Eve and the Devil, who is in the physical form of a serpent, it is only a matter of time before the Devil attempts to have Eve question the very substance and true form of God's Eternal Word. Herein we witness the infirmity of human reason in action. Eve innocently entertains the Devil's ignominious and absurd idea, that observing God's Eternal Word is detrimental and disadvantageous to her greater good.

The infirmity of our natural reason questions and considers false, what it cannot comprehend, nor affirm as a theological fact. We must be careful, that we employ our natural reason within its limits. There are phenomena that are forever beyond the capacity of our natural reason to logically comprehend. Such phenomena remain matters of faith, personal affirmation, and belief. For example, consider the question: What happens to our spirit after death? God's Eternal Word is neither art or science. God's Eternal Word is God's Eternal Word.

In all else that we do, we must utilise our natural reason, judgement, moral conscience, and discernment to make informed decisions that are morally and ethically right. We must not attempt to justify our immoral conduct through the limited power of natural reason. In doing so, we only mislead ourselves, and tread the ill-fated path of sin. It is not the case, that God has provisioned humanity with divine commands for God's personal satisfaction. Rather, God has given humanity commands, that are to be observed for our well-being, prosperity, success, happiness, and the greater good of humanity.

In the final analysis, the instrument of natural reason is a double-edged sword. The moral obligation is upon us to utilise our natural reason for the advancement of social justice, respect, equality, human dignity, peace, community service, benevolence, and tolerance. It is through our reasoned and informed actions that we accrue virtue and merit. The cultivation of our good character is solely in our hands.

> *'Queen of this Universe. Do not believe, those rigid threats of death. You shall not die. How should you? By the fruit? It gives you life to knowledge. By the threatener? Look on me. Me who have touched and tasted. Yet, both live, and life more perfect have attained than fate meant me, by venturing higher than my lot. Shall that be shut to man, which to the beast is open? or will God incense His ire for such a petty trespass, and not praise rather your dauntless virtue, whom the pain of death denounced. Whatever thing death be. Deterred not from achieving what might lead.'*[145]

Herein we witness the Devil, in all his splendour and power, in action within the Garden of Eden. The Devil attempts to deviate Eve's pious thoughts away from God's Sovereign Command. Milton cleverly employs eloquent language to colourfully articulate how the Devil manipulates Eve's mind. In referring to Eve, Milton selectively uses the words 'Queen of this Universe'. Unequivocally, the Devil is appealing to Eve's ego, pride, glory, esteem, and honour. The Devil is tempting Eve to consume the Forbidden Fruit.

---

145 Milton, John. (Darbishire, Helen, Ed.) (1958). *The Poetical Works of John Milton*. London: Oxford University Press, p. 199.

As the aforementioned dialogue illustrates, in unsuspecting discourse with the Devil, it is extremely perplexing to distinguish representations of fact from representations of fiction. The Devil has misconstrued reality, in order for the performance of sin to appear favourable to Eve's flawed reasoning and perception.

With the good benefit of hindsight, we conclusively ascertain that all of the Devil's assertions are categorically false and definitively misleading. In every case, all intrusive thoughts that the Devil attempts to infiltrate our mind with must be rejected from our life narrative. What God's Eternal Word has provided and rendered unto humankind, is alone sufficient for our life journey. The challenge with putting these aspirational statements into practice, is that during the vulnerable moments of our life, during the darkest days of our life, our thoughts become clouded, our judgement becomes dysfunctional. Not to mention, in the resolution of complex moral and ethical dilemmas, we cannot correctly distinguish the right course of action from the wrong course of action.

The Biblical event of Satan tempting Eve in the Garden of Eden, serves as categorical proof, that God has honoured humanity with the especial gift of free will. For humanity has been provisioned with absolute free will. That is to infer, free will to the fundamental and absolute extreme, that humanity is at liberty to transgress God's Eternal Word.

It is a fact of our existence, that with the exercise of our free will comes the undeniable and irrefutable personal responsibility for the consequences that are intrinsically and inevitably attached to our voluntary and conscious actions. This personal responsibility includes, and it extends to incorporate, the unfavourable dimensions and unintended consequences of our free willed actions. God had explicitly forewarned Adam and Eve, that to consume the Forbidden Fruit from the Tree of the Knowledge of Good and Evil, results in the just punishment of death.

In spite of Adam and Eve's transgression, God remains boundless in mercy, forgiveness, compassion, benevolence, and love. Let us not forget, that God provided for the ultimate sacrifice for the penalty of Original Sin. The Son of God atoned for humanity's guilt, damnation, pain, suffering, and punishment that was the direct result of Original Sin.

It is not by our righteousness, initiative, willpower, virtue, personal effort, natural reason, intellectual capacity, agency, or physical strength that we are saved from our sins. Our salvation is only possible through God's Mercy, Favour, Compassion, and Grace. The opportunity for salvation is open to every person on Earth. Salvation is not purchased, traded, earnt, found, retained, stored, or lost. Salvation is God's exceptional gift to humanity.

'Soon as the force of that fallacious fruit, that with exhilarating vapour bland about their spirits had played, and inmost powers, made err, was now exhaled, and grosser sleep bred of unkindly fumes, with conscious dreams encumbered. Now had left them. Up they rose as from unrest, and each the other viewing. Soon found their eyes how opened, and their minds how darkened. Innocence, that as a veil had shadowed them from knowing ill, was gone. Just confidence, and native righteousness, and honour from about them. Naked left to guilty shame. He covered, but his robe uncovered more.'[146]

Regrettably, Adam and Eve fell into the dark abyss of temptation. Adam and Eve engaged in sinful conduct during their time in the Garden of Eden. The duo willingly and of their own superficial understanding consumed the Forbidden Fruit. While the duo was tempted and misled by the Devil, in the physical form of a serpent,

---

146 Milton, John. (Darbishire, Helen, Ed.) (1958). *The Poetical Works of John Milton*. London: Oxford University Press, pp. 208–209.

the fact remains, that God had categorically forewarned them against consuming the Forbidden Fruit. Adam and Eve cannot deny that they knew, consuming the Forbidden Fruit constituted a direct and immediate transgression against God's Eternal Word. In addition, Adam and Eve had been categorically forewarned that death was the high penalty for this immoral action.

Needless to say, Original Sin entered the Garden of Eden and the world. The Fall of Man has forever destroyed the original perfection of the human condition. The harmony of human life, once defined by innocence, purity, chaste love, faith, blessing, happiness, compassion, joy, hope, peace, and virtue was destroyed. Ever since the effectuation of Original Sin, human civilisation possesses the knowledge of good and evil. Furthermore, humanity has also experienced existence defined by pain, fear, sadness, anger, shame, guilt, violence, frustration, anxiety, confusion, envy, hopelessness, poverty, jealousy, conflict, suicide, war, denial, depression, and death.

'Shorn of his strength. They destitute and bare of all their virtue. Silent, and in face confounded long they sat. As strucken mute. Till Adam, though not less than Eve abashed, at length gave utterance to these words constrained. O Eve, in evil hour thou didst give ear to that false worm, of whomsoever taught to counterfeit man's voice. True in our fall. False in our promised rising. Since our eyes opened. We find indeed, and find we know both good and evil. Good lost and evil got. Bad fruit of knowledge. If this be to know, which leaves us naked thus. Of honour void. Of innocence. Of faith. Of purity. Our wanted ornaments now soiled and stained, and in our faces evident the signs of foul concupiscence. Whence evil store.'[147]

Adam and Eve finally come to terms with their newfound reality. The duo accept the dreaded and disgraceful realisation of how their sinful, scandalous, and shameful conduct has contravened God's Eternal Word. Fallen, Adam and Eve now consciously and carefully reflect upon their error in judgement. Adam and Eve have no choice, but to come to terms with the consequences of their immoral actions. The duo lament at their present condition. An inferior condition that is defined by sin and the knowledge of good and evil. Adam and Eve must now repent for their immoral actions. From that inauspicious day forward, a day marked by disobedience to God's Eternal Word, the world has been marred by the powerful curse of Original Sin.

Despite our positive intentions and good endeavours, humanity cannot escape the far-reaching consequences of Original Sin. In fact, Original Sin has destroyed the once picture-perfect Paradise found within the Garden of Eden. Original Sin has given rise to a broken world on Earth. Therefore, we must turn to

---

147 Milton, John. (Darbishire, Helen, Ed.) (1958). *The Poetical Works of John Milton*. London: Oxford University Press, p. 209.

God to secure our undeserved salvation, redemption, forgiveness, peace, mercy, favour, blessing, and grace. Humanity has lost all of its virtue. Humanity is now defined by conflict, concupiscence, covetousness, confusion, greed, passion, anger, jealousy, pride, guilt, despondency, discouragement, fear, envy, and despair. Through God's Grace, humanity purifies its spirit, heart, and mind. Thereafter, humanity secures union with God's Spirit.

The Fall of Man and the effectuation of Original Sin confirms, that more likely than not through the course of human life, our employment of personal agency and freedom of thought are often misappropriated. Personal agency and freedom of thought are positive attributes of the human condition, however, we are prone to error in their application.

Adam and Eve's direct and immediate experience, all but confirms that we are always better off navigating our life's journey in accordance with God's Eternal Word. We ought to desist from permitting our ego to direct our life trajectory. For our reliance upon natural reason to self-determine our principles, ideologies, beliefs, thoughts, desires, attitudes, doctrines, and values, only deviates us away from traversing the path of righteousness.

The chequered course of human history has demonstrated, time and time again, that the exercise of free will by humanity leads to the incidence of endless chaos, instability, destruction, and conflict in the world. When our life has come full circle, when our time on Earth is nearing its end, we realise that from the beginning, God knew what was best for our life. Therefore, in the present moment, it is solely incumbent upon us that we make the right choice, when it comes to obedience or rebellion to God's Eternal Word. We must remain conscious that while we remain resident in the flesh, our ego suggests to us among many things, a life of disobedience to God's Eternal Word.

The *Messiah* understood the principle of obedience to God's Eternal Word. During the *Messiah's* time on Earth, while he was in the flesh, he affirmed the noble principle, 'Not my will, but yours be done.'[148] Through the unmatched power of prayer, penance, and petition, the *Messiah* made himself subservient to God's Sovereign Will. Not only does the righteous speech and conduct of the *Messiah* demonstrate, that he placed his unwavering faith in God, but his inspirational life story also illustrates, that God knows what is the best course of action for our life. From time to time, when we pause and reflect on our life, when we put our life into context, we ought to ask ourselves the question: How often do we consult God, before we make our life-changing decisions?

'With feathered cincture, naked else and wild. Among the trees on isles and woody shores. Thus fenced, and as they thought, their shame in part covered. But not at rest or ease of mind. They sat them down to weep. Nor only tears rained at their eyes. But high winds worse within began to rise. High passions. Anger. Hate. Mistrust. Suspicion. Discord. And shook sore their inward state of mind. Calm region once and full of peace. Now tossed and turbulent. For understanding ruled not, and the will heard not her lore. Both in subjection now to sensual appetite. Who from beneath usurping over sovereign reason claimed.'[149]

The greatest asset that humanity possesses in life is equanimity of mind. To live a tranquil life is a profound blessing. Humanity is endowed with the higher faculties of rational understanding, intuition, imagination, perception, reason, memory, and free will. Therefore, humanity must assume personal responsibility for the good and evil consequences that arise from the exercise of these higher faculties. If we utilise our personal agency and willpower

---

148 The Holy Bible (ESV). (2016). The Gospel of Luke. Chapter 22, Verse 42.
149 Milton, John. (Darbishire, Helen, Ed.) (1958). *The Poetical Works of John Milton*. London: Oxford University Press, p. 210.

to misappropriate the higher faculties of our mind, then we suffer the known and unknown consequences of their misemployment. Our freedom is not an insignificant matter.

The greater we contemplate and reason, the more we come to the true realisation, the inevitable realisation, that God is the best counsel and guide on our life journey. In vain, we boast of the superiority of our natural reason, intellect, insight, knowledge, understanding, and wisdom. However, truth be told, we cannot even resolve all of our own problems and issues. Such is the formidable power of the ego upon our state of being, that we cannot even objectively perceive our own existential reality. We do not even know what are the best choices to make in life. We cannot lay claim that we are righteous and true in our judgements. The unconscious mind is more often than not deceived, even with the enlightened realisation of its many faults, errors, biases, prejudices, fallacies, and limitations. Peace be with you.

None of us are immune from the lifelong psychological and physical struggle with sin. The telling story of Paul the Apostle indisputably confirms, that even this prominent figure of the faith confronted his own struggle with sin. In the Holy Bible, within the New Testament, Paul shares his profound personal experience with us, when he writes, 'For we know that the law is spiritual, but I am of the flesh, sold under sin. For I do not do what I want, but I do the very thing I hate. Now if I do what I do not want, I agree with the law, that it is good. So now it is no longer I who do it, but sin that dwells within me. For I know that nothing good dwells in me, that is, in my flesh. For I have the desire to do what is right, but not the ability to carry it out. For I do not do the good I want, but the evil I do not want is what I keep on doing. Now if I do what I do not want, it is no longer I who do it, but sin that dwells within me.'[150]

---

150 The Holy Bible (ESV). (2016). The Book of Romans. Chapter 7, Verses 14–20.

Paul the Apostle's struggle with sin is a universal human struggle. Saint Paul's remarkable theological writing and life experience defines the very core of our human nature. That is to say, the Self struggles against our human nature. Regardless of human civilisation's variation across sex, race, colour, age, gender, occupation, culture, religion, personal income, vocation, private property, private wealth, ethnicity, education, heritage, language, or any other distinguishing factor, our human nature is guided by the corrupt and sinful dictates of the flesh. It is difficult to deny, that our sinful nature performs an influential and inordinate role in our behaviour. It is in part, due to the presence and function of our moral conscience, that in hindsight, we reflect upon our sinful conduct and express the emotions of regret, guilt, anger, and remorse for our immoral actions.

We must never fall into the trap of thinking we are self-righteous. In fact, we are all sinners. No person is better than any other person. In spite of the immense social, political, legal, private wealth, economic, and educational divide across the modern world, we are all created equal. Every person has the inalienable right to expression of personality, employment of liberty, and exercise of capacity.

In fact, the universal principle of human dignity is the most basic and fundamental premise of all human relations. The presence of inequality does not diminish the first-order principle of human dignity. Human dignity is the foundation stone upon which natural law secures its legitimacy and credibility. Without the affirmation of human dignity and social justice for every person on Earth, there is no lasting peace on Earth.

Now, if we manage to perform good actions, this is solely due to the strength of the spirit that is within us. In all that we do, it is in our best interests that we seek God's Wisdom. God never fails humanity in its noble quest to live a wholesome, honourable, and productive life. The obligation is upon humanity, to effectuate into practice the eternal principles and timeless lessons that God has established. These eternal principles include: faith, charity, forgiveness, mercy, social justice, peace, equality, benevolence, community service, human dignity, and love.

In closing, we must never ponder over the two illegitimate questions: Is God waiting on me? Alternatively, am I waiting on God? Instead, we must seize the initiative to put God's Timeless Principles and Eternal Word into action. Only then we witness transformative change in our lifetime. In all respects, unwavering faith in God is our greatest guide for a truly blessed life. Peace be with you.

CHAPTER 10

PARADISE LOST: BOOK TEN

'My journey strange. With clamorous uproar.
Protesting fate supreme. Thence how I found the new
created world. Which fame in Heaven long had foretold.
A fabric wonderful of absolute perfection.
Therein, man placed in Paradise. By our exile made happy.
Him by fraud, I have seduced from his Creator,
and the more to increase your wonder.'

MILTON

BOOK TEN of *Paradise Lost* is the unfortunate story of Satan's triumph over God's newest Creation—man and woman. In accordance with God's Sovereign Will, the Guardian Angels are unable to prevent Satan's sinister complot of corrupting Adam and Eve in the Garden of Eden. God declares the illegitimate entry of Satan into the Garden of Eden could not have been prevented by the Guardian Angels. For it was God's Sovereign Will, that Adam and Eve's moral conscience, free will, and rational understanding be put to the ultimate test. Indeed, Adam and Eve were wholly and truly free to self-determine their actions. Regrettably, Adam and Eve selected the path of temptation and desire. Adam and Eve's immoral actions resulted in the foretold consequences— sin and death.

Following this devastating disaster and terrible tragedy, Adam blames God and Eve for his consumption of the Forbidden Fruit. Eve does no better. In turn, Eve casts the blame for her immoral actions onto the Serpent. For all practical purposes, neither Adam or Eve accept personal responsibility for their voluntary and conscious action of consuming the Forbidden Fruit. Now having discerned the knowledge of good and evil, the duo lament at their sinful conduct. Adam and Eve mourn, rather than rejoice for their newfound knowledge of good and evil. In Adam and Eve's exercise of personal agency and employment of free will, in this particular instance their loss far outweighs their gain.

This newfound worldly knowledge has deprived Adam and Eve of their innocence, purity, righteousness, merit, and chaste love. Adam and Eve now realise the immense burden of the knowledge of good and evil. Not to mention, this gain of knowledge has exposed them to the dismal reality of the human condition. Indeed, it was better for Adam and Eve not to have known evil. As the duo come to terms with their undesirable reality, denial soon enough turns into anger, followed by resentment, and fear. Finally, Adam and Eve repent. They earnestly pray to God for mercy, salvation, redemption, and forgiveness.

'Meanwhile the heinous and despiteful act of Satan done in Paradise, and how he in the Serpent had perverted Eve. Her husband she, to taste the fatal fruit, was known in Heaven. For what can escape the eye of God all-seeing, or deceive His heart omniscient? God, in all things, wise and just, hindered not Satan to attempt the mind of man. With strength entire, and free will armed, complete to have discovered and repulsed whatever wiles of foe or seeming friend. For still they knew, and ought to have still remembered. The high injunction, not to taste that fruit.'[151]

We must not attempt to reason with the formidable force of temptation. Almost always, our implication in temptation results in the performance of sin. The Devil possesses the supreme power to assume a variety of feelings, thoughts, ideas, and sensations, however, in underlying substance, Satan is inherently evil. Satan harbours demonic, dishonourable, deceitful, deadly, and destructive intentions. In all things, the Devil's malevolent will is never to be trusted. No matter how distressing our personal circumstances, we must fight the good fight of faith. In the hour of need, we ought to appeal to God's Mercy and Grace.

Humanity has been given the requisite instruments to withstand the ferocious power of temptation. These faith-ordained instruments include the Helmet of Salvation,[152] the Breastplate of Righteousness,[153] the Sword of the Spirit,[154] the Shield of Faith,[155] the Belt of Truth,[156] and the Shoes of Peace.[157] Collectively, these instruments constitute the Spiritual Armour

---

151 Milton, John. (Darbishire, Helen, Ed.) (1958). *The Poetical Works of John Milton*. London: Oxford University Press, p. 213.
152 The Holy Bible (ESV). (2016). The Book of Ephesians. Chapter 6, Verse 17.
153 The Holy Bible (ESV). (2016). The Book of Ephesians. Chapter 6, Verse 14.
154 The Holy Bible (ESV). (2016). The Book of Ephesians. Chapter 6, Verse 17.
155 The Holy Bible (ESV). (2016). The Book of Ephesians. Chapter 6, Verse 16.
156 The Holy Bible (ESV). (2016). The Book of Ephesians. Chapter 6, Verse 14.
157 The Holy Bible (ESV). (2016). The Book of Ephesians. Chapter 6, Verse 15.

of God. We must remind ourselves, that all spiritual battles are first won or lost in the mind.

We must safeguard our mind from intrusive, irrational, and impulsive thoughts. In effect, negative thoughts which lead our thinking astray and misinform our judgement. By aligning our values, thoughts, principles, doctrines, actions, beliefs, and morals with God's Eternal Word, we become confident in our ability to stand firm and fight the good fight of faith. With God's Favour upon our life, we begin and end our life journey on the side of righteousness.

'Assembled Angels, and ye powers returned from unsuccessful charge. Be not dismayed. Nor troubled at these tidings from the Earth. Which your sincerest care could not prevent. Foretold so lately what would come to pass. When first, this tempter crossed the gulf from Hell. I told ye then, he should prevail and speed on his bad errand. Man should be seduced and flattered out of all. Believing lies against his Maker. No decree of mine concurring to necessitate his fall, or touch with lightest moment of impulse his free will. To her own inclining left in even scale. But fallen he is, and now what rests, but that the mortal sentence pass on his transgression. Death denounced that day.' [158]

Milton employs colourful and poetic language to demonstrate that men and women are the true authors of their lives. In the antithesis of the aforementioned statement, we posit that God has the Final Judgement. God is the Ultimate Arbitrator of the trajectory of the Universe. Having said that, God has permitted Adam and Eve unconditional free will to determine their destiny.

---

158 Milton, John. (Darbishire, Helen, Ed.) (1958). *The Poetical Works of John Milton.* London: Oxford University Press, p. 214.

In the hypothetical scenario, if Adam and Eve were not free to choose to consume, or not to consume the Forbidden Fruit, or alternatively, God had overridden their self-determination to consume the Forbidden Fruit, then God knowing what was the best course of action, would have acted to prevent this dismal tragedy from occurring in the Garden of Eden.

In the hypothetical scenario, God would have ensured Adam and Eve did not consume the Forbidden Fruit. That is to say, in the counterfactual sense, God would have annulled Adam and Eve's free will, to prevent them from partaking in the act of Original Sin. Yet, God did not intervene in Adam and Eve's destiny, nor did God annul their free will. Therefore, Adam and Eve freely sealed their fate in the Garden of Eden. The duo succumbed to the temptation and weakness of the flesh. Adam and Eve did not adhere to God's Eternal Word. The known consequence of this moral transgression was death. Not to mention, the loss of Paradise was all but inevitable.

The Fall of Man has given rise to a broken world. An inferior world that is defined by sin, guilt, war, fear, greed, punishment, conflict, anger, jealousy, confusion, envy, damnation, prejudice, suicide, discrimination, destruction, depression, and death. How can we live in a world that is characteristic of Paradise, when we do not obey God's Eternal Word?

'Where art thou, Adam, wont with joy to meet. My coming seen far off? I miss thee here. Not pleased. Thus, entertained with solitude. Where obvious duty erewhile appeared unsought. Or come I less conspicuous? Or what change absents thee? Or what chance detains? Come forth. He came, and with him, Eve, more loth, though first to offend. Discountenanced both, and discomposed. Love was not in their looks, neither to God, nor to each other. But apparent guilt and shame. Perturbation and despair. Anger and obstinacy. Hate and guile.'[159]

When God asks us a question, any question, it is put to us for our greater benefit. God already knows the answer, however, God purposefully inquires of us, to prompt our self-reflection and conscious awareness. In the Holy Bible, within the Book of Genesis, we are made privy to God questioning Adam's whereabouts, 'But the LORD God called to the man and said to him, "Where are you?"'[160]

To say the least, Adam and Eve are undoubtedly troubled with the unpleasant thoughts of shame, anger, denial, regret, guilt, and remorse. These undesirable thoughts have arisen due to their sinful conduct. If we reflect carefully on the aforementioned verse of scripture, there is a lasting significance of these words: 'Where are you?' They demonstrate to us, that we cannot indefinitely escape the real consequences of our voluntary and conscious actions. Sooner or later, we are forced to confront reality. A reality of our own making.

God's Eternal Word continues, 'For Adam replies to God, "I heard the sound of you in the Garden, and I was afraid, because I was naked, and I hid myself."'[161] Adam and Eve's minds are now burdened with anxiety, anger, resentment, sadness, confusion,

---

159 Milton, John. (Darbishire, Helen, Ed.) (1958). *The Poetical Works of John Milton*. London: Oxford University Press, p. 216.
160 The Holy Bible (ESV). (2016). The Book of Genesis. Chapter 3, Verse 9.
161 The Holy Bible (ESV). (2016). The Book of Genesis. Chapter 3, Verse 10.

denial, and fear. In hindsight, Adam and Eve have come to the enlightened realisation, that it would have been beneficial for them to have obeyed God's Sovereign Command. In the exercise of their free will, Adam and Eve caused an upheaval, which forever shattered the picturesque serenity found within the Garden of Eden. Since the ill-fated Fall of Man, the human condition has never been, nor will it ever be the same.

'*Least on my head, both sin and punishment, however insupportable, be all devolved. Though should I hold my peace. Yet, thou wouldst easily detect what I conceal. This woman, whom thou madest, to be my help, and gavest me, as thy perfect gift. So good. So fit. So acceptable. So divine. That from her hand, I could suspect no ill, and what she did, whatever in itself, her doing seemed to justify the deed. She gave me of the tree, and I did eat.*'[162]

Regrettably, Adam blames God and Eve for his self-determined actions. In effect, Adam demonstrates a lack of personal accountability and responsibility for his conscious and voluntary conduct. How can Adam be genuinely remorseful for his sinful conduct, when his thoughts, speech, and actions indicate otherwise? Milton's literary writing brings to the forefront of our conscious mind, the undeniable weakness of the human condition. In the flesh, the temptation is ever-present for us to absolve ourselves of the unintended consequences of our immoral actions.

Without a second thought, we often transfer personal responsibility for our sinful conduct onto the change of circumstance, the defence of necessity, the operation of fate, the presence of a challenging condition, the undue influence of a third party, entity, association, organisation, or corporation.

---

162 Milton, John. (Darbishire, Helen, Ed.) (1958). *The Poetical Works of John Milton*. London: Oxford University Press, p. 217.

Rarely do we assume complete personal responsibility for our voluntary decisions and self-determined actions. In particular, when the outcomes of our conscious and voluntary actions do not eventuate as we had intended, it is always a more convenient method of redress, to retrospectively justify our actions, in order to deflect the responsibility for our sinful conduct.

If natural reason was perfect, then Adam ought to have exercised his powers of natural reason not to have consumed the Forbidden Fruit. Given that Adam has consumed the Forbidden Fruit, in the least he ought not to have blamed God or Eve, for his immoral actions. Adam's reprehensible conduct exposes the frailties of the human condition. Our judgement gives rise to mistakes and errors in our life. Having said that, we have a moral obligation to learn from our past experiences, both the good and the not so good. Life is an iterative and experiential process. In order to move onward and upward, we must learn from our past successes and failures. To learn is to understand. To learn is to mature. To learn is to make progress. Without the process of learning, we cannot improve ourselves.

All of our experiential reality of being starts with the acceptance of the cold hard truth—we are imperfect. Progress starts with acknowledging the facts, for what they truly are. Any misrepresentation or distortion of the facts, pertaining to our life, only misleads us further down the path of sin and evil. We are all mortal. We cannot escape our destined date with death. Therefore, let us confront the facts of our life. This includes both the favourable and the unfavourable facts. So that we make the most out of our brief lifetime on Earth. In all circumstances, we ought not to delay acknowledging our imperfections and weaknesses. For what we do not acknowledge as a problem, we never search for a solution.

Returning to the Biblical story of Adam and Eve. Adam's immoral conduct illustrates that it is best we ensure agreement between the exercise of our free will and adherence to God's

Sovereign Command. Often times, when we exercise our free will, we do not carefully and methodically consider the multitude of possible consequences that can eventuate from our actions. Sometimes the consequences are known, other times we confront unintended, or unforeseeable consequences of our conscious and voluntary actions. However, if the employment of our free will is subservient to God's Sovereign Command, then we have greater faith and utmost confidence in our significant decisions. To learn by trial and error is a costly and onerous endeavour. Practical wisdom is learning from the timeless lessons of history.

'Adventurous work. Yet, to thy power and mine not unagreeable. To found a path over this main from Hell. To that new world, where Satan now prevails. A monument of merit. High to all the infernal host. Easing their passage hence. For intercourse, or transmigration, as their lot shall lead. Nor can I miss the way. So strongly drawn by this new felt attraction and instinct.'[163]

At the end of our lifetime, it is the cumulative effect of our voluntary and conscious actions, that we have performed during our time on Earth, which determine whether we are drawn closer or further away from God's Sovereign Kingdom in Heaven. While we are confined to the flesh, we confront many temptations, tests, tragedies, tribulations, and trials. We have to overcome a multitude of vices. We have to improve our few virtues.

During the course of our lifetime, we must ensure our integrity, doctrines, values, principles, beliefs, character, and moral conscience remain intact. We are not assured that the journey of our life is a convenient, good, joyful, and pleasant endeavour. However, keeping and advancing the faith is not an inconsequential aspiration.

---

163 Milton, John. (Darbishire, Helen, Ed.) (1958). *The Poetical Works of John Milton*. London: Oxford University Press, p. 220.

The *Messiah* was correct beyond any trace of doubt, when he asserted the profound statement, 'My kingdom is not of this world.'[164] This broken world is plagued by the negative externalities of sin, conflict, pain, suffering, war, concupiscence, greed, confusion, envy, depression, destruction, damnation, guilt, suicide, and death. Satan prevails in this material world. However, we have the unprecedented opportunity, quite literally the opportunity of a lifetime, to refine our soul, to enlighten our spirit, and to achieve our sanctification. Only by God's Grace, we overcome the weaknesses of the flesh and strengthen our spirit.

In the final analysis, the ways of this world and God's Eternal Word are incongruent. The value system, the fashion trends, the ever-changing elements of popular culture, the competing worldly priorities, the legal conventions, the social customs, and the secular ideologies of the world are always in a state of flux. Yet, in all respects, God's Word is Constant, Eternal, and Perfect. Therefore, we must self-determine which way is our way. Shall we tread the way of this world? Alternatively, shall we tread the matchless path that God has ordained for us?

---

164 The Holy Bible (ESV). (2016). The Gospel of John. Chapter 18, Verse 36.

'The growing miseries. Which Adam saw already in part, though hid in gloomiest shade. To sorrow abandoned, but worse felt within, and in a troubled sea of passion tossed. Thus, to disburden sought with sad complaint. O miserable of happy! Is this the end of this new glorious world, and me so late, the glory of that glory, who now become accursed of blessed? Hide me from the face of God, whom to behold was then my height of happiness. Yet well, if here would end the misery. I deserved it, and would bear my own deservings; but this will not serve. All that I eat or drink, or shall beget, is propagated curse.'[165]

Following Adam and Eve's fatal consumption of the Forbidden Fruit, the negative consequences of their sinful conduct are apparent. Adam comes to the inevitable and painful realisation, that the pursuit of sin has meant the irreplaceable loss of Paradise. The once timeless beauty, peace, pleasure, serenity, happiness, joy, love, and innocence of the Garden of Eden has been forever tarnished. As a logical consequence, Adam possesses the worldly knowledge of good and evil. A most inferior exchange. The acquisition of the knowledge of good and evil has caused Adam to distance himself from God's Love and Presence.

Within the Holy Bible, in the Book of Genesis, we are reminded of the disastrous consequences of the Fall of Man, 'Then the eyes of both were opened, and they knew that they were naked. And they sewed fig leaves together and made themselves loincloths. And they heard the sound of the LORD God walking in the Garden in the cool of the day, and the man and his wife hid themselves from the presence of the LORD God among the trees of the Garden. But the LORD God called to the man and said to him, "Where are you?" And he said, "I heard the sound of you in the Garden, and I was afraid, because I was naked, and I

---

165 Milton, John. (Darbishire, Helen, Ed.) (1958). *The Poetical Works of John Milton*. London: Oxford University Press, p. 231.

hid myself."[166] The aforementioned scripture verse ends with the profound words, 'and I hid myself.' We too have engaged in sinful conduct. That is not the question under consideration. Sinful conduct is a fact of human life. The question we ought to direct our attention to is: What are we hiding from?

The Book of Genesis teaches us the paramount importance of distinguishing temporal knowledge from eternal wisdom. God has given us wisdom, conscience, knowledge, insight, discernment, and understanding in order to live our life on higher moral principles. To live a righteous and honourable life is for our greater benefit. Knowledge is inferior to wisdom. Empirical knowledge obtained by the five senses allows us to learn more about the natural world around us. Having said that, we secure no lasting peace, nor absolute certainty in our endless quest for knowledge. Worldly knowledge is always a means to an end. Wisdom is the end.

> *'But natural necessity begot. God made thee of choice*
> *His own, and of His own to serve Him. Thy reward was*
> *of His Grace. Thy punishment then justly is at His Will.*
> *Be it so. For I submit. His doom is fair. That dust I am,*
> *and shall to dust return. O welcome hour whenever!*
> *Why delay His hand, to execute what His Decree.'*[167]

We witness Adam give voice to the stark poverty of the human condition. A persistent and immaterial poverty of our being, which is all too self-evident when one is engulfed in sin. In the world, we are never satisfied with our state of being, period. Without God's Presence, the human condition is dejected, unsatisfactory, and incomplete. God has created humanity, starting with Adam and Eve, as a symbolic expression of God's

---

166 The Holy Bible (ESV). (2016). The Book of Genesis. Chapter 3, Verses 7–10.
167 Milton, John. (Darbishire, Helen, Ed.) (1958). *The Poetical Works of John Milton.* London: Oxford University Press, pp. 232–233.

Creative Power. Human civilisation has no ulterior purpose, aside from bringing God glory and honour. Our performance of righteous and honourable actions is only secured by God's Grace, Mercy, and Favour. Those select individuals, who align their free will with God's Sovereign Will, they obtain peace during their lifetime on Earth. In all respects, God's Judgement and Divine Providence cannot be circumvented.

> *'Yet one doubt pursues me still. Least all, I cannot die. Least that pure breath of life. The spirit of man, which God inspired, cannot together perish with this corporeal clod. Then in the grave, or in some other dismal place. Who knows, but I shall die a living death? O thought horrid, if true! Yet why? It was but breath of life that sinned. What dies, but what had life and sin? The body properly hath neither. All of me then shall die. Let this appease the doubt. Since human reach no further knows.'*[168]

Our present and immediate existence constitutes two distinct components—the material and the immaterial. The material dimension of our being is the human body, including the sense organs of perception. That is to say, the entirety of our corporeal dimension of being in the world. On the other hand, the immaterial dimension of our temporal being includes the soul, spirit, intellect, mind, and moral conscience. This is described as the entirety of our metaphysical and spiritual dimension of being in the world. With the constant passage of time, the human body perishes. The old gives way to the new. This is the supreme way of nature. The reality of our being cannot be superseded or altered by our reason or willpower.

When we disassociate the nexus between the body and the spirit. That is to infer, we intellectually segregate these two

---

168 Milton, John. (Darbishire, Helen, Ed.) (1958). *The Poetical Works of John Milton*. London: Oxford University Press, p. 233.

concepts. Then we come to the realisation that the phenomenon of our spirit endures the finite existence of the human body. The spirit is not confined to the fixed limitations and deterioration that the human body, by the strict and constant necessity of time, is subject to. For example, consider the human body is subject to sickness, disease, ageing, loss of skeletal muscle strength, the inability to utilise select nerves or muscles (i.e., neuromuscular disorders), hearing loss, cataracts, refractive errors, and the onset of dementia. Therefore, it is reasonable to assert that the spirit transcends the inherent limitations of the flesh. The spirit endures what the flesh cannot. The spirit surpasses the fixed and known capacities of the flesh.

Ultimately, the final destination of our spirit is union with God. This lifetime presents us with a rare opportunity to further our final and ultimate cause. With that final and ultimate cause being to refine our character, improve our virtues, and cultivate our spirit. Sanctification is only received by God's Grace. Having said that, there are several practical initiatives that we must effectuate in order to live a good and honourable life. For example, consider charitable works, the performance of penance, acts of forgiveness, or earnest prayer to God. While salvation is not achieved by merit or good works, through our wholesome actions, we bring our spirit ever closer to God's Spirit.

The totality of human thought is inadequate to comprehend God's Power, Grace, and Glory. The human intellectual capacity cannot ascertain a reality that is beyond the real boundaries of the five senses. For the five senses are only sufficient to provision humanity with empirical knowledge of the natural world. All doctrines and theories pertaining to the fields of metaphysics, theology, philosophy, and spirituality, are beyond verification, confirmation, or absolute proof. Therefore, it is only by faith, and not by knowledge, that our belief in God is affirmed and reaffirmed.

Without qualification, what we place our trust in defines our life. We ought to ensure that our highest trust is not committed to our vocation, private property, employment, relationships, marriage, children, private wealth, or the countless material phenomena of this world, but only to God.

'For though the LORD of all be infinite, is His wrath also? Be it. Man is not so. But mortal, doomed. How can He exercise wrath without end on man whom death must end? Can He make deathless death? That were to make strange contradiction. Which to God Himself impossible is held. As argument of weakness, not of power. Will He draw out, for anger's sake, finite to infinite? In punished man, to satisfy His rigour, satisfied, never? That were to extend His sentence, beyond dust and nature's law, by which all causes else according still to the reception of their matter act. Not to the extent of their own sphere. But say that death be not one stroke, as I supposed. Bereaving sense. But endless misery.' [169]

We all have to run our race in order to fulfil our destiny on Earth. Just as there is a beginning marked by birth, thus, according to the laws of nature, there is also an end, defined by death. Humanity cannot escape the fixed cycle of birth and death. It is not the duration of the human life span that matters, but rather what we accomplish with our finite lifetime on Earth.

Ultimately, even if we live a long life reaching 120 years, still we cannot outrun the Grim Reaper. Nonetheless, we can live a beneficial, purposeful, productive, and meaningful life. It is by living an enriching, rewarding, productive, good, and wholesome life, that we harbour no regrets, when our destined time to confront death arrives.

---

169 Milton, John. (Darbishire, Helen, Ed.) (1958). *The Poetical Works of John Milton.* London: Oxford University Press, p. 233.

We must always remember that the human capacity for love, imagination, thought, curiosity, compassion, gratitude, joy, hope, benevolence, and creativity is remarkable. Therefore, we ought to utilise our talents, gifts, ideas, principles, doctrines, expertise, wisdom, knowledge, and lived experience, to leave the world in a better place than how we found it. There is an indisputable moral imperative upon us, to ensure that each succeeding generation has a better life than the preceding generation. This is the ultimate litmus test of a life well-lived. The lasting legacy of our life ought to be the enrichment and advancement of the human civilisation. This is a lofty and transcendental endeavour, one which keeps us preoccupied for the entirety of our lifetime.

During our limited time on Earth, our unique perception of events, crises, peace, war, justice, injustice, grief, loss, bereavement, gain, trust, betrayal, love, indifference, prejudice, discrimination, and forbearance, and indeed, our perception of life itself, all cumulatively serve to define our lived experience. We must not permit the contours of our personal experience to be defined by misery, grief, jealousy, pain, envy, confusion, loss, fear, anxiety, hate, apprehension, guilt, and suffering.

We must transcend the privation, struggle, loss, pain, envy, grief, tragedy, remorse, suffering, heartache, trauma, and issues associated with our life. During the tests, tragedies, tribulations, and trials of our life, we must hold steadfast to the positive perception of happiness, joy, hope, grace, gratitude, mercy, love, peace, benevolence, forgiveness, and faith. In as much as our worldly reality defines our perception, our perception defines our worldly reality.

Within the Holy Bible, in the Book of Psalms, King David demonstrates the practical wisdom of positive affirmations. David went through life-changing ordeals, struggles, wars, and conquests, but in the midst of all this turmoil, when situations or circumstances were not always advantageous, he reassured himself, 'my cup overflows.'[170]

We too must employ the indescribable power of positive affirmations. For our external reality of being commences with our internal thoughts. When we understand this assertion, then we ought to consciously analyse our thoughts. What are we thinking? What are we associating with? What are we identifying with? For what we think, associate, and identify with, these factors influence our present and immediate state of being in the world.

'So disinherited. How would you bless me? Me, now your curse! Ah, why should all humankind for one man's fault thus guiltless be condemned? If guiltless? But from me, what can proceed, but all corrupt, both mind and will depraved, not to do only, but to will the same with me? How can they then acquitted, stand in sight of God?'[171]

Our conscious and voluntary actions bring about blessings and curses in the world. Therefore, it is important that we act with prudence, foresight, sensibility, understanding, and wisdom. The significant consequences of a person's actions last far beyond their immediate and present lifetime. Consequences are passed down the family lineage, that is to say, on to future generations. Future generations that have nothing to do with the actions of their predecessors, whom gave rise to such consequences. History is harsh. The future descendants of a family lineage can stand condemned for their predecessor's immoral conduct. If and when we follow God's Eternal Word, then we are assured that we are on the path of righteousness.

---

170 The Holy Bible (ESV). (2016). The Book of Psalms. Chapter 23, Verse 5.
171 Milton, John. (Darbishire, Helen, Ed.) (1958). *The Poetical Works of John Milton.* London: Oxford University Press, p. 234.

God never deceives humanity. God always honours sacred covenants. This theological assertion holds true, even when we fall short in upholding our sacred beliefs and keeping our personal commitments. In the Holy Bible, consider the following Biblical verse in the Book of Genesis. God enters into a covenant with Abram, even though Abram does not agree to anything in return, nor has Abram been bound by a solemn oath to the same covenant, however, God honoured the sacred promise.

Concerning God and Abram's Covenant, the specific passage of scripture informs us, 'When the Sun had gone down and it was dark, behold, a smoking fire pot and a flaming torch passed between these pieces. On that day the LORD made a covenant with Abram, saying, "To your offspring I give this land, from the river of Egypt to the great river, the river of Euphrates, the land of the Kenites, the Kenizzites, the Kadmonites, the Hittites, the Perizzites, the Rephaim, the Amorites, the Canaanites, the Girgashites, and the Jebusites."'[172]

The aforementioned passage of scripture demonstrates to us, that God desires our prosperity, success, wealth, joy, abundance, and happiness. We must not permit the voice of temptation, doubt, confusion, fear, or envy to mislead our life journey. As the Biblical narrative of Adam and Eve in the Garden of Eden demonstrates, temptation is ever-present. Temptation to transgress God's Eternal Word is a serious problem. We are periodically tested during our lifetime. The primary responsibility is upon us to exercise our free will in accordance with God's Sovereign Will. In life, the flesh is always tempted to travel by the most convenient route. On the contrary, the spirit is willing to traverse the arduous journey.

---

172 The Holy Bible (ESV). (2016). The Book of Genesis. Chapter 15, Verses 17–21.

'Him after all disputes forced. I absolve. All my evasions vain and reasonings, though through mazes, lead me still but to my own conviction. First and last on me. Me only. As the source and spring of all corruption. All the blame lights due. So might the wrath. Fond wish! Couldst, thou support that burden heavier than the Earth to bear. Than all the world much heavier, though divided with that bad woman? Thus, what thou desire, and what thou fearest, alike destroys all hope of refuge, and concludes thee miserable, beyond all past example and future. To Satan, only like both crime and doom. O Conscience, into what abyss of fears and horrors hast thou driven me? Out of which I find no way. From deep to deeper plunged!'[173]

The immense burden of guilt is too onerous to sustain for an entire lifetime. This is why the act of confession is of paramount importance. Confession allows us to be absolved of our countless sins. Our life journey is not a linear and harmonious trajectory. We make mistakes. We demonstrate several errors of judgement. Occasionally, we fall short in the execution of our duties. Most importantly, our performance is not everything. What truly matters is our intentions, doctrines, motivations, values, ideals, beliefs, and principles. Confession allows us the opportunity to accept responsibility for our faults. We all have our faults. Therefore, confession is for everyone.

From time to time, the application of human effort is inexact. This is a cold hard truth. A universal reality which we must accept. Where human thought, intuition, action, intention, free will, judgement, intellect, memory, reason, and determination are imperfect, we ought to position our reliance upon God. Through faith, we have God's Spirit alongside our life journey. God's Spirit embodies the capacity to guide, counsel, and support us.

---

173 Milton, John. (Darbishire, Helen, Ed.) (1958). *The Poetical Works of John Milton*. London: Oxford University Press, p. 234.

Ultimately, God delivers us from temptation, sin, evil, vice, and error. In order for our faith to be truly lived, we must give witness of our affirmation to God.

Experience, knowledge, and wisdom inform us that the deflection or assignment of blame to our spouse, or another significant person in our life, does not achieve any productive purpose. In all situations, we must be willing to listen and exchange different points of view in a respectful and courteous manner. When and where disagreements arise, the chain of communication must be kept open at all times. Most importantly, the fine art of communication involves both listening and speaking, not just the performance of one component at the expense of the other.

The greatest gift we give our spouse, is to understand them. The greatest gift our spouse gives to us, is to be understood. As long as two parties are communicating, the opportunity remains open that an issue is resolved amicably. Our relationships define our life, therefore, we need to carefully consider how we treat each other. Distrustful and dysfunctional relationships are developed on the art of manipulation. Successful and healthy relationships are developed on the art of articulation.

As moral agents, we are all personally responsible for our conscious and free willed actions in the world. Thus, we have an obligation to carefully think through the [known] consequences of our [voluntary] actions, before we effectuate them. We must permit the righteousness of reason, rather than the permissive power of passion, to guide our voluntary actions. We ought not to permit our mind to be misguided by the undesirable emotions, or the intrusive thoughts of fear, doubt, anger, passion, horror, guilt, confusion, envy, jealousy, uncertainty, or vengeance. We must discipline our mind to hold steadfast to the attributes of humility, gratitude, temperance, moderation, serenity, patience, faith, diligence, love, peace, joy, equanimity, benevolence, and charity. We have a moral obligation, to ensure that we perform our significant and constructive role in the protracted battle between good and evil.

When all is said and done, we have surety in God's Eternal Promises. For God creates, preserves, and destroys all life on Earth. Without God there is no hope, faith, harmony, victory, joy, love, peace, or happiness in the world. When we have gone astray in our thought, speech, and conduct, then it is incumbent upon us to beseech God for mercy. No person is beyond God's Sovereign Power to forgive. It is only by God's Grace that we are redeemed from the negative consequences of sin. God can utilise any person on Earth to perform God's Sovereign Will.

No individual is too far gone, to be an integral part of God's Ministry. Humanity is quick to judge an individual from their appearance, athletic accomplishments, attainments, aspirations, assets, accolades, awards, abilities, and academic achievements. On the contrary, God searches the heart, spirit, intentions, thoughts, motives, and desires of a person, before accrediting them as fit and proper for the advancement of God's Sovereign Kingdom on Earth. God's Grace can accredit any person for the fulfilment of God's Divine Purpose on Earth.

'If prayers could alter high decrees. I to that place would speed before Thee, and be louder heard, that on my head all might be visited. Thy frailty and infirmer sex forgiven. To me committed and by me exposed. But rise. Let us no longer contend. Nor blame each other. Blamed enough elsewhere, but strive in offices of love. How we may lighten each other's burden in our share of woe.'[174]

When we pray to God, we must hold on to hope, that God answers our prayers. While sometimes we are disappointed with the immediate results of our prayers, the greater point to remember

---

174 Milton, John. (Darbishire, Helen, Ed.) (1958). *The Poetical Works of John Milton*. London: Oxford University Press, p. 237.

is that through the act of prayer our perseverance, patience, faith, commitment, trust, belief, and hope are strengthened. All of these character-building traits ultimately benefit our life, and the people around us, in one way or another.

It is true, sometimes our prayers are not answered as soon as we had envisaged. It is also true, sometimes our prayers are not answered how we had envisaged. In all cases, we must remain hopeful that God has a better and brighter future planned for us. We have to trust in God's Timing. After all, God's Ways are not our ways. For our part, we must strengthen our confidence in God, to direct our journey towards a blessed, wholesome, and productive life.

Once we acknowledge and reflect upon the brevity of human life, we arrive at the undeniable and irrefutable conclusion, that forgiveness is the most appropriate method to deal with our disagreements and misdeeds. To blame a third party for the consequences of our actions, even where the liability for error is mutual, never resolves a quarrel, quagmire, or quandary. To move forward, one must set aside the apportionment of blame. Any attempt to assign blame, only leads to a hardened heart and much resentment in our spirit. It is true, a heart replete with love requires the generous dispensation of forgiveness.

'Part of our sentence. That thy seed shall bruise the Serpent's head. Piteous amends. Unless be meant. Whom I conjecture, our grand foe Satan, who in the Serpent hath contrived against us this deceit. To crush his head, would be revenge indeed. Which will be lost by death brought on ourselves, or childless days, resolved. As thou proposest. So, our foe shall escape his punishment ordained, and we instead shall double ours upon our heads. No more be mentioned then of violence against ourselves, and wilful barrenness. That cuts us off from hope, and savours only rancour and pride. Impatience and despite. Reluctance against God and His just yoke. Laid on our necks.'[175]

Justice and mercy go hand in glove. We must not do unto others, what we would not accept done unto ourselves. God's Justice is perfect and final. Given that we are all sinners, we ought to fear God's Righteous Judgement. We must not take the law into our own hands. The performance of a wrong never rights another wrong. For two wrongs never made a right. We must let God determine justice and execute punishment. The powerful Devil is not beyond the jurisdiction or mandate of all-powerful God to punish. Indeed, the Devil periodically tests, troubles, torments, and tempts us in the flesh. This is the fine test of our character. A test that we all must confront.

Within the Holy Bible, the Book of Job is a remarkable demonstration of how the Devil tested Job's loyalty to God. Specifically, what were the motivations and assumptions underlying Job's faith, commitment, and trust in God? Did Job only place his confidence in God, for God had provisioned grace, love, prosperity, abundance, and favour upon Job's life? Alternatively, did Job love God, in spite of his blessed life? Did Job still trust in God, in spite of all the gifts, talents, children,

---

175 Milton, John. (Darbishire, Helen, Ed.) (1958). *The Poetical Works of John Milton*. London: Oxford University Press, p. 239.

private wealth, private property, and good health that Job possessed? It was the Devil's misconceived proposition, that Job only loved and remembered God, due to the fact the God had blessed Job's life with prosperity, success, private wealth, happiness, and abundance.

The Devil ignorantly alleged, that in the absence of God's Blessing, Grace, and Favour, Job will not love, let alone remember God. In order to affirm or refute the Devil's misconceived assertion, God gave the Devil permission to test His faithful servant, Job. The Biblical narrative portrays the losses and setbacks that Job endured throughout his lifetime. However, Job kept his faith in God till the end of the battle between good and evil. Job overcame the dark forces of evil with a heart replete of goodness and unconditional love. Job kept his hope in God. Job was tested to his psychological, spiritual, and physical limits; however, Job did not relent or waver in his faith. In spite of all the heartache, grief, trauma, loss, and pain that Job endured in his lifetime, Job affirmed his belief in God, till the very end of his agonising ordeal.

In the Book of Job, the verses of scripture narrate the following discourse, 'For I know that my Redeemer lives, and at the last He will stand upon the Earth. And after my skin has been thus destroyed, yet in my flesh I shall see God, whom I shall see for myself, and my eyes shall behold, and not another. My heart faints within me!'[176] Towards the final passages of scripture within the Book of Job, we learn how God generously rewarded Job for his unwavering courage, determination, faith, loyalty, love, and belief. Job's fortunes were restored. Job prospered in the final phase of his life, 'And the LORD restored the fortunes of Job, when he had prayed for his friends. And the LORD gave Job twice as much as he had before.'[177]

---

176 The Holy Bible (ESV). (2016). The Book of Job. Chapter 19, Verses 25–27.
177 The Holy Bible (ESV). (2016). The Book of Job. Chapter 42, Verse 10.

For our part, we ought to select our battles with discernment. While the Devil tempts us with countless desires, ideas, and thoughts, not every battle is worth our time, energy, effort, resources, and attention. The imperative is upon us, to selectively and strategically engage in the battles that advance our God-given destiny. We ought to fight the crucial battles that move us forward on the righteous path towards our God-given destiny. On the contrary, if we fail to act, if we fail to exercise our personal agency to secure a decisive victory on the battles that decide our destiny, then we are deprived of the opportunity to self-determine our fate.

Within the Holy Bible, consider King David's exceptional life story. A story which is a telling and illustrative example of faith. At the request of his father Jesse, David went to deliver food to his brothers in the Valley of Elah. Now one of David's brothers resented him. Nonetheless, David did not get entangled in a pointless argument or meritless fight, 'Now Eliab his eldest brother heard when he spoke to the men. And Eliab's anger was kindled against David, and he said, "Why have you come down? And with whom have you left those few sheep in the wilderness? I know your presumption and the evil of your heart, for you have come down to see the battle."'[178] David turned around and walked away from the temptation to reprimand his eldest brother.

On the contrary, David made inquiries into the reward for defeating the fierce, ferocious, and formidable Goliath. We learn that the reward for defeating Goliath was, 'the King will enrich the man who kills him with great riches and will give him his daughter and make his father's house free in Israel.'[179] This was a destiny-defining moment for David. This was a strategic battle that would change David's life trajectory in a substantial manner.

---

178 The Holy Bible (ESV). (2016). The First Book of Samuel. Chapter 17, Verse 28.
179 The Holy Bible (ESV). (2016). The First Book of Samuel. Chapter 17, Verse 25.

Upon securing the victory against Goliath, David married into royalty. David rightfully received King Saul's beloved daughter, Michal as his wife. In addition, David's father's house was lawfully exempt from the payment of taxes to King Saul.

With the LORD's Grace, Favour, and Blessing, David fought and won this formidable battle against Goliath. David's victory not only changed and defined the course of history for his people; however, David's victory secured him his God-given destiny. It was with the correct and proper employment of discernment, that David self-determined which battles to fight, and equally, which battles to withdraw from. There is a fine line between courage and recklessness. In this respect, David faultlessly realised the exact contours of personal agency.

In the final analysis, our lifetime on Earth is not without end. Therefore, we must also be prudent in how we utilise our finite energy, resources, expertise, talents, knowledge, and abilities. We must select our battles wisely. We must not become enmeshed in quarrels that do not advance our God-given destiny. We must know what is worth fighting for. We must know what is worth dying for. Only then is it worth living.

'*To evils which our own misdeeds have wrought. He will instruct us praying, and of grace beseeching Him. So, as we need not fear to pass commodiously this life. Sustained by Him with many comforts. Till we end in dust. Our final rest and native home. What better can we do. Then to the place repairing where He judged us. Prostrate fall before Him reverent, and there confess humbly our faults and pardon beg.*'[180]

Our voluntary and conscious actions determine our life trajectory. This is true, both for the good and evil conduct that we partake

---

180 Milton, John. (Darbishire, Helen, Ed.) (1958). *The Poetical Works of John Milton*. London: Oxford University Press, p. 240.

in during our finite lifetime on Earth. We must keep our distance from the falsehood and misrepresentations that the Devil assails our mind with. We are not on Earth for eternity. The end of life is identical for all people—an end defined by death of the flesh. However, the spirit lives on. The immortal soul endures the materiality of our short-lived Earthly existence. During our life journey, we must not forget to worship, pray, remember, trust, love, and serve God. This approach to living grants us the unmerited opportunity to cleanse our soul of its countless sins.

CHAPTER 11

PARADISE LOST: BOOK ELEVEN

'For dissolution wrought by sin. That first distempered
all things, and of incorrupt corrupted.
I at first with two fair gifts created him endowed.
With happiness and immortality. That fondly lost.
This other served but to eternise woe. Till I provided death.
So, death becomes his final remedy.'

MILTON

BOOK ELEVEN of *Paradise Lost* is the narrative of the Son of God interceding to save humanity from the foretold consequences of Original Sin. The Son of God presents earnest prayers to God. In all respects, the Son of God seeks God's Sovereign Will be done, both in the Kingdom of Heaven and on Earth. The Son of God is merciful in his gracious endeavour to absolve Adam and Eve from the disastrous consequences of their sinful conduct in the Garden of Eden. God accepts the Son's faithful prayers and sincere petitions on behalf of Adam and Eve. However, as atonement for their sins, Adam and Eve are banished from the Garden of Eden.

There is a transcendent and spiritual discourse between Adam and the Archangel, Saint Michael. Saint Michael candidly informs Adam, that it is God's Sovereign Will, that Adam and Eve immediately depart the Garden of Eden. Upon the receipt of this sombre news, Eve is distressed and she laments. Adam pleads to God for mercy and forgiveness. In the end, Adam and Eve submit to God's Sovereign Will. Book Eleven is a classic example of the fundamental principle underlying all human conduct—our voluntary and conscious actions have profound and unintended consequences. Therefore, humanity must reason appropriately. Humanity must assume personal responsibility for its collective and universal conduct.

'By the waters of life. Wherever they sat. In fellowships of joy. The sons of light hasted, resorting to the summons high, and took their seats. Till from His Throne Supreme, the Almighty thus pronounced His Sovereign Will. O Sons, like one of us, man is become to know both good and evil. Since his taste of that defended fruit. But let him boast his knowledge of good lost, and evil got. Happier, had it sufficed him, to have known good by itself, and evil not at all.' [181]

Herein we learn of the tragic fate that awaits not only Adam and Eve, but all of human civilisation. The wearisome burden of the knowledge of good and evil is now upon the shoulders of humanity. We have come to the unfaithful realisation, through Adam and Eve's immoral actions, that it is always best to observe God's Eternal Decree, rather than employ our finite power of natural reason. We must not supersede God's Divine Command.

Ever since the transgression of Adam and Eve in the Garden of Eden, the application of human reason has led us astray from God's Eternal Word. Our free will has been misemployed to further the aims, aspirations, and ambitions of our ego.

---

181 Milton, John. (Darbishire, Helen, Ed.) (1958). *The Poetical Works of John Milton*. London: Oxford University Press, p. 244.

How, in our rational, measured, and reasoned mind, could we have perceived that we equal God in all respects, let alone in the possession of knowledge?

From that cursed time, at which Original Sin was effectuated by Adam and Eve in the Garden of Eden, the knowledge of good and evil has tormented human civilisation. In fact, this newfound knowledge of good and evil continues to torment humanity, until the end of human civilisation. With the power of hindsight, we would have been more fortunate observing God's Divine Commandment. To defer our imprecise and fallible judgement to God is true wisdom. Not to mention, the prolonged and tiresome search for the accumulation of worldly knowledge has no rest in sight. There is no relief in store. There is no respite in supply.

The endless and irrational quest for knowledge has destroyed the peace, serenity, joy, hope, faith, happiness, and equanimity of humanity. The insatiable desire to obtain ever greater empirical knowledge has diminished the pleasure and happiness of living our life characterised by faith, love, hope, grace, belief, tolerance, respect, contentment, joy, acceptance, equality, security, integrity, and human dignity.

> *'But infinite in pardon was my judge. That I, who first brought death on all, am graced the source of life. Next favourable thou, who highly thus to entitle me vouchsafest, far other name deserving. But the field to labour calls us now with sweat imposed. Though after sleepless night. For see the morning. All unconcerned with our unrest, begins her rosy progress smiling. Let us forth. I never from thy side henceforth to stray. Where our day's work lies. Though now enjoined laborious. Till day droop. While here we dwell. What can be toilsome in these pleasant walks? Here let us live. Though in fallen state. Content.'*[182]

Unfortunately, as a direct and immediate consequence of Original Sin and the Fall of Man, humanity exists in a fallen state. This is our newfound reality of being. A comfortless reality in a broken world. A conventional reality that is enmeshed in the bounds of pain, suffering, guilt, sin, punishment, domestic violence, crime, illicit substance addictions, alcohol use disorder, anger, envy, suicide, confusion, denial, depression, damnation, and death. So long as we exist in the flesh, we encounter issues, problems, challenges, and calamities in this broken world. We must seek God to secure our peace, hope, salvation, forgiveness, love, faith, compassion, and mercy.

Albeit we are not resident in Paradise during our finite tenure on Earth, we have the opportunity to ensure that we live our life characterised by contentment, equality, peace, justice, respect, human dignity, love, and equanimity. Our state of mind is for us to self-determine. No matter what our circumstances, we ought to self-determine our actions, so that we are at peace with our worldly reality. Once we understand that perfection in this broken world is beyond attainment, then we ought to reconcile

---

182 Milton, John. (Darbishire, Helen, Ed.) (1958). *The Poetical Works of John Milton*. London: Oxford University Press, p. 246.

ourselves with our best effort to run our race. For the [ideal] state of perfection cannot be obtained within our [present] state of being.

Despite the struggles, upheavals, and tragedies that we experience during our lifetime, we must preserve our hope in God. For God's Loving, Merciful, and Compassionate nature is beyond doubt. If we were all judged according to the outcomes of our voluntary and conscious actions, none of us would have performed perfectly on Earth to be permitted entry into the Kingdom of Heaven. Even when we make mistakes and fall short in our conduct, it is the expression of God's Forgiving Nature, Goodness, and Righteousness, that God pardons our [unintentional] sinful conduct.

In the Holy Bible, within the Book of Hebrews, let us examine the following scripture verse, 'For I will be merciful toward their iniquities, and I will remember their sins no more.'[183] In addition, we are also reminded of God's Compassionate Nature in the Book of Isaiah, 'I, I am He who blots out your transgressions for My own sake, and I will not remember your sins.'[184] Therefore, we ought to place our faith, trust, confidence, and reliance upon God, so that we are forgiven, even when we are not deserving of such divine forgiveness. God's Compassion, Favour, Love, and Mercy are boundless.

It is the way of this world, it is the way of human life, that we must toil in society to earn our living. To labour and earn one's living is an essential attribute of living a good and honourable life. Work provides us with the opportunity to live a productive and wholesome life. In addition, the performance of work ensures that we make a meaningful contribution to civil society. The right to work is a universal human right. Not to mention, there are many social and economic benefits associated with work.

---

183 The Holy Bible (ESV). (2016). The Book of Hebrews. Chapter 8, Verse 12.
184 The Holy Bible (ESV). (2016). The Book of Isaiah. Chapter 43, Verse 25.

When it comes to work, true sensibility resides in finding our vocation. Our vocation consists of what we are good at and what we enjoy doing. Reconciling our vocation with our employment, provisions us with the intrinsic motivation to put our heart, body, soul, spirit, and mind into our work.

Genuine satisfaction and good pleasure from our work is secured by the engagement in our labour of love. Work that brings us meaning, purpose, happiness, and joy, always feels effortless and rewarding, no matter the sacrifices that it entails. When our work incorporates our passion, the hours seem short and the satisfaction is long-lived. The performance of work is also fundamentally a part of what makes us human. Work is as much a part of our constitution, as is our requirement to obtain sufficient sleep, to socialise with our friends, ingest nutritious food, and consume adequate water. After all, our life consists of work, rest, and leisure. The key to a harmonious and blessed life is to do all three in their right measure.

Given that we dedicate the majority of our adult lifetime engaged in some form of paid employment, it is essential that we provision proper consideration to what type of work we would like to be engaged in across our working age life. The answer to this question, in equal measure, resides in being attuned to one's heart and mind. When both the intellect and our passion determine our vocation, we know that we have found something that we enjoy being occupied and absorbed in. To find and wholeheartedly pursue one's calling, this is a blessing of a lifetime.

'O Eve, some further change awaits us nigh. Which Heaven, by these mute signs in nature shows forerunners of his purpose, or to warn us, haply too secure, of our discharge from penalty, because from death released some days. How long? What till then our life? Who knows? Or more than this, that we are dust, and thither must return, and be no more?'[185]

No man or woman circumvents the laws and principles of nature. Human life is marked by the fixed cycle of birth and death. During our limited lifetime on Earth, we must earnestly strive to align our life's worldly purpose with God's Higher Purpose. If we follow God's Eternal Word, we are assured of a blessed and prosperous life. Too often, in the exercise of our free will and personal agency, we make decisions that are fundamentally not in our best interest. God knows what is best for our life. We ought to humble ourselves before God. We ought to place our trust and confidence in God. When we position our ego and pride aside, we arrive at the insightful realisation, that God best directs our life journey.

Given the unquestionable jurisdiction of mortality on every human life, one day we shall no longer remain on Earth. Upon the inevitable and rapid approach of death, no person desires to be consumed with the unpleasant feelings of guilt, denial, remorse, regret, and repentance. Therefore, it is the present time alone, which provisions us with the invaluable opportunity to create our desired reality. If we live our life defined by productivity, love, generosity, social justice, faith, work, respect, tolerance, human dignity, equality, community service, forgiveness, mercy, compassion, joy, and charity, then we have negligible cause to experience contrition, for the manner in which we have utilised our lifetime on Earth.

---

185 Milton, John. (Darbishire, Helen, Ed.) (1958). *The Poetical Works of John Milton*. London: Oxford University Press, p. 247.

As the well-known saying goes, 'actions always speak louder than words.' Literally, this human life is a once-in-a-lifetime opportunity, for us to fulfil our inherent potential. It is through the right combination of thought, speech, and conduct, that we create the conventional reality of our mind's desire.

'Yet, doubt not, but in valley and in plain, God is, as here; and will be found alike present, and of His Presence many a sign, still following thee. Still compassing thee round. With goodness and paternal love, His face express, and of His steps, the track divine. Which that thou mayest believe, and be confirmed.'[186]

During both the high and low moments of our life, we always depend upon God to be present and supportive along our life journey. The Devil's ambitious and ill-intentioned objective is to sever the powerful bond between humanity and God's Eternal Word. The Devil is a grand master of deception and manipulation. The Devil is advanced in the methods of psychological, spiritual, emotional, and physical warfare. The sole purpose of the Devil is to deceive humanity into embracing intrusive thoughts of fear, shame, worry, denial, guilt, envy, confusion, jealousy, doubt, incompleteness, anger, loneliness, pride, arrogance, conceit, depression, suicide, and temptation. With God's Spiritual Armour, we strengthen our resolve to fight the good fight of faith.

In the final analysis, our thoughts and beliefs define every dimension of our being. Our thoughts and beliefs create our living reality on Earth. We can, and we shall overcome the pitfalls, lies, deception, and temptations that the Devil directs our way. The origins of the material world begin within our mind. Our mind is where all our novel ideas, concepts, principles, ideologies, doctrines, and philosophies are formulated.

---

186 Milton, John. (Darbishire, Helen, Ed.) (1958). *The Poetical Works of John Milton.* London: Oxford University Press, p. 251.

The epic spiritual battle of good and evil is won or lost in our mind. If we conquer our mind, then we have effectively prevented the Devil from securing a foothold in the formation of our thoughts. We must ensure that this epic spiritual battle results in the definitive victory of good over evil. In this, and all our endeavours, we must remember that God's mercy is unassailable. To God belongs the glory of victory!

'Alas, both for the deed and for the cause! But have I now seen death? Is this the way I must return to native dust? O sight of terror! Foul and ugly to behold. Horrid to think. How horrible to feel! To whom thus Michael replied. Death thou hast seen in his first shape on man. But many shapes of death, and many are the ways that lead to his grim cave. All dismal. Yet, to sense, more terrible at the entrance, than within.'[187]

Our death can eventuate from countless causes. Yet, despite what the cause of our death may or may not be, the occurrence of our death is inevitable. In so far as human life is concerned, we cannot debate the fixed reality of our mortality. We have no choice in the matter, but to live our life in accordance with the laws and principles of nature. In all living species, death cannot be denied its rightful and proper place. Since death cannot be prevented, there is no utility in fearing our certain existential demise. It is illogical and irrational to focus on the fixed biological reality of birth and death. The unchanging reality of our being is beyond our control.

Rather, we must concentrate our thoughts, time, endeavours, resources, and energy on what we can control in this lifetime. Now if we proceed to utilise our finite lifetime on Earth with sensibility, rationality, understanding, and the exercise of our

---

187 Milton, John. (Darbishire, Helen, Ed.) (1958). *The Poetical Works of John Milton*. London: Oxford University Press, pp. 253–254.

natural reason, then at the end of our lifetime, we ought to be filled with a sense of achievement. A sense of accomplishment. A sense of having lived a purposeful, productive, and passionate life. In all respects, we must remember that yesterday is no more. The present day is all that we have in our possession. Tomorrow is not guaranteed. Whatever we intend to actualise in the world, it must be accomplished in the present time.

> *'O miserable humankind! To what fall degraded! To what wretched state reserved! Better end here unborn. Why is life given, to be thus wrested from us? Rather, why obtruded on us thus? Who if we knew what we receive, would either not accept life offered, or soon beg to lay it down. Glad to be so. Dismissed in peace. Can thus the Image of God in man created once, so goodly and erect, though faulty since, to such unsightly sufferings be debased, under inhuman pains? Why should not man, retaining still divine similitude in part, from such deformities be free, and for his Maker's Image sake, exempt?'*[188]

It is an undeniable fact that the human condition is full of imperfections, flaws, inadequacies, and defects. We are not perfect. This does not mean that we ought to accept everything about ourselves and our life as it currently stands. We ought to engage in the timeless art of self-improvement. We ought to strive to cultivate our virtues. With the benefit of time, effort, tenacity, and practice, we improve our character, abilities, knowledge, expertise, virtues, and commitment to God. It is within the genesis of our intention, that the fruits of our action are sown.

---

188 Milton, John. (Darbishire, Helen, Ed.) (1958). *The Poetical Works of John Milton*. London: Oxford University Press, pp. 254–255.

'But is there yet no other way, besides these painful passages? How we may come to death, and mix with our connatural dust? There is, said Michael. If thou well observe the rule of not too much, by temperance taught in what thou eat and drink. Seeking from thence due nourishment. Not gluttonous delight. Till many years over thy head return. So mayest thou live. Till, like ripe fruit, thou drop into thy mother's lap, or be with ease gathered. Not harshly plucked, for death mature. This is old age. But then, thou must outlive thy youth. Thy strength. Thy beauty. Which will change to withered weak and grey. Thy senses then obtuse. All taste of pleasure must forgo. To what thou hast, and for the air of youth hopeful and cheerful, in thy blood will reign. A melancholy damp of cold and dry. To weigh thy spirits down, and last consume, the balm of life.'[189]

We must not focus our thoughts upon the inevitably of death. Rather, we ought to consider and inquire how to live a good life during our brief lifetime on Earth. Milton suggests moderation, abstinence, and homeostasis are the golden keys to living a good life. Milton's eloquent writing expresses the undeniability of the human condition. Even though we attain greater longevity through the application of self-control, one day we must all grow old and pass away. Our very existence in the world is fleeting and uncertain. A wise person makes their peace with nature's laws and principles.

During our lifetime, we experience countless highs and lows. We endure many positive and negative experiences. We experience the best of joy and the worst of pain. In order to endure life, there must be hope in times of tragedy. But there is also tragedy in times of hope. While it is extremely difficult

---

189 Milton, John. (Darbishire, Helen, Ed.) (1958). *The Poetical Works of John Milton.* London: Oxford University Press, p. 255.

to keep a balanced mind throughout the entirety of one's life, we must strive to ensure that sensibility and rationality prevail in our life. We must earnestly attempt to live by the motto—mind over matter. As change cannot be denied during our lifetime, we must come to terms with letting go. We must let go of the fictitious representation, or the false sense impression of permanency in the world. We are situated on Earth for a momentary period of time. All of life is a process of becoming and dissolution.

God's Eternal Word reminds us of the brevity of human life. In the Holy Bible, within the Book of James, we are acquainted with the following Biblical verse, 'What is your life? For you are a mist that appears for a little time and then vanishes.'[190] In all respects, we must accept God's Sovereign Will. This includes the acceptance of our mortality on Earth.

How we utilise our precious lifetime on Earth is what matters most. We must make a conscious and determined effort, to ensure that our lifetime on Earth is not diminished in the pursuit of inconsequential, trivial, and frivolous endeavours. Life is too short to run our race a second time. Therefore, we must act with prudence, so that we achieve our endeavours and fulfil our aspirations, within the limited time that we have on Earth. In our lifetime, we lose and gain many things, for example, consider private wealth, personal assets, and private property, but we never recoup lost time or missed opportunity.

'Nor love thy life, nor hate. But what thou livest, live well. How long, or short permit to Heaven: and now prepare thee for another sight.'[191]

We must never pursue the two extreme psychological states of attraction or aversion associated with our state of being. For our

---

190 The Holy Bible (ESV). (2016). The Book of James. Chapter 4, Verse 14.
191 Milton, John. (Darbishire, Helen, Ed.) (1958). *The Poetical Works of John Milton.* London: Oxford University Press, p. 256.

existence, lived experience, and material body are all temporary phenomena. We must live in the present time. We ought to live our life to its greatest capacity, inherent potential, and the full employment of our natural endowments. Ultimately, this lifetime represents the preparatory assignment for what eventuates after our death.

During our lifetime, we ought to self-determine the principles, doctrines, theories, values, beliefs, ideals, and ideologies that we subscribe to. We all need to have fundamental and immovable principles in our life. Principles that not only define who we are, but also guide our thought, speech, and conduct. When we consciously affirm our personal identity, then our thought, speech, and conduct become congruent.

When we resolutely affirm our personal identity, when we consciously affirm who we are, then we withstand the many conflicting viewpoints, contemporary opinions, ideologies, doctrines, values, customs, beliefs, cultures, fashion trends, and perspectives of the modern world. The reality is that we choose to be influenced and moulded into what society expects of us. Alternatively, we choose to self-determine the trajectory of our life. We have a choice, either we conform to society, or we reform society. We must always remember, that if we do not make the difficult decisions in our life, then they will be made for us. It is the case, that either we exercise our personal agency in our best interests, or a third party exercises the requisite agency on our behalf.

During our lifetime, we cannot deny our duty concerning the personal responsibility for the good governance of our personal affairs in the midst of civil society. We must assume complete accountability for our sense of well-being, health, state of mind, personal finances, spouse, children, contractual undertakings, commitment to work, fulfilment of our obligations, professional and personal commitments, sporting endeavours, and formal education. It is in and though the assumption of personal responsibility, that we live a sensible, well-governed, and reasoned life. When a person acts with complete accountability for the consequences of their actions, such a person has the fate and destiny of their life in the palm of their hands.

> *'Just men they seemed, and all their study bent to worship God aright, and know His works. Not hid. Nor those things last, which might preserve freedom and peace to men.'*[192]

The most important endeavour we have in our lifetime is to love God. During our lifetime, we have a higher duty to worship God, and to reflect upon God's Eternal Word. Once we reflect upon God's Eternal Word, the succeeding step is to put into practice God's Timeless Principles. Both men and women can know and experience God's Illuminating Presence.

All people on Earth possess the fundamental and inalienable right to liberty, peace, equality, respect, human dignity, love, justice, joy, happiness, and prosperity. When we treat every person on Earth with human dignity, equality, and respect, then we create a superior world. Through the exercise of our personal agency, we self-determine what type of world we desire to create during our lifetime.

---

192 Milton, John. (Darbishire, Helen, Ed.) (1958). *The Poetical Works of John Milton*. London: Oxford University Press, p. 256.

> *'True opener of my eyes. Prime Angel blessed. Much better seems this vision, and more hope of peaceful days portends, than those two past. Those were of hate and death, or pain much worse. Here nature seems fulfilled in all her ends. To whom thus Michael replied. Judge not what is best by pleasure. Though to nature seeming meet. Created, as thou art, to nobler end. Holy and pure. Conformity divine.'*[193]

It is through our mind that we construct our worldly reality, and thereby, we choose to affirm either a vision of Heaven or Hell on Earth. We must not let the Devil tempt and delude our mind into harbouring evil thoughts. While nature is indifferent to our personal suffering, we must self-determine to live a meaningful, purposeful, productive, and harmonious life. The irrational pursuit of pleasure is not our primary objective in life. Too often, the countless temptations of the flesh guide our life towards the unsatisfactory pleasure of sin. Yet, when we reflect and ponder on the temporal bliss of sinful pleasure, we realise that it is a superficial, unfulfilling, and trivial bliss.

The presence of pleasure in our life is usually an artificial and ineffective antidote to us not living a fulfilling and productive life. Pleasure is a brilliant masquerade that functions very effectively to distort our accurate perception of reality. In many instances, the pursuit of pleasure seeks to fill a void in our life. Pleasure clouds our sharp judgement. Pleasure inhibits the exercise of our natural reason.

When we pursue pleasure, as an end in and of itself, this usually signifies that some desirable quality, attribute, trait, relationship, or achievement is absent in our life. This deficiency in our life could be due to a lack of love. No meaningful work. No spiritual life. A weakness of faith. The absence of hope.

---

193 Milton, John. (Darbishire, Helen, Ed.) (1958). *The Poetical Works of John Milton*. London: Oxford University Press, p. 257.

The inability to maintain quality relationships. Not feeling a sense of accomplishment. The undesirable feeling of boredom. Uncertainty surrounding our employment contract. Experiencing financial hardship. A strong sense of discontent with our personal and professional achievements. A dysfunctional marriage. The distressing experience of trauma. Loss of a loved one. Family issues. A personal crisis. Navigating a divorce. Having been diagnosed with a debilitating medical condition. Raising children with rare genetic disorders. Being a party to protracted legal proceedings. Navigating the ins and outs of being a single parent. Last but not least, personal regret concerning unfulfilled sporting or scholarly endeavours.

In all the aforementioned examples and many more, the pursuit of pleasure only serves to fill an inherent void in our life. Regardless of the personal circumstances that we confront in our life, this immense void of the incompleteness of our being innately exists due to our spiritual poverty. Only God's Spirit eradicates such an innate void in our life. In all cases, indulgence in pleasure is not the antidote to our life's real and perceived challenges. Pleasure is only a delusion.

The [desirable] presence of pleasure represents a diversion to an objective assessment of our life. The pursuit of pleasure keeps us distracted from an accurate perception of worldly reality. Pleasure only serves to entangle and warp our mind. Pleasure satisfies and enraptures our five senses, but it never appeases our mind, nor does it satisfy our spirit. Needless to say, pleasure does not promote genuine and true contentment with our state of being in the world.

'Of human glory, and for glory done of triumph. To be stilled great conquerors. Patrons of humankind. Gods and Sons of Gods. Destroyers rightlier called, and plagues of men. Thus, fame shall be achieved. Renown on Earth, and what most merits fame, in silence hid. But he, the Seventh from thee, whom thou beheldest. The only righteous in a world perverse, and therefore, hated. Therefore, to beset with foes for daring single to be just, and utter odious Truth. That God would come to judge them with His Saints. Him the Most High, rapt in a balmy cloud with winged steeds. Did as thou sawest receive, to walk with God, high in salvation and the climes of bliss. Exempt from death. To show thee, what reward awaits the good. The rest, what punishment.'[194]

Our intentional and free willed actions on Earth define our proximity to God. We cannot escape the consequences of our self-determined actions. God judges every person in accordance with God's Just and Righteous Law. This lifetime serves as an unprecedented opportunity for us to bring ourselves ever closer to God. We must make God the centre of our life through sincere acts of worship, love, mercy, reflection, faith, community service, belief, forgiveness, prayer, charity, social justice, and devotion. The attribute of free will is a positive aspect of human life, however, this proposition only holds true and constant, subject to one condition. That condition being, if we utilise our free will to further productive and constructive endeavours during our lifetime on Earth.

On the contrary, if we perform countless evil deeds during our lifetime on Earth, what hope shall we hold on to, in order to secure our salvation? Destruction, damnation, and death awaits that person who employs this lifetime to further the

---

194 Milton, John. (Darbishire, Helen, Ed.) (1958). *The Poetical Works of John Milton.* London: Oxford University Press, pp. 259–260.

illegitimate cause of evil on Earth. We must always remember the Devil exploits our countless weaknesses, in order to make us conveniently traverse the path of evil. The Devil always finds the means, motives, and methods to make humanity perform his bidding on Earth. We must not be so naive to think, that we permanently escape punishment for the destructive outcomes of our unconscionable conduct on Earth.

The administration of justice on Earth is imperfect. This undesirable reality is due to the sinful and corrupt nature of humanity. Having said that, the scales of justice in God's Sovereign Court are always perfect and precise. God's Eternal Word forewarns us, 'Do not be deceived. God is not mocked. For whatever one sows, that will he also reap. For the one who sows to his own flesh, will from the flesh reap corruption, but the one who sows to the Spirit, will from the Spirit reap eternal life. And let us not grow weary of doing good, for in due season we will reap, if we do not give up. So then, as we have opportunity, let us do good to everyone, and especially to those who are of the household of faith.'[195]

Our actions are either in the pursuit of good or evil. Whichever path we select, we are held accountable for the consequences of our conscious and voluntary actions. Therefore, it is essential that we carefully think through the intentions that inform our actions, before we act, so that we are in a position to fully appreciate the consequences of our conduct.

In the contemporary era, we inhabit an interconnected world. A multiracial, multicultural, and multilingual world. A world that is simultaneously defined by the attributes of globalism and pluralism. However, regardless of the multitude of differences in our customs, beliefs, values, ideologies, and principles, we all agree on the centrality of good over evil.

---

195 The Holy Bible (ESV). (2016). The Book of Galatians. Chapter 6, Verses 7–10.

Every person on Earth has a duty to ensure that good prevails over evil. A duty to ensure that justice prevails over injustice. A duty to ensure that prosperity prevails over poverty. A duty to ensure that fairness prevails over inequity. A duty to ensure that dignity prevails over indignity. A duty to ensure that peace prevails over war. A duty to ensure that love prevails over hate. A duty to ensure that tolerance prevails over discrimination. A duty to ensure that mercy prevails over inhumanity. These are common and universal duties that must be upheld by all members of human civilisation.

'O visions, ill foreseen! Better had I lived ignorant of the future! So had borne my part of evil only. Each day's lot, enough to bear! Those now, that were dispensed the burden of many ages. On me, light at once. By my foreknowledge, gaining birth abortive. To torment me ere their being. With thought, that they must be! Let no man seek henceforth to be foretold, what shall befall him or his children. Evil he may be sure. Which neither his foreknowing can prevent, and he the future evil shall no less in apprehension then in substance feel. Grievous to bear. But that care now is past. Man is not whom to warn. Those few escaped famine and anguish, will at last consume wandering that watery desert. I had hope. When violence was ceased, and war on Earth, all would have then gone well. Peace would have crowned with length of happy days the race of man. But I was far deceived. For now I see, peace to corrupt no less, than war to waste.'[196]

Foreknowledge and certainty of the future is forever denied to humankind. Therefore, we must exercise our personal agency and initiative in the present moment, with appropriate consideration

---

196 Milton, John. (Darbishire, Helen, Ed.) (1958). *The Poetical Works of John Milton.* London: Oxford University Press, p. 261.

for the resources, traits, talents, skills, expertise, knowledge, and abilities that God has graced us with. We must act with firmness, conviction, boldness, and determination to achieve our practical objectives within the structures, institutions, rules, processes, policies, and laws of our civil society and sovereign nation-state.

We cannot leave the all-important accomplishment of our endeavours to the probability of chance, or to the whim of fate. If we strive, sacrifice, and struggle in the present time, then we ensure for ourselves that we secure every possible opportunity, to accomplish our desired endeavours, rather than depend upon circumstance, timing, luck, or fortune, as the four high arbitrators to determine our fate.

During our life journey on Earth, we all have our personal obligations and particular burdens to carry in this lifetime. One must not forget that even the *Messiah* had to carry the immense weight of the Cross on his shoulders. In the Holy Bible, within the Gospel of John, we are reminded of the human suffering of the *Messiah*, 'So they took Jesus, and he went out, bearing his own Cross, to the place called The Place of a Skull, which in Aramaic is called Golgotha.'[197] Case in point, life is not always perfect, joyful, and serene. The human condition and our unique lived experience is consumed with much discomfort, suffering, trauma, grief, tragedy, and pain. Having said that, we are never alone in our hour of need. God always creates provision in our difficult time of privation.

The good news is that help is always near at hand. For even the *Messiah* relied upon a sincere helping aid during his hour of need, 'And they compelled a passerby, Simon of Cyrene, who was coming in from the country, the father of Alexander and Rufus, to carry his Cross.'[198] The Biblical message here is that even in the midst of the dark, disastrous, dejected, and disillusioned times,

---

197 The Holy Bible (ESV). (2016). The Gospel of John. Chapter 19, Verses 16–17.
198 The Holy Bible (ESV). (2016). The Gospel of Mark. Chapter 15, Verse 21.

we witness the best of humanity. No matter the circumstances, we must always affirm our faith.

The upholding of universal human dignity is obligatory for every person on Earth. The legitimate expectation to treat every person on Earth with equality, respect, human dignity, compassion, equity, and love is what makes the world a blessed, better, and brighter place for human civilisation.

In the brief course of human life, one cannot deny the undesirable incidence of misfortune, bad luck, or pure evil. We have to accept the world consists of both the good and the evil dimensions. Regrettably, much of human history demonstrates how the world is defined by famine, war, conflict, hate, disease, illiteracy, prejudice, injustice, war crimes, natural disasters, discrimination, and systemic poverty.

In spite of the evil in the world, we must hold on to hope. Hope that we construct the world into a better representation of humanity. Hope that we leave the world in a better place. Hope that good overcomes evil. Hope that our obstacles, challenges, and privations are surmountable. Hope that God's Sovereign Kingdom reigns on Earth forever.

Human nature has its countless flaws, known imperfections, and inherent weaknesses. Peace amongst humanity is the most desirable state of existence; however, it is always difficult to secure a lasting peace in the world. Every person desires peace on their particular terms, and the crystallisation of this ideal reality is far-fetched. It is not always feasible, to secure a lasting peace on our precise terms. To advance the noble cause of peace on Earth, there must be a just compromise between all the belligerents. There must be justice for peace to prevail. Whereas, the protracted state of war and conflict is always possible.

The cold hard truth is that the just and noble cause of peace not only requires the presence of inexhaustible patience, the perfection of human understanding, and the art of emotionally-intelligent negotiation; however, peace also requires the setting aside of historical grievances. True peace acknowledges that the indescribable pain of loss, and the ineradicable wounds of hurt must be set aside, in order to move forward.

Now, peace is only possible when all parties cease focusing on the bitter memory of the fixed past, and they actively work towards the creation of a blessed, brighter, and better future. Peace on Earth is an ideal representation. Having said that, peace is an ideal representation that we ought to strive to transform into our living reality. Any progress towards the path of peace is commendable.

'In triumph and luxurious wealth, are they first seen in acts of prowess. Eminent and great exploits. But of true virtue void. Who having spilt much blood, and done much waste subduing nations, and achieved thereby fame in the world. High titles and rich prey. Shall change their course to pleasure, ease, sloth, surfeit, and lust. Till wantonness and pride, raise out of friendship, hostile deeds in peace.'[199]

Almost all of human action is futile. Victory and conquest over foreign nations and the possession of vast amounts of gold, private property, private wealth, treasure, and territory is all in vain. The passing fame and fleeting recognition of the world is valueless. Fame and fortune diminish in value with the constant passage of time. Too often we place an immense worth on securing a favourable worldly opinion. In reality, true good fame, honourable standing, and noble character are derived from God's approval of us, not the superficial approval of humanity.

Till the end of time, till the extinction of the human race, humanity's erratic ego and war-like will is always in a state of conflict with one another. Each person's ego and will is attempting

---

199 Milton, John. (Darbishire, Helen, Ed.) (1958). *The Poetical Works of John Milton*. London: Oxford University Press, p. 262.

to exercise domination and control, in an attempt to enforce their unique perception of reality onto the natural world. Amongst humanity, there is ever-present a greater mutual basis for conflict, rather than the desirable basis for an equitable and eternal peace.

This material world of our being is a battleground of our will, against the will of countless people in the world, so that we impress upon it, our [unique] representation of being. This is the root cause of all conflict amongst humanity; the expression of each person's individuality, the unique representation of ourselves.

> *'Worldly and dissolute. On what their Lords shall leave them to enjoy. For the Earth shall bear more than enough. That temperance may be tried. So, all shall turn degenerate. All depraved. Justice, temperance, truth, and faith forgot. One man except, the only Son of Light. In a dark age. Against example good. Against allurement, custom, and a world offended. Fearless of reproach and scorn, or violence. He of their wicked ways, shall them admonish, and before them set the path of righteousness. How much more safe, and full of peace, denouncing wrath to come on their impenitence; and shall return of them derided. But of God observed, the one just man alive.'*[200]

The *Messiah* is the saviour of the world. For our part, we ought to utilise our lifetime on Earth, to cultivate our virtues and to improve our character. It is through faith, and not through merit, virtue, or the performance of good works, that we secure our undeserved salvation. The *Messiah*, as the Son of God, is perfect in all respects. The *Messiah* is an ideal model for humanity on how to live a blessed and good life on Earth.

---

200 Milton, John. (Darbishire, Helen, Ed.) (1958). *The Poetical Works of John Milton*. London: Oxford University Press, p. 262.

God's Grace is the distinguished and esteemed attribute that we must obtain during our lifetime. God's Grace is an unsurpassable blessing. God's Grace is a gift that is freely given by God, without regard to our sex, gender, occupation, colour, race, ethnicity, age, personal income, class, private property, private wealth, social status, nationality, vocation, or any other discriminatory factor. God is at liberty to bestow divine gifts to any person. God's Grace is not obstructed by worldly factors or temporal considerations.

With God's Grace, we accomplish our greatest endeavours and achievements, that are otherwise not possible through our superior faculties of willpower, intuition, self-determination, initiative, intellect, perseverance, natural reason, judgement, understanding, or the exercise of personal agency. It is by God's Grace, that we fulfil our destiny and purpose on Earth. God's Grace cannot be earnt, purchased, traded, stored, or exchanged, for it is not ours to give. The Creator bestows grace upon any individual that God deems worthy of this especial gift. We cannot reason ourselves into securing God's Grace. The dispensation of God's Gift of Grace is beyond human comprehension.

There is no methodical or intellectual basis, to understand or rationalise how God dispenses the gift of grace upon humanity. In the Holy Bible, within the Book of Exodus, consider the following Biblical narrative in relation to Aaron and the golden calf, 'So Aaron said to them, "Take off the rings of gold that are in the ears of your wives, your sons, and your daughters, and bring them to me." So, all the people took off the rings of gold that were in their ears and brought them to Aaron. And he received the gold from their hand and fashioned it with a graving tool and made a golden calf. And they said, "These are your gods, O Israel, who brought you up out of the land of Egypt!"'[201]

---

201 The Holy Bible (ESV). (2016). The Book of Exodus. Chapter 32, Verses 2–4.

One theological interpretation of the aforesaid Biblical narrative is that Aaron flagrantly violated God's Eternal Word. However, in God's Infinite Mercy, God showed Aaron unmerited grace. For God responded to Aaron, with the following words, 'I give your priesthood as a gift.'[202]

Aaron's striking example illustrates, that sometimes in our life there is no justification or explanation for God's Gift of Grace to us. In such circumstances, we have not received God's Gift of Grace due to our goodness, righteousness, merit, virtue, character, or the performance of honourable deeds. Rather, we have received God's Gift of Grace due to the unequal qualities and unrivalled attributes of the Creator. The Creator is never dependent or contingent upon Creation, when it comes to the dispensation of grace, favour, blessing, or mercy.

As the aforementioned Biblical narrative pertaining to Aaron and the golden calf demonstrates, it is well-nigh impossible to understand God's Mysterious Thoughts. This proposition is especially true, when it comes to how and why grace is granted to select people, but it is not secured by other individuals, who according to our principle of natural reason, may be equally, if not more deserving of God's Grace. In the final analysis, to employ human understanding to comprehend God's Gift of Grace, this is akin to an attempt to square the circle.

---

202 The Holy Bible (ESV). (2016). The Book of Numbers. Chapter 18, Verse 7.

CHAPTER 12

PARADISE LOST: BOOK TWELVE

*'That all this good of evil shall produce, and evil turn
to good. More wonderful than that which by Creation
first brought forth light out of darkness! Full of doubt
I stand. Whether I should repent me now of sin by me
done and occasioned, or rejoice much more.
That much more good thereof shall spring.
To God more glory. More good will to men.'*

MILTON

BOOK TWELVE of *Paradise Lost* represents the account of
Archangel, Saint Michael's philosophical, moral, theological,
and spiritual discourse with Adam. The two towering figures
discuss doctrinal matters pertaining to God that are of lasting
significance. Saint Michael and Adam's dialogue includes
the Biblical events concerning the Flood, Incarnation, Death,
Resurrection, Ascension, and the Second Coming of Christ.
Adam is content with the divine knowledge that Saint Michael
has relayed to him. Shortly thereafter, Adam wakes Eve from her
troubled sleep.

Despite Adam and Eve's strong protest, the duo had no choice,
but to submit to God's Sovereign Will. Adam and Eve accept

God's Just Punishment for their sinful conduct. Consequently, Adam and Eve are banished from Paradise. At the close of this book, Saint Michael escorts Adam and Eve out of the Garden of Eden. God's faithful Angels take their post, and they stand guard at the entrance to Paradise. This book is the epilogue to Milton's *Paradise Lost*.

One of the most important lessons that we derive from Book Twelve of *Paradise Lost* is that we cannot escape the consequences of our conscious and voluntary actions. Adam and Eve incorrectly presumed, that the knowledge of good and evil positioned their existence in a better place. In fact, Adam and Eve's possession of the knowledge of good and evil constituted a curse. This newfound knowledge was to their great detriment. God's Blessing of living in the Garden of Eden was forever lost.

While not without the presence of temptation, and the influence of evil, Adam and Eve's fall from grace was of their own volition. In the end, we cannot circumvent the reality, that what God has decreed as favourable and unfavourable, is for our greater benefit. When we misappropriate our free will, and transgress God's Eternal Word, then we ought to expect undesirable consequences to follow our immoral actions.

'Authority usurped, from God not given. He gave us only over beast, fish, fowl, dominion absolute. That right we hold, by His donation. But man over men, He made not Lord. Such title, to Himself reserving. Human left from human free. But this usurper his encroachment proud stays not on man. To God, his tower intends siege and defiance. Wretched man! What food will he convey up thither, to sustain himself and his rash army? Where thin air above the clouds will pine his entrails gross, and famish him of breath, if not of bread?'[203]

God's Sovereign Commands have been given to humanity. These sacred commands must be observed for our own welfare. God gave humanity dominion over the Earth, and the creatures of this Earth. Having said that, God reserved dominion over man and woman for God's Higher Purpose. Regrettably, the disappointing record of human history affirms the dismal reality of oppression, domination, discrimination, war, conflict, forced labour, chattel slavery, human trafficking, hate crime, child labour, indentured servitude, child soldiers, and capital punishment. Through the exercise of personal agency and free will, humanity engages in actions that self-sabotage the peace, prosperity, and perfection of God's Creation. By the forces of vice, evil, sin, and the insatiable desire for profit, humanity has lost its moral conscience.

Who are we to judge, degrade, and demonstrate indignity towards our fellow brothers and sisters? Humanity has only one True Master—God. Man and woman were never ordained to have dominion over each other. The world, and all that is contained within it, is God's Creation. Therefore, it is only God's rightful and proper place, to pass judgement and command obedience from humanity. Humanity must not be so arrogant, as to assume

---

203 Milton, John. (Darbishire, Helen, Ed.) (1958). *The Poetical Works of John Milton.* London: Oxford University Press, p. 267.

the improper authority of exercising God's Prerogative Power over Creation.

In all respects, it is the presence and function of our ego, which leads us astray in the world. The ego positions our experience of being at the centre of the world. The ego positions ourselves as the beginning and end of conventional reality. We must not be so naive to disregard the long-lasting consequences of our voluntary and conscious actions. Consequences that reverberate and create enduring effects for the future of humanity.

In the modern world, too often we witness the majority of people entertain the presence of countless vices in their life. Many members of humanity live their life characterised by hate, greed, envy, concupiscence, pride, avarice, anger, jealousy, and covetousness. Not to mention, the majority of humanity are engrossed in the excessive pursuit of pecuniary gain, profit maximisation, private property, and private wealth creation.

We all desire the better life. We all desire the creation of the good life. Having said that, we are quick to ignore that it is the principles, doctrines, ideologies, beliefs, values, emotions, and thoughts, that we permit to define us, in as much as it is the endeavours and objectives which we pursue, that ultimately determine the content, capacity, and character of our life.

In the illegitimate endeavour of entertaining the sinful pleasures of the flesh and partaking in the reprehensible deeds of evil on Earth, men and women exercise callous control and demeaning domination over one another. This unreasonable exercise of control and domination is witnessed through a number of different principal-agent relationships in modern society. For example, consider the following relationships: doctor-patient, director-shareholder, trustee-beneficiary, lawyer-client, employer-employee, executor-the beneficiaries of a deceased estate, and government-citizen. What all these relationships have in common is a power imbalance between the parties.

Within principal-agent relationships, there is a self-evident dependence of the principal upon the agent. This dependence arises due to the knowledge, resources, expertise, learning, experience, qualification, talent, abilities, skill, and reputation of the agent. The sombre reality of power asymmetry cannot be denied or ignored in relationships throughout modern society. Self-interest is ingrained in human nature.

In the final analysis, God creates, sustains, and destroys Creation. Was it not for God's Sovereign Act of bringing the Universe into existence, we would not possess human life. Thus, everything in and of the world, rightfully belongs to God. Without God's Grace, Mercy, Blessing, and Favour, we would not exist at this present moment, or at any other point in time. The private wealth, personal income, political power, prestige, influence, good health, prosperity, well-being, social status, personal relationships, spouse, friendships, children, and private property that we possess, all of it is merely and temporarily on loan from God.

In the Holy Bible, the remarkable Biblical story of Job demonstrates that we can lose everything that we possess in our life in a tragic turn of events. Job, a faithful servant of the LORD was put to the ultimate test by Satan. In all the struggles that Job confronted, he did not forget his Creator, 'Then Job arose and tore his robe and shaved his head and fell on the ground and worshipped. And he said, "Naked I came from my mother's womb, and naked shall I return. The LORD gave, and the LORD has taken away. Blessed be the Name of the LORD." In all this Job did not sin or charge God with wrong.'[204]

It is the reality of the world, that evil occupies its legitimate place and powerful influence amongst humanity. The jurisdiction of evil is all-encompassing on Earth. As the aforementioned Biblical story of Job illustrates, it is incumbent upon humanity

---

204 The Holy Bible (ESV). (2016). The Book of Job. Chapter 1, Verses 20–22.

to correctly distinguish good from evil. It is incumbent upon humanity not to relinquish God's Grace during times of privation, heartache, grief, trauma, and loss. The Devil's sole purpose herein was to turn Job away from God. An evil endeavour, one in which the Devil failed.

Unfortunately, the presence of evil inflicts its destruction and chaos upon the good people of the world. In spite of the Devil wreaking havoc on Earth, we must weather the storm. The extraordinary life story of Job has shown us, that it is possible to overcome evil and ensure goodness prevails on Earth. When we perform righteous actions in the world, the presence of evil along our life journey is evidently unjust and unfair, however, we cannot deny the operation of God's Eternal Word, 'For He makes His Sun rise on the evil and on the good, and He sends rain on the just and on the unjust.'[205] We cannot always secure a complete theological explanation, to account for all the twists and turns that eventuate in our lifetime. However, we must keep our trust and confidence in God's Providence to guide our life trajectory.

'Such trouble brought. Affecting to subdue rational liberty. Yet, know withal, since thy original lapse, true liberty is lost. Which always, with right reason dwells twinned, and from her hath no individual being. Reason in man obscured, or not obeyed, immediately inordinate desires and upstart passions. Catch the government from reason, and to servitude reduce man till then free. Therefore, since he permits within himself unworthy powers to reign over free reason, God in judgement just, subjects him from without to violent Lords. Who oft as undeservedly enthral his outward form. Tyranny must be. Though to the tyrant, thereby no excuse.'[206]

---

205 The Holy Bible (ESV). (2016). The Gospel of Matthew. Chapter 5, Verse 45.
206 Milton, John. (Darbishire, Helen, Ed.) (1958). *The Poetical Works of John Milton.* London: Oxford University Press, p. 267.

We have a choice, either we employ our liberty in a constructive or destructive manner. Our God-given freedom is inherently a positive attribute of human life. However, with the power of freedom comes the undeniable duty of personal responsibility. We have an overriding responsibility to utilise our freedom with prudence, good judgement, and practical reason. In life, the push and pull of our passions must be subservient to the principle of natural reason. We cannot provision free rein to our unchecked passions.

While we remain subject to the limitations and weaknesses of the flesh, the phenomenal force of temptation remains strong and powerful in our life. Yet, our free willed actions must be guided by the remarkable qualities of the spirit, and not by the irrational demands of the flesh.

As long as we are resident in the flesh, we daily confront the battle between passion and reason. The Holy Bible, within the Book of Galatians, shares profound wisdom with us on the enduring battle between the flesh and the spirit, 'But I say, walk by the spirit, and you will not gratify the desires of the flesh. For the desires of the flesh are against the spirit, and the desires of the spirit are against the flesh, for these are opposed to each other, to keep you from doing the things you want to do.'[207]

It is only when the pure, peaceful, and perfect power of the spirit rules our entire experience of being, that we live a superior life. An exemplary life that is based on incontrovertible moral principles. When we sincerely obey the commands of the spirit, God's Blessing and Favour guide our life journey.

During our lifetime, the greatest battle we confront is the psychological battle against the Self. If we truly conquer ourselves, then we have conquered far more than the world. If we master ourselves and make reasonable, balanced, and sensible decisions with our personal agency, then we have mastered the art

---

207 The Holy Bible (ESV). (2016). The Book of Galatians. Chapter 5, Verses 16–17.

of life. Too often, we do not seriously grapple with the difficult existential questions that confront our state of being in the world.

The only true and tested method to realise our inherent potential is to resolve the challenges, pitfalls, and issues that confront our life. Too often, we unconsciously permit the problems that we confront to define our living reality. Yet, the resolution resides in working through and resolving the multitude of social, moral, legal, political, historical, economic, medical, and ethical issues that impede the realisation of our inherent potential.

If we do not resolve our personal challenges, then we become confined to an inferior reality. We end up living our life defined by our burdens, dilemmas, and problems, rather than living our life defined by our ambitions, dreams, and aspirations. If we do not secure the personal initiative and positively act for our betterment, then the important decisions concerning our life are determined for us. In the absence of the exercise of our personal agency, a third party advertently exercises agency on our behalf. No matter how difficult, we must always make our life-changing decisions, otherwise, they will be determined for us.

> *'Of me and all humankind. But now I see his day. In whom all nations shall be blessed. Favour unmerited by me, who sought forbidden knowledge by forbidden means. This yet I apprehend not. Why to those among whom God will deign to dwell on Earth so many and so various laws are given? So many laws argue so many sins among them. How can God with such reside?'*[208]

We are all sinners. No person on Earth is perfect. Even with complete knowledge of God's Sovereign Commands, all of us fall short in our ability to observe them. It is the sin that is living

---

208 Milton, John. (Darbishire, Helen, Ed.) (1958). *The Poetical Works of John Milton*. London: Oxford University Press, p. 272.

within us, that tempts us to turn our heart and mind away from God's Eternal Word. Our sinful nature, in connection with the weakness of the flesh, makes us partake in vice and reprehensible conduct. As problematic as our Earthly battle with sin is, we must persevere to be true and faithful to God's Eternal Word. All of God's Just Laws are provisioned for our benefit, however, we constantly fail to ensure God's Sovereign Will is performed on Earth.

Throughout the course of our life, we perceive that we know ourselves better than our Creator. We incorrectly infer that we must live our life in the manner and choice that we desire. This unenlightened approach to living is not in our best interest. The ignorance of our many flaws and limitations is a sure recipe for a disastrous life. As we have witnessed throughout the course of human history, when humanity disobeys God's Sovereign Command, there is conflict, chaos, confusion, crime, war, envy, jealousy, prejudice, poverty of spirit, discrimination, suicide, depravity, depression, destruction, and death.

Despite our sinful nature, God's Spirit resides within us, because of God's overwhelming goodness and perfection. Even though our thoughts, actions, beliefs, principles, doctrines, values, and ideals fall short of God's Expectations, it is by God's Grace, Compassion, Love, Forgiveness, Blessing, and Mercy that we come closer to God and experience God's Presence in our life. This is God's unmerited favour. To receive such divine favour is God's special gift to humanity.

God's Favour cannot be earnt, stored, traded, purchased, or redeemed. God's Favour cannot be commoditised. Not to mention, we cannot secure God's Favour by the application of human effort, the performance of good works, or through the exertion of our finite willpower. The receipt of God's Favour is only possible by God's Grace.

'Doubt not. But that sin will reign among them. As of thee begot; and therefore, was law given them to evince their natural pravity. By stirring up sin against law to fight. That when they see, law can discover sin, but not remove. Save by those shadowy expiations weak. The blood of bulls and goats. They may conclude, some blood more precious must be paid for man. Just for unjust. That in such righteousness, to them by faith imputed. They may find justification towards God, and peace of conscience. Which the law, by ceremonies, cannot appease. Nor man, the mortal part perform, and not performing, cannot live.'[209]

So long as we remain in the flesh, we are subject to the confines of sin. It is extremely difficult to live a pure, honourable, morally righteous, and chaste life. The flesh presents humanity with a myriad of temptations and unproductive desires. The permanent marks of sin upon the soul simply cannot be eradicated by means of superficial sacrifices. For the ordinary animal sacrifices referred to in the Old Testament are insufficient recompense to atone humanity for its sinful conduct. As conscious and moral agents, we must assume personal responsibility for our conduct.

When we pause and carefully examine each of the Ten Commandments, we fall short in our ability to observe every one of them, throughout the entire course of our lifetime. If we cannot observe God's Sovereign Command, how can we be assured of our salvation? It is the case, that the Son of God is the way to redemption and eternal life. Within the Holy Bible, in the Gospel of Luke we are reminded, 'For the Son of Man came to seek and to save the lost.'[210] Within and of ourselves, all our secular thoughts, speech, and conduct fall short to secure

---

209 Milton, John. (Darbishire, Helen, Ed.) (1958). *The Poetical Works of John Milton*. London: Oxford University Press, p. 272.
210 The Holy Bible (ESV). (2016). The Gospel of Luke. Chapter 19, Verse 10.

our own salvation. Our true salvation is only secured by God's Grace, Favour, Blessing, Compassion, and Mercy.

> *'Be sure they will, said the Angel. But from Heaven, He to His own a comforter will send. The promise of the Father, who shall dwell His Spirit within them, and the law of faith working through love. Upon their hearts shall write. To guide them in all Truth, and also arm them with spiritual armour. Able to resist Satan's assaults, and quench his fiery darts. What man can do against them. Not afraid. Though to the death. Against such cruelties. With inward consolations recompensed.'*[211]

We must constantly remind ourselves of God's Eternal Promises that are given to us. The Devil attempts his level best to torment our mind and distract us from the realisation of our destiny. In this evil quest the Devil utilises intrusive thoughts, such as jealousy, guilt, fear, failure, envy, temptation, resentment, procrastination, discouragement, confusion, worry, anger, doubt, suicide, and loneliness. The Devil's intention is to ensure that we do not become all that we were destined to be. Having said that, there is a Godly remedy for each devilish instrument. When we feel the onset of jealousy, we must remind ourselves that 'The LORD is near to all who call upon Him, to all who call upon Him in Truth.'[212]

When we feel the onset of guilt, we must remind ourselves that, 'As far as the East is from the West, so far has He removed our transgressions from us.'[213] When we feel the onset of fear, we must remind ourselves that, 'Do not be afraid of sudden terror, nor of trouble from the wicked when it comes; for the LORD will

---

211 Milton, John. (Darbishire, Helen, Ed.) (1958). *The Poetical Works of John Milton*. London: Oxford University Press, p. 277.
212 The Holy Bible (ESV). (2016). The Book of Psalms. Chapter 145, Verse 18.
213 The Holy Bible (ESV). (2016). The Book of Psalms. Chapter 103, Verse 12.

be your confidence, and will keep your foot from being caught.'[214] When we feel the onset of failure, we must remind ourselves that 'Let us then with confidence draw near to the Throne of Grace, that we may receive mercy and find grace to help in time of need.'[215]

Furthermore, when we feel the onset of worry, we must remind ourselves that, 'Cast your burden on the LORD, and He shall sustain you. He shall never permit the righteous to be moved.'[216] When we feel the onset of temptation, we must remind ourselves that, 'Submit yourselves therefore to God. Resist the Devil, and he will flee from you.'[217] When we feel the onset of resentment, we must remind ourselves that, 'See to it that no one fails to obtain the Grace of God; that no "root of bitterness" springs up and causes trouble, and by it many become defiled.'[218] When we feel the onset of procrastination, we must remind ourselves that, 'So teach us to number our days, that we may gain a heart of wisdom.'[219]

When we feel the onset of discouragement, we must remind ourselves that, 'So we do not lose heart. Though our outer self is wasting away, our inner self is being renewed day by day.'[220] When we feel the onset of anger, we must remind ourselves that, 'With patience a ruler may be persuaded, and a soft tongue will break a bone.'[221] When we feel the onset of doubt, we must remind ourselves that, 'Behold, the LORD's hand is not shortened, that it cannot save, or His ear dull, that it cannot hear.'[222]

---

214 The Holy Bible (ESV). (2016). The Book of Proverbs. Chapter 3, Verses 25–26.
215 The Holy Bible (ESV). (2016). The Book of Hebrews. Chapter 4, Verse 16.
216 The Holy Bible (ESV). (2016). The Book of Psalms. Chapter 55, Verse 22.
217 The Holy Bible (ESV). (2016). The Book of James. Chapter 4, Verse 7.
218 The Holy Bible (ESV). (2016). The Book of Hebrews. Chapter 12, Verse 15.
219 The Holy Bible (ESV). (2016). The Book of Psalms. Chapter 90, Verse 12.
220 The Holy Bible (ESV). (2016). Book of Second Corinthians. Chapter 4. Verse 16.
221 The Holy Bible (ESV). (2016). The Book of Proverbs. Chapter 25, Verse 15.
222 The Holy Bible (ESV). (2016). The Book of Isaiah. Chapter 59, Verse 1.

When we feel the onset of loneliness, we must remind ourselves that, 'The LORD is near to the broken-hearted, and saves the crushed in spirit.'[223] With God's Eternal Word in our heart, mind, and spirit, with God's Spiritual Armour upon our body, and with God's Grace upon our life, we stand firm in battle against the incalculable power of the Devil.

'Their ministry performed and race well run. Their doctrine and their story written left. They die. But in their room. As they forewarn. Wolves shall succeed for teachers. Grievous wolves, who all the sacred mysteries of Heaven, to their own vile advantages shall turn of lucre and ambition, and the Truth.'[224]

During our lifetime on Earth, we have a higher duty to live our life to its inherent potential. We have a moral obligation to ourselves, that we make full use of our superior faculties of being. Every person leaves behind their unique story; the incredible legacy of one's lifetime. Therefore, we must consciously and actively work towards ensuring that our lifetime is a productive, positive, purposeful, passionate, and prosperous one.

Our journey on Earth is not a linear and convenient path. We are tempted by falsehood, evil, tragedy, and disaster. Having said that, we must live our life to transcend these inferior and ignoble characteristics of the world. No person realises their destiny without surmounting setbacks, obstacles, losses, heartache, trauma, or grief along their life journey.

In the Holy Bible, the Biblical narrative of Joseph is an exceptional account of how Joseph transcended the tragedies, tests, temptations, and tribulations of the world. In every problematic situation that Joseph encountered, he always held

---

223 The Holy Bible (ESV). (2016). The Book of Psalms. Chapter 34, Verse 18.
224 Milton, John. (Darbishire, Helen, Ed.) (1958). *The Poetical Works of John Milton*. London: Oxford University Press, p. 278.

steadfast onto his faith-based principles and timeless values. In all respects, Joseph placed his paramount trust in God, and 'The LORD was with Joseph, and he became a successful man, and he was in the house of his Egyptian master. His master saw that the LORD was with him and that the LORD caused all that he did to succeed in his hands.'[225]

In spite of the evil intentions of Joseph's brothers, the LORD protected Joseph and assisted him to accomplish his God-given destiny. In the final analysis, we must be vigilant and circumspect in our thoughts, beliefs, and desires, for they ultimately define our living reality on Earth. Joseph had complete trust and confidence in God to deliver him from evil. It was this trust and confidence that empowered Joseph to realise his destiny.

'The Spirit of God. Promised alike and given to all believers, and from that pretence, spiritual laws by carnal power shall force on every conscience. Laws which none shall find left them inrolled, or what the spirit within shall on the heart engrave. What will they then but force the spirit of grace itself, and bind his consort liberty? What, but unbuild his living temples? Built by faith to stand. Their own faith, not another's? For on Earth, who against faith and conscience can be heard infallible? Yet many will presume. Whence heavy persecution shall arise on all who in the worship persevere of spirit and Truth. The rest, far greater part, will deem in outward rites and specious forms religion satisfied. Truth shall retire, bestuck with slanderous darts. Works of faith, rarely be found. So shall the world go on.'[226]

---

225 The Holy Bible (ESV). (2016). The Book of Genesis. Chapter 39, Verses 2–3.
226 Milton, John. (Darbishire, Helen, Ed.) (1958). *The Poetical Works of John Milton*. London: Oxford University Press, (p. 278).

There is nothing greater in this temporal world than God's Uncreated, Timeless, and Infinite Spirit. The Supreme Spirit of God is always accessible to humanity, no matter where we are in the world, what circumstances we confront, or what condition our life is in. The transcendent Spirit of God supports us to overcome any and all obstacles in our life. The power of the Spirit of God is unrivalled, unstoppable, and unparalleled. The Spirit of God dwells everywhere on Earth. The Spirit of God is universally accessible to every person. Only by God's Grace we experience God's Spirit reside within us.

During our lifetime on Earth, we must endeavour to hold steadfast to the faith. For the faith is the most important aspect of living. Every day, we must strengthen our faith, which supports, sustains, and survives our spirit. Let there be no doubt, we confront many trials, tribulations, tragedies, and tests, which challenge the foundation of our faith, but we must overcome these challenges and take heart in being courageous, sincere, grateful, loving, generous, compassionate, merciful, benevolent, and forgiving to one another.

The mere observance of religious traditions, beliefs, norms, cultures, principles, doctrines, and practices does not demonstrate that we love God. These unconscious acts are merely symbols, the superficial performance of rituals, the unquestioned acceptance of custom, and the trivial expression of formality.

How then do we express our sincere love for God? It is by our conscious actions of love, worship, charity, prayer, petition, penance, intercession, community service, human dignity, forgiveness, respect, tolerance, giving, social justice, peace, and humanity, that we demonstrate our faith and love for God.

There are rare spirits in the world, which only by God's Mercy and Grace accomplish remarkable works of faith. For example, consider the inspirational life story of Saint Paul the Apostle, who authored thirteen of the twenty-seven books contained within the New Testament of the Holy Bible. Yet, if any person does accomplish some great work of faith, this was not due to their individual merit, talent, genius, expertise, or intellect. Rather, such a fine achievement was only possible through God's Grace.

Despite the presence of our troubled, ignorant, and misinformed ego, we must not permit the Devil to misconstrue any invaluable accomplishment as a reflection of our talent, goodness, effort, personal agency, willpower, or intellect. When we recognise our dependence upon God for our life, health, personal income, private wealth, purpose, vision, well-being, and destiny, we affirm our rightful place in the world.

Life is not all about us. Life starts when we position our self-interest aside. Life starts when we factor ourselves out of the equation. Life starts when we position God in first place. When we set aside seeking our happiness, and pursue the furtherance of God's Sovereign Will, we have made a conscious choice that brings us a profound and unexplainable joy. The joy of living is beyond the confines of our superficial self-interest.

When we begin to live beyond the pursuit of self-interest, then we create a fulfilling life. A life that has meaning, purpose, vision, passion, and hope for the betterment of humanity. All the goodness living within us originates from God's Eternal Spirit. When we realise this reality as a fact of our being, then we become enlightened to God's Providence. All of our work on Earth, and the dividends that flow from our earnest work, are for the benefit and advancement of God's Glory and Honour. It is an unmerited blessing to contribute to the advancement of God's Sovereign Kingdom on Earth.

'Measured this transient world. The race of time. Till time stand fixed. Beyond is all abyss. Eternity. Whose end, no eye can reach. Greatly instructed, I shall hence depart. Greatly in peace of thought, and have my fill of knowledge. What this vessel can contain; beyond which was my folly to aspire. Henceforth I learn. That to obey is best, and love with fear the only God. To walk as in His Presence. Ever to observe His Providence, and on Him sole depend. Merciful over all His works. With good still overcoming evil, and by small, accomplishing great things. By things deemed weak, subverting worldly strong, and worldly wise by simply meek. That suffering, for Truth's sake is fortitude, to highest victory.'[227]

The world and everything contained within it is flawed, broken, marred, and temporal. Nothing in and of this world is capable of granting us everlasting peace, serenity, equanimity, or genuine happiness. Everything within this natural world is measured, quantified, and obtained, only to be stolen, lost, or destroyed. We can traverse the entire Earth, and explore it with the fullness of our senses. Yet, for some reason or another, we remain genuinely unsatisfied with our life.

This undesirable condition of discontent still remains in the background of our life. This inherent and universal unsatisfactoriness with the human condition presents us with a protracted sense of incompleteness, apathy, indifference, despair, and boredom. A dejected feeling of loneliness. An apprehension surrounding the uncertainties and vicissitudes in our life. A persistent unhappiness with our personal limitations, shortcomings, and inadequacies.

---

227 Milton, John. (Darbishire, Helen, Ed.) (1958). *The Poetical Works of John Milton*. London: Oxford University Press, p. 279.

In the greater scheme of things, we all harbour an underlying fear of unbecoming, by the uncertain, unknown, and unpredictable occurrence of our death, before we have truly become. Truly become, in the sense that we have realised our inherent potential. We have reached our highest limit of self-actualisation. We have accomplished our endeavours, before our permanent and irreversible existential demise on Earth.

To attain this transcendent state of being is a profound experience of a lifetime. In this unrivalled state of being, the mind has not only conquered the world, but it has precisely defined our living reality on Earth. The mind has defined our living reality, to such a degree and depth, that nothing disturbs the peace of our being. The mind is no longer perturbed by the clutter, conflict, and chaos of our being. If and when, we attain this transcendent state of being, then we have come to the *realisation* of the true nature of our being, to the *acceptance* of the impermanence of our being, and to the *peace* of our present state of being.

In our life, the persistent, problematic, and pernicious feeling of despondency is only eradicated by God's Eternal Word. The spiritual dimension of our life is never fulfilled with the material dimension of life on Earth. No quantum of formal education, empirical knowledge, personal experience, profit, private wealth, concupiscence, illicit substance abuse, alcohol consumption, private property, self-medication, or sensual pleasure satisfies the inherent disposition of our soul.

The soul only achieves a permanent state of satisfaction once its primordial purpose has been fulfilled, which is to reunite with God's Uncreated, Timeless, and Infinite Spirit. We entertain our life with a multitude of experiences, events, and ecstasy. Having said that, nothing in and of this material world, forever satisfies our immediate and present [seemingly permanent] spiritual poverty.

Due to our sinful nature, we constantly struggle against the Self. We struggle to conquer our world and to conquer our mind. However, we are never alone in this formidable struggle against the Self. For we are to place our total reliance and faith upon God's Spirit for assistance. By traversing the path of righteousness, the path that God has appointed for us, we subdue the infinite inclinations, expectations, desires, and hopes of the will, which are all in vain and present us with trivial endeavours that distract our mind.

All too often, we engage in worldly pursuits, through which we do not secure our lasting contentment, tranquillity, peace, happiness, or joy. It is only by our obedience to God's Sovereign Command, and our supplication to God's Sovereign Will, that we overcome the endless pursuit of our erratic ego and the irrational inclinations of our will.

Those select individuals that perform God's Sovereign Will, they secure a lasting peace in this troubled and transitory world. This enlightened reality cannot be achieved by the exertion of human effort or willpower, it is only secured by God's Grace. The exalted state of being in the world, which encompasses peace, joy, and happiness is only obtained on Earth, if we surrender our will to God's Sovereign Will.

Unfortunately, to the contrary we witness how our reliance upon natural reason and understanding leads to much suffering, pain, war, envy, jealousy, destruction, chaos, confusion, and conflict on Earth. Any person who desires to become the master of their life, must first recognise who their true master is, and without qualification that is God.

All too often, we are prepared to defer gratification in the present moment, or to proceed without the satisfaction of some desire, to achieve our grand mission or noble purpose in life. Yet, even this delayed gratification is the epitome of self-interest, where we indoctrinate our thoughts and condition our behaviour, to accomplish our intended long-term objectives, dreams, ambitions, endeavours, and hopes. If we perform, with the same dedication and commitment to holding onto and advancing the

Eternal Truth, then we gain an everlasting victory. A victory not of this world, but a victory of God's Eternal Kingdom.

Too often, after the passage of an entire lifetime, we are left with nothing in this world, but a lived experience that is comprised of regret, remorse, rage, resentment, and revenge. With remarkable consistency and determination, we always follow the logic of our ego and the inclination of our will, however, towards the end of our lifetime, we come to the inevitable realisation, that we did not know better.

With the priceless lived experience of a lifetime, we now perceive all too clearly, the stark limits of our natural reason, judgement, logic, discernment, and intellect. Despite our best intentions, we fall short in living a good life, only to feel contrite about our countless flaws and mishaps. It is the undeniable case, that the pursuit of self-interest is a life truly lived in vain. A life lived for the sole purpose of our self-interest is a selfish life. Such a mediocre life does not render our spirit with everlasting satisfaction. Peace be with you.

'Thus, having learnt. Thou hast attained the sum of wisdom. Hope no higher. Though all the stars thou knewest by name, and all the ethereal powers. All secrets of the deep. All nature's works, or works of God in Heaven, Air, Earth, or Sea. All the riches of this world enjoyed. All the rule. One empire. Only add deeds to thy knowledge answerable. Add faith. Add virtue. Patience. Temperance. Add love. By name to come called charity. The soul of all the rest. Then will thou not be loath to leave this Paradise. But shall possess a Paradise within thee. Happier far.'[228]

True wisdom resides in living the good life. True wisdom resides in living our life based upon honourable principles and timeless values. True wisdom is found in God's Eternal Word. To hope any higher is simply the boasting of our ego, and the demonstration of the shallow depth of our intellect. The ego and the intellect are ignorantly infatuated with the pleasures, desires, substances, private wealth, profit, private property, and priceless treasures of the world. Not to mention, knowledge of the natural world cannot satisfy our soul, nor can it grant us an eternal and immovable peace.

All the riches, pleasures, substances, political power, status, fame, influence, prestige, honour, private wealth, treasure, wine, concupiscence, knowledge, and private property of the world is incapable of creating a blessed, serene, and peaceful life. The pursuit of ecstasy, enjoyment, and entertainment in this material world are superficial endeavours. These worldly pursuits are forever incapable of permanently appeasing our mind.

All human endeavours that do not further God's Glory and Honour are representative of vanity. In the Holy Bible, within the Book of Ecclesiastes, we directly confront the sheer emptiness of

---

228 Milton, John. (Darbishire, Helen, Ed.) (1958). *The Poetical Works of John Milton*. London: Oxford University Press, p. 280.

human effort and worldly accomplishments, 'Vanity of vanities, says the Preacher, vanity of vanities! All is vanity. What does man gain by all the toil at which he toils under the Sun? A generation goes, and a generation comes, but the Earth remains forever. The Sun rises, and the Sun goes down, and hastens to the place where it rises. The wind blows to the South and goes around to the North. Around and around goes the wind, and on its circuits the wind returns. All streams run to the sea, but the sea is not full; to the place where the streams flow, there they flow again. All things are full of weariness; a man cannot utter it; the eye is not satisfied with seeing, nor the ear filled with hearing. What has been, is what will be, and what has been done, is what will be done, and there is nothing new under the Sun.'[229]

Indeed, our lasting peace, sanity, spiritual prosperity, and contentment are secured, when we concentrate our mind upon living our life characterised by restraint, temperance, grace, mercy, community service, forgiveness, charity, benevolence, compassion, social justice, tolerance, human dignity, respect, and love. In our virtuous quest to live a good life, the moderation of our desires and the acceptance of reality are two methods, by which we secure greater contentment and fulfilment with our present state of being. Every person on Earth is seeking something. If we do not search in the right place, we will never find what we seek. Peace be with you.

---

229 The Holy Bible (ESV). (2016). The Book of Ecclesiastes. Chapter 1, Verses 1–9.

CHAPTER 13

PARADISE REGAINED: BOOK ONE

'By one man's disobedience lost.
Now sing recovered Paradise to all humankind.
By one man's firm obedience fully tried.
Through all temptation, and the tempter foiled.
In all his wiles, defeated and repulsed.'

MILTON

BOOK ONE of *Paradise Regained* is the story of the redemption of humanity by the Son of God. This book foretells of the coming of the *Messiah* to save humanity. Almighty God has blessed and destined the *Messiah* to conquer the powerful archnemesis—Satan. The *Messiah's* triumph is not without Satan's towering tests, temptations, trials, and tribulations. However, it is by God's Grace, Mercy, Blessing, and Favour, that the *Messiah* prevails over the presence of darkness and evil. The restoration and salvation of humankind is near at hand. To God belongs the eternal glory of this epic battle.

The moral of *Paradise Regained* is that God's Sovereign Will cannot be obstructed. In all respects, God has the Final Judgement. All that is contained within Creation proceeds according to God's Providence. To God belongs the honour, glory, and victory of good over evil. In *Paradise Lost,* we witnessed the Devil, in the form of a serpent, successfully deceive Eve in the Garden of Eden. This tragic event was followed by the banishment of Adam and Eve from the Garden of Eden. In *Paradise Regained*, we witness the *Messiah's* decisive victory over Satan.

Satan won the battle against Adam and Eve in the Garden of Eden. However, the *Messiah* secures total victory in the war against Satan on Earth. Among the many positive messages contained within *Paradise Regained*, above and beyond all, we learn that our belief in God's Goodness is never unfounded. For during the all-important time that the *Messiah* was on Earth, he took away 'the keys of Death and Hades'.[230]

'How many ages. As the years of men. This Universe we have possessed, and ruled in manner at our will the affairs of Earth. Since Adam and his facile consort Eve lost Paradise. Deceived by me. Though since, with dread attending when that fatal wound shall be inflicted by the seed of Eve.'[231]

The Devil is deception, lies, falsehood, half-truths, and empty promises. Within the Holy Bible, the Old Testament narrates the timeless Biblical story of Adam and Eve situated in the Garden of Eden. Through God's Eternal Word, we learn how the Devil successfully manipulated Eve. Thereafter, Eve misleads Adam to the performance of sin, by his ignorant consumption of the Forbidden Fruit. The negative consequence of Adam and Eve's transgression against God's Eternal Word was the remarkable loss of Paradise in the Garden of Eden. Through the Devil's Machiavellian deed, the state of perfection in Paradise was forever shattered.

---

230 The Holy Bible (ESV). (2016). The Book of Revelation. Chapter 1, Verse 18.
231 Milton, John. (Darbishire, Helen, Ed.) (1958). *The Poetical Works of John Milton.* London: Oxford University Press, p. 286.

With the proper exercise of our rationality and sensibility, we cannot transfer the personal responsibility of Adam and Eve's actions onto God. For Adam and Eve were given concise, clear, and categorical commands, one of them being not to consume the Forbidden Fruit from the Tree of Knowledge of Good and Evil. Nonetheless, the Devil succeeded in his evil scheme to deceive Adam and Eve. As the Book of Genesis teaches us, our natural reason, even at the best of times, is deceived and manipulated. Often, our natural reason is misplaced, misinformed, and misconstrued. Natural reason has the remarkable ability to rationalise what our mind desires.

The Biblical story of Adam and Eve is profoundly important for several reasons. This Biblical story demonstrates the undeniable depravity of the human condition. The fallacy of our personal agency. The incapacity of our free will to always be exercised in a positive and beneficial manner. Last but not least, this Biblical story illustrates the allure and deception of the ego, which misleads Adam and Eve from their true purpose in the Garden of Eden.

The moral of this Biblical story concerning Adam and Eve's tragic fall from grace is eternal and timeless. The important lessons and practical wisdom, which are deduced from this Biblical story have not changed. This proposition is true, because the human condition is fixed and static. There is no progress to be made in human nature, affairs, or behaviour, so to speak. Regardless of the vast industrial, economic, medical, scientific, and technological advances within the modern world, our human nature has remained the same since God created Adam and Eve.

Since the beginning of Creation, which is not the beginning of time, since the advent of Adam and Eve, right up to the present moment, we have already witnessed the high-water mark of human tragedy. That is to say, the effectuation of Original Sin and the Fall of Man. The negative externalities of Original

Sin and the Fall of Man continue to reverberate throughout the contemporary world.

Human civilisation continues to perpetuate sin, vice, and evil. God's Sovereign Will is ignored on Earth. Therefore, the Devil reigns supreme on Earth. Equally, both men and women, fail to learn the fundamental lesson from the Biblical story of Adam and Eve. That lesson being, the pivotal importance of living our life in complete agreement with God's Sovereign Will. Rather, humanity has imposed its own imperfect will on Earth, with devastating consequences.

Throughout the modern world, human civilisation has remained engulfed with immediate and pressing issues, such as civil war, ethnic conflict, capital punishment, refugees, internally displaced people, systemic poverty, sexual assault, famine, death from preventable and curable diseases, genocide, illicit drugs, terrorism, money laundering, the employment of child labour, the proliferation of nuclear weapons, economic inequality, racial discrimination, illiteracy, social class inequality, hate crime, domestic violence, war crimes, social injustice, child abuse, alcohol use disorder, food insecurity, and water scarcity.

These aforementioned international and national issues only represent a select sample of the vast challenges that humanity confronts. Through the voluntary and conscious exercise of our personal agency, natural reason, intellect, and free will, through organising human affairs in accordance with our capacity for rational and deliberate thought, through the act of self-determination, what have we truly achieved on Earth? The true depth of natural reason is remarkably shallow. In fact, so shallow is the depth of our natural reason, that the human civilisation cannot live in peace, dignity, respect, civility, and harmony on Earth.

'Thou and all Angels conversant on Earth with man or men's affairs. How I begin to verify that solemn message late. On which I sent thee to the virgin pure in Galilee. That she should bear a son great in renown, and called the Son of God. Then toldest her. Doubting how these things could be to her a virgin. That on her should come the Holy Ghost. The power of the Highest overshadow her. This man, born and now upgrown. To show him, worthy of his birth divine.'[232]

Fate and destiny guide the purpose of each person's life. The *Messiah* came to Earth to fulfil God's Sovereign Command and Divine Purpose. The *Messiah* had fixed his purpose and vision to the pursuit of fulfilling God's Vision—the redemption of humanity from Original Sin. At all times, the *Messiah* remained absorbed in God's Spirit. Therefore, the *Messiah* did not waver in his personal beliefs and convictions. The *Messiah* knew his mission with clarity, 'When the days drew near for him to be taken up, he set his face to go to Jerusalem.'[233] The *Messiah* knew the atoning sacrifice he was called to perform on Earth. The *Messiah* did not question or doubt his sole mission on Earth. The *Messiah* was preordained to accomplish his grand objective on Earth.

To further God's Glory and Honour, the *Messiah* 'set his face' when his hour had come, to fulfil his divinely preordained mission on Earth. The *Messiah* did not waver in the performance of his divine duty. Within the Holy Bible, the Gospel of John informs us that the *Messiah* accomplished his prime objective on Earth, 'After this, Jesus, knowing that all was now finished, said (to fulfil the scripture), "I thirst." A jar full of sour wine stood there, so they put a sponge full of the sour wine on a hyssop branch and held it to his mouth. When Jesus had received the

---

232 Milton, John. (Darbishire, Helen, Ed.) (1958). *The Poetical Works of John Milton*. London: Oxford University Press, p. 288.
233 The Holy Bible (ESV). (2016). The Gospel of Luke. Chapter 9, Verse 51.

sour wine, he said, "It is finished," and he bowed his head and gave up his spirit.'[234]

What had to be done was done, in order that the *Messiah* fulfilled God's Divine Plan. It is due to God's boundless mercy, compassion, and forgiveness, that humanity was absolved of its sin. Without the *Messiah's* Crucifixion, humanity would have no atonement. Without the *Messiah*, humanity would not be absolved from the blemish of sin.

During the time that the *Messiah* was in the flesh on the Earth, the Devil put the *Messiah* to the ultimate test on three separate occasions. On the first occasion, the Devil tempted the *Messiah* after forty days and nights of fasting, to turn stones into bread. The *Messiah* responded, 'Man shall not live by bread alone, but by every word that comes from the mouth of God.'[235] On the second occasion, the Devil tempted the *Messiah* to throw himself down from the Temple in the Holy City, in the belief that God's Angels will rescue him. The *Messiah* responded, 'You shall not put the LORD your God to the test.'[236]

On the third and final occasion, the Devil tempted the *Messiah* with all the Earthly kingdoms of this world. The *Messiah* responded to this worldly temptation, 'Be gone, Satan! For it is written, "You shall worship the LORD your God and Him only shall you serve." Then the Devil left him, and behold, Angels came and were ministering to him.'[237] Thus, on all three occasions, the *Messiah* did not concede to the worldly temptations of the flesh. The *Messiah* was preordained to fulfil God's Divine Plan on Earth. With God's Grace, Favour, Blessing, and Mercy, the *Messiah* accomplished his divine purpose.

The *Messiah's* remarkable life narrative informs us of the paramount importance of keeping our mind focused on our

---

234 The Holy Bible (ESV). (2016). The Gospel of John. Chapter 19, Verses 28–30.
235 The Holy Bible (ESV). (2016). The Gospel of Matthew. Chapter 4, Verse 4.
236 The Holy Bible (ESV). (2016). The Gospel of Matthew. Chapter 4, Verse 7.
237 The Holy Bible (ESV). (2016). The Gospel of Matthew. Chapter 4, Verses 10–11.

grand endeavours and objectives. The *Messiah's* exceptional life story reminds us, that we must not let our life purpose be diminished, by our engagement in trivial distractions and the pursuit of worldly temptations during our lifetime on Earth.

If and when we allow ourselves to fall into the tragic trap of sin, we ultimately lose our peace of mind, we become detached from our life's true purpose. The sinful temptations of the flesh are many. These worldly temptations are profoundly addictive, as they are pleasurable. The pleasures of the flesh are difficult to eradicate from our life. As the formidable battle between the spirit and the flesh rages on, for the supremacy of our mind, this protracted conflict is only won by our earnest performance of prayer, penance, and petition.

> *'To Satan. Let him tempt and now assay his utmost subtlety, because he boasts and vaunts of his great cunning to the throng of his Apostasy. He might have learnt less overweening. Since he failed in Job, whose constant perseverance overcame whatever his cruel malice could invent. He now shall know I can produce a man of female seed. Far more able to resist all his solicitations, and at length all his vast force, and drive him back to Hell. Thereby, winning by conquest, what the first man lost.'*[238]

The Biblical story of Job is a testimony to the sheer greatness of our spirit to endure suffering, privation, loss, grief, heartache, misery, tragedy, trauma, and tribulation. Job's remarkable life experience educates humanity of the spirit's tenacity, to overcome formidable odds in our unwelcome confrontation with adversity. Indeed, Job transcended the Self.

Most importantly, we must never forget that our spirit is endowed with the exceptional capacity to transcend the

---

238 Milton, John. (Darbishire, Helen, Ed.) (1958). *The Poetical Works of John Milton*. London: Oxford University Press, p. 288.

traumatising, tragic, terrifying, and terrible troubles of the flesh. However, we must always remember, in so far as it concerns our personal affairs, that such a triumph over tragedy is only possible through God's Grace. We do not secure a victory over our troubles, tragedies, and trials through our sinful nature, but only by securing the invaluable assistance of God's Spirit, which operates through and within us.

Throughout the highs and lows of our life, personal losses, errors of judgement, missed opportunities, and mistakes of fact are inevitable. The ebbs and flows of human life are unavoidable. The key to our success in life, is to confront the undesirable situations, and navigate the difficult conversations. In all respects, the process of letting go and moving forward is of paramount importance. For one day, we will not have any time in the remainder. The Devil would have us constantly dwell upon the negative experiences in our life. The Devil intends to keep us bound to a life of tragedy, pain, suffering, guilt, shame, confusion, anger, denial, regret, remorse, and trauma.

The good news is that we exercise control over our mind. We have the inherent freedom to associate or disassociate from select thoughts, in order to create our desired reality. To persevere in the irrational and finite struggle of life, one must have hope for a better and brighter future, unwavering faith in God, the opportunity to participate in meaningful and purposeful work, compassion and love for humanity, and a sense of non-delegable duty to one's family. The ability to remain optimistic, positive, and hopeful during turbulent times is a great blessing.

If we carefully reflect and consider the reality of human life, all of life is a process of integration and disintegration. In this cognitive dissonance and flux of life, the only phenomenon worth holding onto in the world is God. We ought to construct our reality and identity around God.

Regrettably, we cause ourselves great distress by holding onto past experiences, both the good and the traumatising experiences that no longer exist, but continue to define our life narrative, because we permit them to do so. If we realise the immense power of our mind, then we consciously and selectively determine to leave the past in the past. Those people who live in the present, without thought of the past, and without a burdensome concern for the future, they are truly blessed. For the fullness of life is only experienced in the present moment.

'Of his great warfare, here I send him forth. To conquer sin and death, the two grand foes. By humiliation and strong sufferance. His weakness shall overcome Satanic strength and all the world, and mass of sinful flesh. That all the Angels and ethereal powers, they now, and men hereafter may discern. From what consummate virtue I have chosen this perfect man. By merit called My Son. To earn salvation for the sons of men.'[239]

The *Messiah* came to Earth and he conquered the two greatest opponents of humanity—sin and death. In the Holy Bible, within the Book of Revelation, we bear witness to the authenticity of the *Messiah* as the true saviour of humanity, 'fear not, I am the first and the last, and the living one. I died, and behold I am alive forevermore, and I have the keys of Death and Hades.'[240] The *Messiah* did not overcome death and Hades through the sheer demonstration of his power, but rather by his wisdom of total reliance upon God's Strength, Spirit, and Sovereignty.

There is a profound Biblical lesson that we deduce from the aforementioned scripture verse, and that is through faith, we eradicate our fear of death and hell. Since time immemorial, the Devil has employed the instruments of death and hell to victimise humanity. However, since the *Messiah* has taken away

---

239 Milton, John. (Darbishire, Helen, Ed.) (1958). *The Poetical Works of John Milton.* London: Oxford University Press, p. 289.
240 The Holy Bible (ESV). (2016). The Book of Revelation. Chapter 1, Verses 17–18.

this power from the Devil, then our fear of death and hell is misconceived. It is in and through faith, that we secure our peace on Earth.

Furthermore, in the Gospel of Matthew, we learn how the *Messiah* did not employ force, but ensured God's Sovereign Will was done on Earth, 'Do you think that I cannot appeal to my Father, and He will at once send me more than twelve legions of Angels? But how then should the scriptures be fulfilled, that it must be so?'[241] In the end, the *Messiah* overcame the weaknesses and limitations of the flesh, by his complete faith in the power of the spirit.

The spirit ventures where the flesh cannot. The spirit endures what the flesh cannot. The spirit overcomes what the flesh cannot. The spirit grants peace where the flesh cannot. In the final analysis, what we place our faith in ultimately defines our life. We need to think twice about whom we affirm our trust in, so that are soul returns to its final destination—the eternal and timeless Kingdom of Heaven.

It is important to highlight herein, that God places the emphasis squarely on the *Messiah's* merit, as opposed to an emphasis on his birth right. The *Messiah* was the Chosen One, not merely because he was the Son of God, but rather because he had earnt his merited place in Heaven by righteousness. The profound distinction between birth right and merit is of great significance and consequence.

With God's emphasis squarely on merit, it demonstrates to all of humanity, that every person is inherently capable of cultivating their own merit by the performance of righteous actions on Earth. The rigid considerations of birth right do not define our life trajectory. It is not the case, that a person who originates from a wealthy, affluent, famous, astute, educated, elite, noble,

---

241 The Holy Bible (ESV). (2016). Gospel of Matthew. Chapter 26, Verses 53–54.

or privileged family, possesses some greater advantage in securing God's Grace.

God alone predetermines the higher purpose and divine mission of each person's sacred life. God is not bound by the superficial worldly distinctions, biological variations, and artificial barriers of socio-economic inequality that are prevalent in the world. Some of these human-made distinctions, biological variations, and factors of inequality include genetic differences, biological distinctions, private property, private wealth, race, university education, colour, gender, social status, nationality, sex, and personal income.

These aforementioned distinctions, variations, and factors, function to segregate, marginalise, and discriminate against, otherwise equal members of human civilisation. Every person is equal, solely by the universal attribute of human dignity. In the final analysis, every person by the virtue of human dignity, is capable of securing salvation on Earth through repentance, atonement, prayer, petition, and acceptance of God's Sovereign Will. No person is lesser or greater than any other person. Before God, all people are judged equally.

'Victory and triumph to the Son of God, now entering his great duel. Not of arms, but to vanquish by wisdom, hellish wiles. The Father knows the Son; therefore, secure. Ventures his filial virtue, though untried.'[242]

The *Messiah* came to Earth to redeem humanity. The *Messiah* came to Earth for the sake of humanity. The *Messiah's* victory and triumph over the Devil were preordained by God. The *Messiah* placed his unwavering trust and unquestionable belief in God when it came to the Great Duel of Good and Evil. The *Messiah* confronted and prevailed against the formidable

---

242 Milton, John. (Darbishire, Helen, Ed.) (1958). *The Poetical Works of John Milton*. London: Oxford University Press, p. 289.

power of Satan. The *Messiah* relied upon God's Eternal Word, and not his own strength, to vanquish Satan.

On three separate occasions, the Devil tempted the *Messiah*, however, on all three occasions, the *Messiah* was triumphant. Through the unmatched power of faith, through an unwavering belief in God's Eternal Word, the *Messiah* overcame Satan—a powerful and terrible foe. Satan is a deadly foe, whose sole mission on Earth is to promote destruction, depression, suffering, conflict, confusion, envy, doubt, anger, revenge, disobedience, denial, suicide, jealousy, chaos, war, and death.

> '*O what a multitude of thoughts at once awakened in me swarm. While I consider what from within. I feel myself, and hear what from without comes often to my ears. Ill sorting with my present state compared. When I was yet a child. No childish play to me was pleasing. All my mind was set. Serious to learn and know, and thence to do what might be public good; myself I thought. Born to that end, born to promote all Truth. All righteous things. Therefore, above my years. The Law of God I read, and found it sweet. Made it my whole delight, and in it I grew.*'[243]

The human condition is complex, in as much as it is multifaceted. People are infused with a diverse spectrum of feelings, emotions, inclinations, instincts, temperaments, passions, and sensations, which are enmeshed within the defining presence of our personality, genetic material, parentage, childhood, history, lived experience, knowledge, education, language, literature, folklore, nationality, religion, nationhood, customs, traditions, beliefs, and culture. To acknowledge and entertain a thought,

---

243 Milton, John. (Darbishire, Helen, Ed.) (1958). *The Poetical Works of John Milton*. London: Oxford University Press, p. 290.

without accepting it and acting upon it, this is the hallmark of self-mastery and intelligence.

In order to develop our practice of mindfulness, we ought to analyse our thoughts and reflect upon the question: Why do we think in the manner that we think? After all, the construction of our reality of being commences with our conscious thoughts. If we understand ourselves better, then we live a wholesome, rational, and productive life. A life that is reflective of our values, endeavours, doctrines, objectives, principles, and beliefs. A life that is characterised by purpose, productivity, and passion. This is the meaning of a life well-lived.

In order to transform this noble idea, of a life well-lived into our living reality, we need to carefully examine our thoughts, beliefs, ideas, doctrines, and principles, that collectively constitute our mindset. The emotionally intelligent art of introspection allows us to better understand our present reality. In all circumstances and situations, our mindset is malleable. Therefore, throughout our lifetime, we need to calibrate and recalibrate our mindset, to ensure that we are receptive to change and conscious of the forces that define our lived experience on Earth. Transformative change always starts with transformative thinking.

'By words at times cast forth, inly rejoiced, and said to me apart. High are thy thoughts O Son, but nourish them and let them soar. To what height sacred virtue and true worth can raise them. Though above example high. By matchless deeds express thy matchless sire.'[244]

Our worldly reality starts with and in the formation of our thoughts. Having said that, it is the summation of our conscious and free willed actions which determine our life. It is a universal

---

244 Milton, John. (Darbishire, Helen, Ed.) (1958). *The Poetical Works of John Milton*. London: Oxford University Press, p. 290.

truth, that our deeds always speak louder than our words. Therefore, we must exercise self-determination, introspection, circumspection, and judgement to perform deeds which are meritorious, constructive, and honourable. In the end, it is our deeds, not our thoughts and not our words, which define our life. It is through volition; the voluntary exercise of our will, that our conscious actions create our experience of being in the world.

When we live our life marked by the remembrance of God's Eternal Word, compassion, prayer, mercy, human dignity, respect, tolerance, petition, benevolence, intercession, universal love for humanity, the deliverance of social justice, participating in work that advances civil society and the just cause of humanity, giving a portion of our private wealth and personal income to the less fortunate people, and furthering the noble cause of peace, then we are living our life truly defined as matchless in deeds. Our thoughts, no matter how positive and original, are only aspirations. It is through the performance of righteous deeds, that we make the world a better, brighter, and blessed place for humanity.

'A pathless desert. Dusk with horrid shades. The way he came not having marked. Return was difficult. By human steps untrod; and he still on was led. But with such thoughts accompanied of things past and to come lodged in his breast. As well might recommend such solitude before choicest society. Full forty days he passed. Whether on hill, sometimes anon in shady vale. Each night under the covert of some ancient oak, or cedar. To defend him from the dew, or harboured in one cave, is not revealed. Nor tasted human food. Nor hunger felt till those days ended. Hungered then at last among wild beasts. They at his sight grew mild. Nor sleeping him. Nor waking harmed. His walk the fiery serpent fled, and noxious worm. The lion and fierce tiger glared aloof.'[245]

The *Messiah* conquered all the trials that were placed before him on his unique journey in the world. The *Messiah* overcame the world. The *Messiah's* divinely preordained accomplishments led to the only plausible understanding that remained, after ascertaining the world for what it truly is, and that exact understanding was, 'My kingdom is not of this world.'[246] The *Messiah* demonstrated a formidable depth of spiritual self-mastery that is rarely seen in the world. For the *Messiah* overcame the Self. The *Messiah* transcended the countless pitfalls of the flesh.

God has also endowed us with free will to exercise our personal agency. The moral imperative is upon us to live our life in accordance with the spirit. Learning from the profound wisdom of the *Messiah*, we too can apply the same time-honoured principles to our life. In this present moment, it is incumbent upon us to overcome the pleasures, temptations, desires, and distractions of the flesh. While our protracted battle with the

245 Milton, John. (Darbishire, Helen, Ed.) (1958). *The Poetical Works of John Milton*. London: Oxford University Press, pp. 292–293.
246 The Holy Bible (ESV). (2016). The Gospel of John. Chapter 18, Verse 36.

flesh is a difficult endeavour, as it is a lifelong endeavour, we must persevere in this struggle. For it is through our perseverance and suffering, that the phenomenal power of the spirit develops within us. When our spirit is constantly cultivated, the power of our flesh gradually diminishes.

> *'By miracle he may, replied the swain. What other way.*
> *I see not. For we here live on tough roots and stubs.*
> *To thirst inured more than the camel, and to drink go far.*
> *Men to much misery and hardship born. But if thou be*
> *the Son of God. Command that out of these hard stones*
> *be made thee bread. So shall thou save thyself, and us*
> *relieve with food. Whereof we wretched seldom taste.'*[247]

The Devil cunningly tempted the *Messiah* to demonstrate his power, for his own worldly honour, reputation, pride, and glory. However, the *Messiah* did not give credence to the devious stratagem of debating with the Devil. The *Messiah* placed his complete faith and reliance upon God's Eternal Word. Within the Holy Bible, in the Gospel of Matthew, the *Messiah* reminds us that, 'Man shall not live by bread alone, but by every word that comes from the mouth of God.'[248] We too confront countless adversities, problems, issues, and challenges during our lifetime.

It is a cold hard truth, human life is a journey that for many of us, is to some degree characterised by privations, clinical diseases, addictions, psychological disorders, social challenges, prescription drug abuse, illicit substance abuse, political disagreements, lengthy legal proceedings, alcohol use disorder, community correction orders, incarceration, the onset of family problems, divorce, child custody arrangements, attempted suicide, periodical unemployment challenges, psychiatric conditions,

---

247 Milton, John. (Darbishire, Helen, Ed.) (1958). *The Poetical Works of John Milton*. London: Oxford University Press, p. 293.
248 The Holy Bible (ESV). (2016). The Gospel of Matthew. Chapter 4, Verse 4.

complications of pregnancy, and intrauterine fetal demise. This is the conventional reality of running our race. We cannot run our race in the absence of worldly impediments.

The key to transcending the aforementioned social, legal, moral, personal, economic, medical, and political issues, is not to let these issues define our personal identity. These issues do not define who we are, rather they represent what we experience in our lifetime. We must never confuse who we are, with what we experience. Highs and lows are a part of every person's life journey. We must keep our issues in perspective.

With the right social support, a plan of action, faith in God's Goodness, and the pursuit of constructive endeavours, we secure a turnaround in our personal affairs. How can we transform this ideal proposition into our real-life narrative? Through belief, hope, prayer, faith, action, love, dedication, commitment, and discipline. Peace be with you.

The Devil utilises the aforementioned life challenges, or unfavourable changes in our circumstances, to tempt us to renounce our faith. The Devil tempts us to believe that God does not exist. This assertion is especially true, when we are at the most vulnerable point in our life. We are most vulnerable, when our heart is heavy, when our mind is distracted, and when our spirit is troubled. It is during these make or break moments that our life is defined. The adversity that we experience in our life is strong, yet where there is love, hope, belief, forgiveness, mercy, and faith, in that place anything is possible.

We must always remember, it is not what happens to us that defines us. Rather, it is how we respond to such crises, events, situations, or circumstances, that ultimately define our character and determine our life trajectory. No matter how negligible the odds appear to us, a turnaround in our life is always possible. On our life journey, surrendering to the Devil is not an option. We cannot lay claim to the defence of plausible deniability, if we consciously permit evil free rein in our life. No matter the losses we endure in our struggle of life, the faith must be kept under all circumstances.

We cannot secure our salvation through the performance of good works. The *Messiah* has directly imparted this knowledge, wisdom, and experience to us. Even the *Messiah* had to suffer in the world. The *Messiah's* most direct and immediate suffering on the Cross was not for his sake, but rather for the universal sake of humanity.

In the Holy Bible, in the Book of First Peter, we are reminded of the *Messiah's* sacrifice, 'For Christ also suffered once for sins. The righteous for the unrighteous. That he might bring us to God, being put to death in the flesh but made alive in the spirit.'[249] In life, we confront two divergent paths when it comes to determining a difficult decision. We can choose the convenient, comfortable, and corrupt path, or the difficult, dedicated, and devoted path. The cumulative consequences of our decisions ultimately determine our destiny.

> *'Companions of my misery and woe. At first it may be. But long since with woe nearer acquainted. Now I feel by proof. That fellowship in pain divides not smart. Nor lightens aught each man's peculiar load. Small consolation then, were man adjoined. This wounds me most (what can it less?) that man. Man fallen shall be restored. I never more.'*[250]

The pursuit and advancement of fellowship is a must in this world. Fellowship helps to support, sustain, and strengthen our common struggle in this world. The protracted struggle between the flesh and the spirit becomes bearable with fellowship. In addition, fellowship strengthens our faith in God. By participating

---

249 The Holy Bible (ESV). (2016). The First Book of Peter. Chapter 3, Verse 18.
250 Milton, John. (Darbishire, Helen, Ed.) (1958). *The Poetical Works of John Milton*. London: Oxford University Press, p. 295.

in fellowship, we feel a greater sense of security in ourselves, society, and state. Fellowship provides us with the opportunity for confession and witness. The seemingly endless worldly burdens of our life become lighter, when we share them and seek good counsel in God's Presence.

Fellowship assists us to become more cognisant of the human condition, by sharing our common lot with grief, loss, trauma, heartbreak, life issues, tragedies, difficulties, concerns, and worries. Fellowship fosters emotional intelligence amongst the members of civil society. Participating in fellowship also makes us more receptive to other people's pressing concerns. Last but not least, fellowship provisions us with an acute awareness of the surmountable challenges confronting civil society.

'From thee I can, and must, submiss, endure. Check or reproof, and glad to escape so quit. Hard are the ways of Truth. Rough to walk. Smooth on the tongue discoursed. Pleasing to the ear, and tunable as sylvan pipe or song.'[251]

The Devil knows our numerous weaknesses. Most concerningly, the Devil is not perturbed with the immorality of using our weaknesses against us. The Righteous Path of Truth is not a convenient endeavour. We must live our life according to the higher principles of honesty, respect, trustworthiness, integrity, human dignity, tolerance, mercy, security, peace, forgiveness, community service, charity, benevolence, compassion, equality, love, and credibility.

Often times, our ego seeks to provision credence to the Devil's temptations, however, there is always an exorbitant price to pay for the performance of sin. We must not allow ourselves to fall into the terrible trap of temptation. The thought of temptation almost always leads us to the performance of sin. The effectuation

---

251 Milton, John. (Darbishire, Helen, Ed.) (1958). *The Poetical Works of John Milton*. London: Oxford University Press, p. 297.

of sin, in turn leads us to the undesirable feelings of remorse, regret, denial, frustration, and anger. Our grand strategy is to defeat temptation at its source. Therefore, we do not permit the thought of temptation to secure refuge in our mind.

Indeed, every person reaps what they sow. For the greater struggle of Truth, we endure our lesser privations. This approach to life cultivates our character, strengthens our spirit, improves our willpower, promotes our moral conscience, and enhances our virtues. The path of faith is not traversed without the incidence of loss, hardship, grief, setback, tragedy, pain, suffering, trauma, and heartache. Therefore, it is important that we strengthen our determination and resolve to keep our faith.

It is by God's Grace, that a minority of predestined people remain steadfast on the path of faith, till the very end of their lifetime. Near the time of our death, if we reflect upon our life, and we genuinely affirm the words, 'I have fought the good fight. I have finished the race. I have kept the faith,'[252] this is an irrefutable personal testimony, to the decisive victory of good over evil.

---

252 The Holy Bible (ESV). (2016). Second Letter of Paul to Timothy. Chapter 4, Verse 7.

CHAPTER 14

PARADISE REGAINED: BOOK TWO

'With more than human gifts from Heaven adorned.
Perfection absolute. Grace divine.
Amplitude of mind to greatest deed.
Therefore, I am returned.
Lest confidence of my success with Eve in Paradise.'

MILTON

BOOK TWO of *Paradise Regained* narrates Satan's three powerful temptations of the *Messiah*. Milton closely follows the well-known Biblical events of the *Messiah's* three major tests at Satan's evil hands. These trials, tests, tribulations, and temptations include: Testing the *Messiah* to turn stones into bread. Attempting to persuade the *Messiah* to fall from the top of the Temple, to be saved by God's faithful Angels. Last but not least, offering the *Messiah* to become the King of all the kingdoms of this world, in exchange for worshipping the Devil. The *Messiah* passes all three tests. At no point does the *Messiah's* belief, trust, and faith in God waver.

This book establishes the true foundation, for how humanity transcends the many temptations, trials, tragedies, tests, tribulations, and troubles of the world. The righteous and good life is not a convenient endeavour. However, the *Messiah* has exhibited a demonstrable and practical example for all people, concerning how to overcome the temptation of evil with the presence of good. In aspiring to lead a noble and honourable life, humanity ought to cultivate its conscience and observe moral principles. Every person can improve their character through the performance of morally righteous conduct. Humanity cannot circumvent the refined and tested process of moral perfection, to achieve the desired final outcome—Eternal Life in the Kingdom of God.

'Alas, from what high hope to what relapse. Unlooked for are we fallen! Our eyes beheld; the Messiah has certainly now come. So long expected of our fathers. We have heard his words. His wisdom full of grace and truth. Now, now, for sure. Deliverance is at hand.'[253]

Since the advent of Adam and Eve, humanity has been unable to honour God's Sovereign Commands. Humanity has and still continues to live life characterised by grief, pain, hate, lust, confusion, envy, sin, pride, anger, jealousy, denial, pleasure, suffering, and death. The Devil has blinded humanity away from a life of dignity, morality, conscience, natural reason, integrity, benevolence, peace, social justice, and righteousness.

Instead, the Devil has successfully lured humanity towards living our life defined by a renowned love for the sinful pleasures of the flesh. An inferior life that is characterised by sin, evil, concupiscence, ignorance, darkness, arrogance, and disobedience. The blessed coming of the *Messiah* transformed human reality. The *Messiah* offered a new pathway forward for human civilisation. The *Messiah* offered a pathway towards complete reconciliation with God. A newfound divine pact. An everlasting

---

253 Milton, John. (Darbishire, Helen, Ed.) (1958). *The Poetical Works of John Milton*. London: Oxford University Press, p. 298.

pact that witnesses humanity wholly absolved of its sin, and therefore, truly redeemed.

> *'For Solomon, he lived at ease. Full of honour, wealth, high fare, aimed not beyond higher design than to enjoy his State. Thence to the bait of women lay exposed. But he whom we attempt is wiser far than Solomon, of more exalted mind. Made and set wholly on the accomplishment of greater things.'*[254]

Within the Holy Bible, in the First Book of Kings, we are made privy to the life of Solomon. Solomon lived a remarkable and grandiose life. King Solomon's life was defined by immense pleasure, private wealth, privilege, fame, political power, riches, worldly glory, royalty, social influence, treasure, prestige, and honour.

The First Book of Kings acquaints us with the finer details pertaining to the magnificent extent of King Solomon's wealth, 'Now the weight of gold that came to Solomon in one year was 666 talents of gold, besides that which came from the explorers and from the business of the merchants, and from all the Kings of the West and from the Governors of the land. King Solomon made 200 large shields of beaten gold; 600 shekels of gold went into each shield. And he made 300 shields of beaten gold; three minas of gold went into each shield. And the King put them in the House of the Forest of Lebanon.'[255]

The First Book of Kings continues with its vivid description of King Solomon's grandiose life, 'The King also made a great ivory throne and overlaid it with the finest gold. The throne had six steps, and the throne had a round top, and on each side of the seat were armrests and two lions standing beside the armrests,

---

254 Milton, John. (Darbishire, Helen, Ed.) (1958). *The Poetical Works of John Milton.* London: Oxford University Press, p. 303.
255 The Holy Bible (ESV). (2016). First Book of Kings. Chapter 10, Verses 14–17.

while twelve lions stood there, one on each end of a step on the six steps. The like of it was never made in any kingdom. All King Solomon's drinking vessels were of gold, and all the vessels of the House of the Forest of Lebanon were of pure gold. None were of silver. Silver was not considered as anything in the days of Solomon. For the King had a fleet of ships of Tarshish at sea with the fleet of Hiram. Once every three years the fleet of ships of Tarshish used to come bringing gold, silver, ivory, apes, and peacocks.'[256]

King Solomon's astounding wealth cannot be denied or disputed. Yet, even with the possession of all this worldly glory, private wealth, and worldly success, true contentment is only secured by the possession of a peaceful mind and the cultivation of an enlightened spirit. The many superficial desires and empty pleasures of the world are temporal. The vain pursuits and empty accomplishments of our heart's desires do not provide us with everlasting satisfaction.

In one sense, the lofty pursuits that we dedicate our life to, and the accomplishments that we secure, these personal endeavours define our lifetime on Earth. Therefore, it is essential that we dedicate our heart and mind to the achievement of extraordinary endeavours that further God's Sovereign Kingdom on Earth.

Let us momentarily digress from the discourse on King Solomon's private wealth, life of extravagance, and worldly fame. In all the things that we do on Earth, it is important that we create the requisite time and space for God in our life. This unmatched approach to living is essential, so that we gain a greater appreciation of the vast expanse of reality that surrounds our life. An unfathomable reality, one that is far greater than the confines of our immediate and proximate self.

---

256 The Holy Bible (ESV). (2016). First Book of Kings. Chapter 10, Verses 18–22.

When we come to the irrefutable and enlightened realisation, that we inhabit a Universe that is far greater than our finite existence, then we must express love for our life, joy for living, and gratitude for our finite sense of being in an infinite Universe. Knowing that each and every one of us constitutes an integral part of God's Creation, and that we possess everything that we require to live a whole, productive, joyous, and good life, thereby, we obtain genuine equanimity within ourselves. An enduring equanimity that cannot be obtained beyond the Self.

During our lifetime on Earth, the secret to our success is to neither entertain the thought of hubris, nor the sense of complacency with our lot in life. We were not created to stand still. Human progress is painstaking work; however, it must be done. Through the course of our endless labour, we must persevere, if we have any chance at securing the dividends of our toil. Our work does not encompass a never-ending sense of joy, satisfaction, or fulfilment. In certain cases, the dividends of our work are not secured within our lifetime. Instead, it may be the cumulative effort of three or four generations, before humanity witnesses the benefits of our labour.

The crucial point herein is to regulate our emotional state of being during the countless ebbs and flows of our work. In managing our emotions, we must be attentive to the undesirable presence of self-pity, which is the worst of all emotions. For self-pity only serves to obstruct the actualisation of our inherent potential. Self-pity degrades the inherent capacity for human flourishing.

We ought to strive to better ourselves, further our personal achievements, and secure our desired accomplishments. We must never stand still and be satisfied with the status quo. Life is all about moving forward and upward to conquer new horizons and uncharted territory. To develop spiritually, emotionally, socially, and intellectually, we must defeat our adversaries. We must not fall into the temptation to be consumed by the presence of trivial distractions, fleeting pleasures, and inconsequential battles. Every person is a work in progress.

The Holy Bible, in the Book of Isaiah reminds us that, 'But now, O LORD, you are our Father; we are the clay, and you are our potter; we are all the work of your hand.'[257] Wisdom, knowledge, skill, ability, talent, and expertise are accumulated after a lifetime's worth of dedication, commitment, and effort towards our work. Each day that we grow and learn, we make progress towards the betterment of ourselves.

In order to live a productive, fulfilling, and wholesome life, it is essential that we set our mind to the achievement of lofty pursuits and towering ambitions. We must rise above and beyond the mundane reality of simply existing within the confines of popular culture, trending ideologies, the contemporary tastes of fashion, the dictates of custom, and the prevailing social norms.

Instead, we must concentrate on the everlasting, eternal, and eminent Glory of God. We must employ our finite lifetime on Earth to live our life to its highest potential. We must dedicate our lifetime to the pursuit of noble-minded endeavours that make our life on Earth a truly worthwhile endeavour. In achieving such an ideal endeavour, we must commit our mind to the task at hand. We must hold ourselves accountable. In fact, we only hold ourselves accountable, when and where we are transparent.

It is through the application of initiative, action, and agency, that we actualise the endeavours that we envisioned. Such a desirable life is only achieved when we consciously live in the lifelong pursuit of the accomplishment of our inherent potential. We ought to strive to live the life that we truly desire. It is morally incumbent upon us, to earnestly accomplish our objectives. If we concentrate our mind towards the achievement of our noble endeavours, then the many pitfalls, setbacks, obstacles, losses,

---

257 The Holy Bible (ESV). (2016). The Book of Isaiah. Chapter 64, Verse 8.

disadvantages, and barriers that we encounter along our life are transcended.

In order to create such an ideal reality, we must cultivate the higher faculties of our mind. These desirable faculties include intuition, imagination, perception, memory, natural reason, and will. We must fixate our mind upon the realisation of our noble ambitions. We must not permit the day-to-day distractions of modern living to lead us astray. If we concentrate our mind towards the accomplishment of our grand objectives, then we consciously create our desired reality. At the end of our lifetime, we only hold ourselves accountable and responsible for our fulfilled and unfulfilled endeavours. Therefore, our present reality of being begs the question: What are we waiting for?

'Where still from shade to shade the Son of God after forty days fasting had remained. Now hungering first, and to himself thus said. Where will this end? Four times ten days, I have passed. Wandering this woody maze, and human food, nor tasted, nor had appetite. That fast to virtue I impute not, or count part of what I suffer here. If nature need not, or God support nature without repast though needing, what praise is it to endure? But now I feel I hunger, which declares, nature hath need of what she asks. Yet, God can satisfy that need some other way.'[258]

The *Messiah* passed the litmus test to submit to God's Sovereign Will. It was by God's Grace that the *Messiah* overcame the limitations of the human condition. Likewise, we too must also live our life characterised by an unconditional love for God's Eternal Word. We must strive to live our life in accordance with God's Sovereign Will. To position God's Eternal Word and

---

258 Milton, John. (Darbishire, Helen, Ed.) (1958). *The Poetical Works of John Milton*. London: Oxford University Press, p. 304.

Sovereign Will ahead of ourselves, we must exercise restraint, good judgement, self-discipline, and discernment in our life.

We must ensure that our life is one of moderation in all things. In part, moderation is secured by the self-regulation of our psychological state of being, and the self-control of our appetites, desires, passions, emotions, inclinations, thoughts, and urges. When we self-regulate our appetites, desires, passions, emotions, inclinations, thoughts, and urges, then we are in control of our physical and psychological state of being. Through the unmatched power of self-control, we create and define our life narrative.

Our desires and passions possess the remarkable capacity to define our life trajectory, for good or evil. We must be vigilant in our thoughts, in order that we engage in the furtherance of good during the temporal reality of our being on Earth. Often, human judgement is prone to error in its capacity to identify the allure of evil. In addition, sometimes the temptation to perform an evil act is perceived as an expeditious resolution to our worldly troubles. Regardless of the immediate context, the specific circumstance, or the pressing situation, we are certain that the Devil misconstrues the facts, so as to enhance the appeal and temptation for us to perform evil actions on Earth. We must not be so naive, as to assume that the fruit of all our actions ripen within our present lifetime. Peace be with you.

'How hast thou hunger then? Satan replied. Tell me.
If food were now before thee set. Wouldst thou not eat?
Thereafter, as I like the Giver, answered Jesus. Why should
that cause thy refusal, said the subtle fiend. Hast thou not
right to all created things? Owe not all creatures. By just
right. To thee duty and service. Nor to stay till bid.
But tender all their power?'[259]

The Devil is tempting the *Messiah* to produce his power. Not only that, the Devil seeks to target the *Messiah* at the most opportune and vulnerable time, being forty days and forty nights after the *Messiah* had abstained from the consumption of food. We deduce invaluable lessons from this Biblical narrative found within the Gospel of Matthew. During a vulnerable moment in our lifetime, the Devil tempts us with an intrusive thought, about what we do not have, or what is missing from our life. The Devil always seeks to exploit our weaknesses and vulnerabilities. The Devil's egregious abuse of spiritual power is a strategic approach, one that is targeted at destroying our faith in God. Simply put, the Devil's spirit is impure and evil.

In the Holy Bible, within the Book of Isaiah, God's Eternal Word has forewarned us of the Devil's insincere and corrupt nature, 'How you are fallen from Heaven, O Day Star, Son of Dawn! How you are cut down to the ground, you who laid the Nations low! You said in your heart, "I will ascend to Heaven; above the stars of God. I will set my throne on high. I will sit on the Mount of Assembly in the far reaches of the North. I will ascend above the heights of the clouds. I will make myself like the Most High."'[260]

The Devil's unchecked pride and ambition was behind his tragic fall from grace. The Devil has not repented, nor has he

---

259 Milton, John. (Darbishire, Helen, Ed.) (1958). *The Poetical Works of John Milton*. London: Oxford University Press, p. 306.
260 The Holy Bible (ESV). (2016). The Book of Isaiah. Chapter 14, Verses 12–14.

expressed remorse for his transgressions against God's Sovereign Kingdom. Rather, the Devil has committed himself to the immoral aims of furthering destruction, conflict, chaos, and war on Earth. Therefore, we must dismiss the Devil's ideas without a second thought.

While we have so much in our life, the Devil endeavours to destroy our peace of mind, by constantly reminding us of the one precious commodity that is absent from our life, but we genuinely and strongly desire that one particular commodity. Now this tangible or intangible commodity that is absent from our life could be marriage, children, education, employment, private wealth, home ownership, important relationships, private property portfolio, or our happiness due to pending legal proceedings. In all these cases and many more, the Devil exerts his utmost influence, to persuade us that God has forgotten about our welfare. The Devil takes advantage of our dreams, desires, and disappointments. The Devil suggests that he has the remedy, if only we switch our allegiance to worship him.

Simply put, the Devil is proffering suggestions to humanity. Why? To persuade us to listen to him. This is the same tried and tested stratagem that the Devil employed against Eve. The Devil successfully deceived Eve from following God's Sovereign Command. If we are to stand firm in the presence of the Devil's incalculable and formidable power, we must place our total reliance on God's Infallible Word. The Devil exploits the weaknesses in our thought processes. The Devil attempts to find discontinuity, discord, or deficiency in our natural reason. The Devil is acutely aware of the frailties associated with human understanding. After all, a chain is only as strong as the weakest link.

Unlike the *Messiah*, it is not possible for us to outmanoeuvre the Devil. We are more likely than not to be outreasoned by the Devil's powerful temptations, such is the frailty of our human condition. It is best counsel that we do not engage the Devil, but remain steadfast adjoined to God's Eternal Word. Thereafter, the Devil's malevolent spirit sooner or later departs from our immediate presence, to return another day. Even if we manage to withstand the assault of the Devil, and are left unscathed, let us not boast that we have achieved anything. This ignorant approach only serves to strengthen our ego. For truly, it was God's Spirit that protected our being from the Devil's unmatched power.

> *'Great acts require great means of enterprise. Thou art unknown. Unfriended. Low of birth. A carpenter. Thy Father known. Thyself bred up in poverty and straits at home. Lost in a desert here and hunger-bit. Which way, or from what hope, dost thou aspire to greatness? Whence authority derives? What followers? What retinue canst thou gain, or at thy heels the dizzy multitude, longer than thou canst feed them on thy cost? Money brings honour, friends, conquest, and realms.'*[261]

The Devil's false discourse with the *Messiah* is truly telling of how the Devil attempts to mislead us. The Devil's prime objective is to create discord, division, and disunity in our life. The Devil furthers this evil objective by separating us from God's Eternal Word. As Milton's aforementioned poetic writing illustrates, the Devil tempts the *Messiah* with what he does not presently have. That is to infer, the Devil tempts the *Messiah* with the riches, fame, private wealth, social status, influence, prestige, political power, and the pleasures of the world.

However, the *Messiah* has no desire for temporal, trivial, and transient phenomena, such as financial capital, private property, private wealth, social status, influence, prestige, political power, fame, and worldly glory. The *Messiah* possesses God's Blessing, Grace, Mercy, and Favour. In fact, the *Messiah* has the rarest

---

261 Milton, John. (Darbishire, Helen, Ed.) (1958). *The Poetical Works of John Milton*. London: Oxford University Press, p. 308.

treasures in his immediate possession; immaterial treasures that are only found within divine, pure, and angelic spirits. Treasures not of this world. Treasures which surpass all the inconsequential riches and worldly prizes that the Devil has proffered to the *Messiah*.

Too often in our life, we become entrapped by the temporary pursuits of life. Worldly pursuits such as private wealth creation, career progression, family planning, the incessant demands of parenting, methodical tax planning, the collection of vintage cars, the pursuit of a university education, real property ownership, travelling the world, planning for our forthcoming retirement, estate planning, and writing our will. Thereby, we lose sight of the permanent and everlasting matters of great consequence, such as our character, integrity, dignity, moral conscience, merit, virtues, beliefs, principles, trust, and credibility.

In the irrational pursuit of pleasure, profit, and power, people exchange fine gold for low-carbon steel. We must remain circumspect in our thoughts, speech, and conduct. We must never surrender the eternal and everlasting Crown, in exchange for the trivial and fleeting possessions of this temporal world.

Throughout the course of our lifetime, we become overly influenced by the popular culture and mainstream media, in order to keep up with the Joneses. Even when we are able to keep up with the Joneses, we are only ever truly happy for a passing moment. When it comes to keeping up with the Joneses, indeterminacy is ever-present. Why then do we pursue the elusive success and shifting expectations of society, only to attain a momentary sense of satisfaction? Is there more to human psychology and behaviour than the desire for acceptance, validation, approval, and social pressure?

In this endless and illogical pursuit of becoming successful by the standards of society, we unconsciously become defined by the very material forces and social constructs that permeate civil society. When we unwittingly follow the ideologies set forth by society, we internalise these secular ideologies into our conscious thoughts. Most of us do not realise, the fact that civil society institutionalises the very ideologies upon which we arrange our private life and organise our personal affairs.

In most cases, our worldly reality and lived experience is constructed for us, it is not one of our conscious design or self-determination. For humanity, the innate desire to be a constituent of the crowd is incredibly strong. A minority of individuals dare to imagine, envision, and be exceptional.

Underlying all social relations are human-made ideologies which define our existential reality for a limited period of time in the chequered history of human civilisation. For example, consider the sixteenth century was defined by ideas of European trade, English and Spanish territorial conquest, Puritanism, and the Protestant Reformation. The seventeenth century was defined by ideas of secularism and enlightenment. The eighteenth century was defined by ideas of republicanism and liberalism. The nineteenth century was defined by ideas of socialism, colonialism, and imperialism. The twentieth century was defined by ideas of capitalism, feminism, communism, Marxism, Leninism, Stalinism, and nationalism. The aforementioned prominent ideologies and many more like them, have defined the lived experience of humanity during select periods of time in world history.

In order for us to live and lead an authentic life, we must transcend the prevailing ideologies found within the epoch of our lifetime. We must not be defined by an unjust social order that is founded on economic, political, monetary, sexual, racial, religious, or legal inequality. Rather, we ought to live our life, and seek to institutionalise a social order that is characterised by the pursuit of timeless and universal principles. Principles such as respect, social justice, equality, duty, integrity, human dignity, love, benevolence, compassion, faith, peace, community service, tolerance, and charity. The application of these higher-order principles is what matters at the end of our lifetime.

> *'Therefore, if at great things thou wouldst arrive. Get riches first. Get wealth. Get treasure heap. Nor difficult, if thou hearken to me. Riches are mine. Fortune is in my hand. They whom I favour thrive in wealth amain. While virtue, valour, and wisdom, sit in want. To whom thus Jesus patiently replied. Yet, wealth without these three is impotent. To gain dominion or to keep it gained. Witness those ancient empires of the Earth. In height of all their flowing wealth dissolved. But men endued with these have oft attained in lowest poverty to highest deeds.'*[262]

The *Messiah* has accurately perceived through the veil of falsehood that the Devil has portrayed to him. To secure the private wealth, glory, social influence, prestige, fame, kingdoms, political power, love, honour, praise, and status of the world is worthless, without the cultivation of our virtues, the possession of valour, and the power of practical wisdom. To hold on to political power, private wealth, social status, influence, prestige, private property, and fame in the world is superficial. These so-called desirable traits that define our conventional reality, they are as fleeting as our uncertain life.

One dimension that defines our worldly existence of being is what we seek in this world. The second, and perhaps the more important dimension is the underlying why, which informs what we seek. When we methodically analyse the why behind the what we seek, then we begin to understand our passions, motivations, inclinations, emotions, drives, intentions, thoughts, sensations, urges, and desires. In order to truly understand ourselves, we need to understand what defines our state of being in the world.

---

262 Milton, John. (Darbishire, Helen, Ed.) (1958). *The Poetical Works of John Milton*. London: Oxford University Press, pp. 308–309.

The phenomenon of our being is an inherently complex and multifaceted reality.

All political power, territory, riches, and private wealth are perishable. None of these phenomena endure the towering test of time. In fact, the history of human civilisation has demonstrated the rise and fall of great empires. For example, consider the Assyrian Empire, the British Empire, the Japanese Empire, the Mongol Empire, the Ottoman Empire, the Persian Empire, the Portuguese Empire, the Roman Empire, and the Spanish Empire. Indeed, no entity, association, person, corporation, nation-state, or phenomenon, in and of this world endures the towering test of time, with the one and only exception being, God.

On the contrary, the absence of wealth is no barrier to the performance of noble deeds, the expression of our moral conscience, the application of morality, the flourishing of our spirit, and the creation of a good life. On the other hand, the absence of wealth positively assists us, to eradicate the well-known worldly distractions that become defining obstacles in our ultimate quest for spiritual growth. There is always the real possibility, that through the absence of prestige, private wealth, fame, social status, political power, influence, and private property, we have been granted a blessing in disguise.

'For I esteem those names of men so poor, who could do mighty things, and could contemn riches, though offered from the hand of kings. And what in me seems wanting, but that I may also in this poverty as soon accomplish what they did, perhaps and more? Extol not riches then, the toil of fools. The wise man's cumbrance. If not snare. More apt to slacken virtue, and abate her edge. Then prompt her to do aught may merit praise. What if with like aversion I reject riches and realms. Yet, not for that a Crown. Golden in show, is but a wreath of thorns. Brings dangers. Troubles. Cares. Sleepless nights to him who wears the Regal Diadem. When on his shoulders each man's burden lies. For therein stands the Office of a King. His Majesty's honour, virtue, merit, and chief praise. That for the public, all this weight he bears.'[263]

The *Messiah* refused to be tempted by the worldly riches, the trivial security of worldly treasure, the power of private wealth, the endless fame of royalty, the strong desire for kingdoms, and the sensual pleasures that the Devil proffered to him. For the noble cause of Truth, the *Messiah* lived his life defined by pain, sacrifice, suffering, denial, and privation.

We must also appreciate that all the riches, fame, prestige, political power, influence, private wealth, social status, private property, and kingdoms of this world are incapable of securing us an everlasting peace and profound sense of security in our lifetime. Not to mention, power, status, wealth, property, fame, royalty, honour, and prestige, these things cannot prevent the unconditional onset of our forthcoming death.

Since the incontestable answer to the philosophical question concerning mortality of the human condition is forever unalterable, we ought to utilise this finite lifetime to improve our

---

263 Milton, John. (Darbishire, Helen, Ed.) (1958). *The Poetical Works of John Milton*. London: Oxford University Press, p. 309.

character and cultivate our virtues. Sometimes, the less we have in our life, this is a blessing in disguise. For the limited possession of private wealth, political power, fame, influence, social status, prestige, and private property, is a formula for a life defined by fewer complications, crises, concerns, and complexities.

Human wisdom resides in turning our attention to the matters of lasting significance. No matter if we live a long life, one that is 120 years in length; nonetheless, this present lifetime is brief. After the here and now, eternity awaits us. This forthcoming eternity is of lasting significance.

'Yet, he who reigns within himself, and rules passions, desires, and fears, is more a king. Which every wise and virtuous man attains. And who attains not, ill aspires to rule cities of men, or headstrong multitudes. Subject himself to anarchy within, or lawless passions in him, which he serves. But to guide nations in the Way of Truth by saving doctrine, and from error lead to know, and knowing, worship God aright. Is yet more kingly. This attracts the soul. Governs the inner man. The nobler part.'[264]

To always demonstrate self-mastery is a rare and exceptional trait. The human condition is fraught with chaotic emotions, powerful inclinations, turbulent feelings, troublesome sensations, irrational passions, strong desires, inescapable instincts, and towering personal endeavours. The desirable and feasible state of homeostasis is not always possible in conventional reality. Through the many highs and lows that we experience throughout the course of our lifetime, if we wisely govern ourselves with rationality, equanimity, sensibility, and objectivity, we find within

---

264 Milton, John. (Darbishire, Helen, Ed.) (1958). *The Poetical Works of John Milton.* London: Oxford University Press, pp. 309–310.

ourselves an immovable peace. In life, our peace of mind is our greatest asset.

To command obedience from other people is only an outward demonstration of one's political power, private wealth, control, social status, prestige, and influence. This is a most superficial affirmation of one's esteemed position in the hierarchical social order of the sovereign nation-state. If we competently govern ourselves, and if we direct our mind to create the conventional reality that we desire, then we have conquered our life. Of course, this is easier spoken than accomplished. In fact, this is a transcendental endeavour, one that we struggle to, and never completely attain in our life.

The conscious, concentrated, and continuous practice of self-mastery ensures that we do not simply live our precious life, unconsciously defined by and helplessly subject to, the countless involuntary physiological processes of life, the biological development of the human body, and the psychological constructs of our social environment. Self-mastery is a transcendental endeavour that we ought to work towards on a daily basis. Self-mastery is an ideal endeavour. Self-mastery keeps us preoccupied for an entire lifetime. In our quest for self-mastery, we stumble and we fall, however, so long as we do not lose heart, we realise the pinnacle of our existence.

The paradox of control is that we expend too much of our time, energy, resources, and effort in an attempt to exert control over what is practically outside of our control. For example, consider the following situations: The uncertainty of the weather. The unreasonable responses or undesirable behaviour of our work colleagues. Navigating the chaos of city traffic. The market price of shares that we own in a listed corporation that is trading on the national stock exchange. The fluctuating market valuation of our real property. The change in political leaders and heads of government. The retirement and appointment of justices to the supreme court. The sporadic movement of our foreign currency holdings on the international currency market. The headline rate of inflation. Last but not least, the spot price of gold. In all these examples and many more, these situations are theoretically and practically beyond our conscious control.

Rather than being overly concerned with the situations and events that we cannot influence or directly control, we ought to limit the adverse influence of such situations and events on our life. Instead, we ought to direct our time, energy, resources, and effort towards controlling what we can change and influence; what is within our personal agency to change. For example, consider our health and well-being. The friendships and important relationships in our life. The profession that we are employed in. The quantum of quality time that we spend with our spouse and children. How we utilise our personal income and private wealth. Which sovereign nation-state we self-determine to be a valued citizen of. What social, legal, economic, humanitarian, or political causes we subscribe to and seek to change, for the betterment of human civilisation. Last but not least, our pursuit of scholarly or sporting endeavours.

When we exert influence and control over what is within the parameters of our personal agency, then we self-determine our life narrative. Practical wisdom is found in knowing where to direct one's time, energy, resources, and effort. Too often, individuals become engaged in an endless concern for what is beyond their inherent capacity to change. In most cases, when we are consumed with what we cannot amend or modify, this only serves to destabilise our equanimity of mind. In the final analysis, by being consumed with what we cannot change, we stand to lose more than we gain.

'Besides to give a kingdom hath been thought greater and nobler done, and to lay down far more magnanimous, than to assume. Riches are needless then. Both for themselves, and for thy reason why they should be sought. To gain a sceptre, oftest better missed.'[265]

Milton cleverly exposes the paradox of sovereignty, using the English symbol of sovereignty—the Sceptre—as an illustration. It is incredibly difficult for a king or queen to willingly cede sovereignty. On the contrary, it is always more convenient for a king or queen to secure sovereignty by the use of force, or the legal-political process of treaty-making between the High Contracting Parties.

Often protracted wars are fought in the royal names of kings and queens to secure the political and legal right to sovereignty over disputed or contested territory. Such civil or foreign wars are immensely expensive, and they require the expenditure of much blood and treasure. Not to mention, the desired victory is never certain in the condition of war. Even if sovereignty is secured by one of the belligerents over contested territory, it is never a permanent and eternal sovereignty. The long and short of human history demonstrates that empires, dukedoms, principalities, republics, and kingdoms always rise and fall.

The illusion of power and sovereignty in this world are temporal phenomena. These concepts, while attractive and appealing in their own right, they are not eternal in and of themselves. The security of the diadem is illusory. If a person relinquishes their desire for power, territory, private wealth, fame, private property, kingdom, dukedom, sovereignty, influence, glory, social status, and prestige, then they are no longer bound to the servitude of such [desirable] worldly phenomena.

---

265 Milton, John. (Darbishire, Helen, Ed.) (1958). *The Poetical Works of John Milton*. London: Oxford University Press, p. 310.

A righteous and noble-minded person is unaffected by the customs and dictates of the world. Such an enlightened person is not motivated by an endless desire to secure what the world recognises as invaluable treasure. Worldly treasure that is left behind, upon the guaranteed and forthcoming event of our death. Within the world our liberty is always conditional, whereas, our death is unconditional. In any case, the endless problems, troubles, issues, and political disagreements that materialise with the possession of power and sovereignty, are perhaps better left uninherited ...

CHAPTER 15

PARADISE REGAINED: BOOK THREE

'I see thou knowest what is of use to know.
What best to say canst say. To do canst do.
Thy actions to thy words accord.
Thy words to thy large heart give utterance due.
Thy heart contains of good, wise, and just.
The perfect shape.'

MILTON

BOOK THREE of *Paradise Regained* consists of a profound discourse between the Son of God and Satan. The two powerful figures exchange diametrically opposing and conflicting views on worldly reality, glory, power, fame, prestige, virtue, social status, private wealth, the higher purpose of human life, and many other profound theological, doctrinal, and philosophical matters. Until the very end, Satan continues to tempt and mislead the *Messiah*. However, unlike Satan's triumph over Adam and Eve, Satan is not victorious in his evil endeavour to deceive the *Messiah*.

This book witnesses the grand victory of good over evil. The *Messiah* conquers his archnemesis—Satan. It is by God's Grace, Mercy, Blessing, Compassion, Love, and Favour that the *Messiah* withstands Satan's powerful temptations and malevolent intentions. The *Messiah's* insightful discourse within this book establishes the true and unshakeable basis for us to accrue genuine merit in our lifetime.

When we carefully reflect upon the *Messiah's* lifetime on Earth, we come to the undeniable realisation, that the most important things that we ought to live our life by are virtue, character, love, honour, peace, integrity, honesty, compassion, forgiveness, community service, benevolence, social justice, and charity. We too have an unprecedented opportunity in the present time, to refine our state of being. To promote good. Also, to create a better and brighter world. Last but not least, this lifetime provides us with the unprecedented opportunity to further God's Sovereign Kingdom on Earth.

> *'These God-like virtues wherefore dost thou hide? Affecting private life, or more obscure in savage wilderness. Wherefore deprive all Earth her wonder at thy acts. Thyself the fame and glory. Glory, the reward that sole excites to high attempts the flame of most erected spirits. Most tempered pure ethereal. Who all pleasures else despise? All treasures and all gain esteem as dross, and dignities and powers? All, but the highest?'*[266]

Satan persuasively tempts the *Messiah* to secure all the worldly glory, fame, prestige, status, private wealth, kingdoms, and honour for himself. Satan attempts to deceive the *Messiah* to forget God, and all of God's Glory, Grace, Goodness, Grandeur, and Greatness. Satan is acutely aware of the privation, pain, and suffering that the *Messiah* has endured on Earth. Therefore, Satan makes a direct appeal to the *Messiah's* ego and pride. The *Messiah* is tempted to reveal himself in all his honour, prestige, glory, power, and virtue, to affirm his individual greatness. The

---

266 Milton, John. (Darbishire, Helen, Ed.) (1958). *The Poetical Works of John Milton*. London: Oxford University Press, p. 311.

Messiah is tested with the ultimate temptation of securing all that this world promises, in exchange for his irreversible betrayal of God. The *Messiah* passes this test with flying colours.

Above and beyond all the privations that the *Messiah* confronts during his lifetime on Earth, the *Messiah* remains true to his belief, faith, and trust in God. Through the *Messiah's* profound discourse and exemplary conduct, he reaffirms his enduring relationship with God.

During our lifetime, we confront physical and psychological ordeals, where the moral composition of our character is tested. Our moral conscience is probed for flaws, imperfections, and weaknesses. Our morality is put to the ultimate test. We have to make significant choices, that accept or reject the presence of God in our life. These fundamental choices position our life on the path of righteousness or evil. We are free to self-determine our choices; however, we are not free from their consequences, both the intended and unintended consequences.

> *'Thou neither dost persuade me to seek wealth for empire's sake. Nor empire to affect for glory's sake. By all thy argument. For what is glory, but the blaze of fame? The people's praise, if always praise unmixed? And what the people, but a herd confused. A miscellaneous rabble, who extol things vulgar, and well weighed, scarce worth the praise? They praise and they admire they know not what, and know not whom. But as one leads the other; and what delight to be by such extolled. To live upon their tongues, and be their talk? Of whom to be dispraised were no small praise?'*[267]

The *Messiah* has invalidated Satan's unfounded claims concerning the irrational pursuit of worldly praise and the people's superficial

---

267 Milton, John. (Darbishire, Helen, Ed.) (1958). *The Poetical Works of John Milton*. London: Oxford University Press, p. 312.

approval. In its fullness, worldly glory is nothing more than momentary fame, and that being the attention, validation, and praise of the billions of people on Earth. The people's praise is as fleeting as the setting of the Sun at the end of each day.

Within the Holy Bible, in the Gospel of Matthew, we witness the reprehensible nature of humankind. As it has been narrated in the enlightening passages of scripture, one day the people were praising the *Messiah*, 'The Disciples went and did as Jesus had directed them. They brought the donkey and the colt and put on them their cloaks, and he sat on them. Most of the crowd spread their cloaks on the road, and others cut branches from the trees and spread them on the road. And the crowds that went before him and that followed him were shouting, "Hosanna to the Son of David! Blessed is he who comes in the Name of the LORD! Hosanna in the highest!"'[268]

Not long after praising the *Messiah*, the people were seeking the *Messiah's* [physical] death. The Gospel of Matthew narrates the following passage, 'Now the Chief Priests and the Elders persuaded the crowd to ask for Barabbas and destroy Jesus. The Governor again said to them, "Which of the two do you want me to release for you?" And they said, "Barabbas." Pilate said to them, "Then what shall I do with Jesus who is called Christ?" They all said, "Let him be crucified!" And he said, "Why? What evil has he done?" But they shouted all the more, "Let him be crucified!"'[269] Indeed, as we have witnessed herein, the scriptures categorically confirm the people are a lost, ignorant, and confused herd. One moment the people exalt the *Messiah*, and the next moment, they seek his [physical] death.

The aforementioned passages of scripture inform us of the depravity of the human condition. Why then, in vain do we strive to secure the people's approval and endorsement? There is no

---

268 The Holy Bible (ESV). (2016). Gospel of Matthew. Chapter 21, Verses 6–9.
269 The Holy Bible (ESV). (2016). Gospel of Matthew. Chapter 27, Verses 20–23.

satisfaction, serenity, or security, to be found in what is temporary and uncertain. Why then, do we direct our finite time, capacity, abilities, resources, knowledge, and expertise to seek worldly praise?

In all cases, worldly praise is as changing as the time-bound trends of contemporary fashion. To position one's trust and confidence in public opinion is a grave mistake. If we self-determine to obey the unpredictable opinions of the unenlightened masses, then we are forever held hostage to a mediocre life that is characterised by an endless keeping up with the Joneses. We must position our trust and confidence in what is everlasting, eternal, and esteemed. This reality is only true of God's Eternal Word. Peace be with you.

'The intelligent among them and the wise are few. Glory scarce of few is raised. This is true glory and renown, when God, looking on the Earth, with approbation marks the just man, and divulges him through Heaven to all His Angels, who with true applause recount his praises. Thus, He did to Job. When to extend his fame through Heaven and Earth. As thou to thy reproach mayest well remember. He asked thee. Hast, thou seen my servant, Job? Famous he was in Heaven. On Earth less known. Where glory is false glory. Attributed to things not glorious. Men not worthy of fame.'[270]

Within the Holy Bible, the Book of Job is a remarkable Biblical account, of God consenting to the Devil putting Job to the ultimate test of faith. Throughout the course of Job's remarkable life, he overcame heartbreak, loss, devastation, grief, bodily suffering, and psychological trauma. Job's powerful perseverance was only possible through his unwavering belief in God.

---

270 Milton, John. (Darbishire, Helen, Ed.) (1958). *The Poetical Works of John Milton*. London: Oxford University Press, p. 312.

Indeed, Job retained the faith throughout his many trials and ordeals. Several times, Job was tested to his physical and psychological limits. Yet, Job did not waver in his steadfast belief that God's Sovereign Will prevails on Earth, as it does in the Kingdom of Heaven. In spite of the major setbacks and struggles, Job reaffirmed his unshakeable belief in God's Providence.

We must take heart in the Biblical story of Job. We too must affirm the importance of hope in our life. Hope, that no matter what diabolic forces come against us, with God's Mercy, Favour, Blessing, and Grace, we withstand the many tragedies, troubles, traumas, and tribulations of the world. When the good fight of faith was finished, Job had conquered his archenemy.

While we closely associate the Book of Job with Job's trauma, loss, grief, pain, and suffering, we must not forget how Job's story concludes. The finality of the Book of Job describes how God blessed Job's life. Indeed, God provisioned Job plenty of resources, blessings, happiness, wealth, success, joy, peace, and prosperity in the final years of his life.

In fact, in the closing lines of the Book of Job, we learn the exact details pertaining to God's Goodness and Blessing on Job's final years on Earth, 'And the LORD blessed the latter days of Job more than his beginning. And he had 14,000 sheep, 6,000 camels, 1,000 yoke of oxen, and 1,000 female donkeys. He had also seven sons and three daughters. And he called the name of the first daughter Jemimah, and the name of the second Keziah, and the name of the third Keren-happuch. And in all the land there were no women so beautiful as Job's daughters. And their father gave them an inheritance among their brothers. And after this Job lived 140 years, and saw his sons, and his sons' sons, four generations. And Job died, an old man, and full of days.'[271] Even though we fall short in the performance of our obligations and duties, God always honours divine promises.

---

271 The Holy Bible (ESV). (2016). The Book of Job. Chapter 42, Verses 12–17.

In our quest to secure ever greater worldly fame, prestige, private wealth, personal income, political power, private property, social status, and the people's praise, too often we are prepared to compromise on our personal values, beliefs, principles, ideologies, virtues, doctrines, character, judgement, faith, integrity, and moral conscience. In effect, we concede ground on what is of fundamental importance in our life, in order to secure the trivial, mundane, and fleeting desires of the world.

We do not consider the far-sighted vision pertaining to the eternal and everlasting Kingdom of God. Instead, we become enmeshed, entrapped, entangled, and engrossed with our immediate and present focus on the temporal phenomena of the world. In this respect, the Book of Job serves as a timely reminder, that when we experience tragedy, grief, pain, suffering, agony, conflict, and loss, it is our primary focus on God, which saves our life. It is our eternal focus on God, which ensures that we are redeemed.

In our fast-paced pursuit of private wealth, fame, success, social status, prestige, power, and influence in the world, we need to understand that our reputation, character, and honour is at stake. We must not forget that our integrity, values, principles, doctrines, and beliefs matter. In our lifetime, there are countless opportunities for a convenient route, backdoor exit, shortcut solution, temporary workaround, or a quick fix, however, over the years and decades of our life, we witness that the poor choices we determine, they inevitably begin to produce a cumulative effect on our life.

The right option in our life is not always synonymous with the most convenient option. When we are presented with a multitude of options and choices in our life, the preferable decision requires sacrifice, patience, self-determination, perseverance, and commitment. We cannot indefinitely ignore the long-term consequences of our actions. Instant gratification brings forth instantaneous results that appear to benefit our today, but what does this approach to living bring for our tomorrow?

> *'Poor Socrates, (who next more memorable?) by what he taught and suffered for so doing. For Truth's sake, suffering death unjust. Lives now equal in fame to proudest conquerors. Yet, if for fame and glory aught be done, aught suffered. If young African, for fame, his wasted country freed from punic rage. The deed becomes unpraised. The man at least, and loses, though but verbal, his reward. Shall I seek glory then, as vain men seek, often not deserved? I seek not mine, but His who sent me, and thereby witness whence I am.'*[272]

The monumental story of Socrates' moral struggle to uphold the Truth is a timeless one. Socrates' profound discourse on the defence of Truth is narrated in *The Apology* written by the Greek philosopher, Plato. Socrates' defence of the Truth has secured him everlasting fame in the Ancient World. Humanity continues to remember Socrates for his unrelenting and defiant stand for the Truth, even when he was confronted with death.

When Socrates was found guilty by his fellow Athenian jurors, he affirmed to accept the fate that he was dealt. Socrates died for the high and noble sake of Truth. Socrates consumed a cup of hemlock; a powerful poison, which led to his tragic death. Socrates exhibited remarkable fortitude in the face of death. Socrates was able to demonstrate remarkable fortitude because of his righteousness. Socrates was secure in the certainty of his convictions and moral conscience. Socrates sacrificed this temporal life for the Eternal Truth. Socrates lived his life on timeless principles, not on the whims and fancies of the people.

---

272 Milton, John. (Darbishire, Helen, Ed.) (1958). *The Poetical Works of John Milton*. London: Oxford University Press, p. 313.

When we perform our actions in the world, our motives and intentions underlying them matters. If we act to secure riches, worldly fame, social status, influence, prestige, private wealth, glory, private property, and personal income, then we diminish the positive externalities associated with our voluntary and conscious actions.

On the contrary, if we act for the advancement of the common struggle of humanity, then we are remembered for our suffering, setbacks, and struggles. For example, consider the individuals who defined world history, such as Susan Brownell Anthony, Charles Nelson Perkins, Mahatma Gandhi, Sojourner Truth, Martin Luther King Jr., Lucy Stone, Nelson Mandela, Eddie Mabo, Rosa Parks, Lucy Burns, Emmeline Pankhurst, Elizabeth Cady Stanton, Lucretia Mott, and Alice Paul.

All of the aforementioned great individuals and countless others, fought for a common struggle concerning the universal advancement of liberty, racial and sexual equality, social justice, economic empowerment, emancipation, human dignity, the civil and political rights of oppressed people, enfranchisement, and representative government throughout the modern world. All of these prominent figures advanced a worthy, just, and noble cause. They advanced humanitarian, political, moral, legal, social, and economic causes far greater than themselves, and for this reason we continue to remember their legacy.

The *Messiah* also engaged in deeply profound acts that promoted equality, human dignity, respect, peace, brotherhood, sisterhood, love, community service, tolerance, benevolence, and social justice on Earth. For example, consider that the *Messiah* did not differentiate amongst people on Earth, regardless of a person's sex, race, ethnicity, colour, nationality, or prevailing cultural norms.

In the Holy Bible, within the Gospel of John, we witness the humanity of the *Messiah*, 'A woman from Samaria came to draw water. Jesus said to her, "Give me a drink." (For his Disciples had gone away into the city to buy food.) The Samaritan woman said to him, "How is it that you, a Jew, ask for a drink from me, a woman of Samaria?" (For Jews have no dealings with Samaritans.) Jesus answered her, "If you knew the gift of God, and who it is that is saying to you, 'Give me a drink,' you would have asked him, and he would have given you living water."'[273]

The *Messiah*, through his profound thoughts, insightful deeds, and eloquent speech demonstrated righteous conduct as an example for humanity on how to live the good life. However, at all times, the *Messiah's* primary focus was on the Divinity of God. The *Messiah* always positioned God in first place. The *Messiah* performed God's Sovereign Will on Earth. For this noble act the *Messiah* is blessed.

Too often, humanity becomes misguided in its way. Humanity relinquishes its focus on God. We witness humanity become entrapped in the worldly pursuits of self-interest, private wealth creation, profit maximisation, pecuniary gain, and private property. The unquestionable vanity of our self-interest is exposed at the exact time of our death, when we come to the enlightened realisation, that all of our actions in the pursuit of self-interest are reduced to naught.

In all respects, it is of paramount importance that we utilise our finite lifetime on Earth to advance God's Sovereign Kingdom. It is incumbent upon us to ensure that we live our life characterised by tolerance, courage, integrity, forgiveness, community service, charity, honesty, respect, love, human dignity, benevolence, faith, social justice, and hope. In our lifelong quest to live a good life, we must not forget that this [ideal] endeavour commences with how we treat one another in society. It is through our association, interaction, and communication with members of civil society, that we consciously create and define our worldly reality. Peace be with you.

---

273 The Holy Bible (ESV). (2016). The Gospel of John. Chapter 4, Verses 7–10.

'But why should man seek glory? Who of his own hath nothing, and to whom nothing belongs but condemnation, ignominy, and shame? Who for so many benefits received turned recreant to God. Ingrate and false. So, of all true good himself despoiled. Yet, sacrilegious, to himself would take that which to God alone of right belongs. Yet, so much bounty is in God. Such grace. That who advance His Glory. Not their own. Them, He Himself to glory will advance.'[274]

Humanity has no factual basis to seek worldly glory and honour for itself. Humanity must advance God's Sovereign Kingdom on Earth. In all cases, it is the rightful and proper place of the unequal Creator to be extolled and exalted. It is due to the grace of the Creator, that Creation and all that is within it, is existent. Humanity's existence is, was, and always will be conditional and contingent upon God. We must not permit our ego to deceive our temporal reality of being in the world. No person willed themselves into being in the world. On what basis then, does humanity seek glory, praise, and honour for itself?

Humanity, perforce, is dependent upon God. When we accept this theological fact, then we live our life defined by reverence for God. It is our highest moral duty on Earth to advance God's Sovereign Kingdom and observe God's Eternal Word. A righteous soldier does not take the place of the Sovereign.

The Angel Lucifer betrayed God. Lucifer made a brazen attempt to usurp God's Sovereign Throne. For this unprecedented transgression in the Kingdom of Heaven, Lucifer was cast out of God's Presence and lost favour in the sight of God. In the Holy Bible, within the Book of Revelation, we are made privy to Lucifer's casting out of Heaven, 'Now war arose in Heaven, Michael and his Angels fighting against the Dragon and his

---

274 Milton, John. (Darbishire, Helen, Ed.) (1958). *The Poetical Works of John Milton*. London: Oxford University Press, p. 314.

Angels fought back, but he was defeated, and there was no longer any place for them in Heaven. And the great Dragon was thrown down, that ancient serpent, who is called the Devil and Satan, the Deceiver of the whole world—he was thrown down to the Earth and his Angels were thrown down with him.'[275]

Just like the Devil, humanity is constantly tempted to misappropriate its free will. Therefore, the personal responsibility is upon us to overcome the vice of temptation, the trap of evil, the arrogance of pride, the allure of intelligence, the pitfalls of political power, the seduction of beauty, the conceit of ego, and the deception of desire. During our temporary tenure on Earth, we must remember our Creator. Not to mention, we must remember our proper place in God's Creation. When we are mindful of God, then this temporal representation of our being in the world does not deceive us. Peace be with you.

'All things are best fulfilled in their due time. Time there is for all things. Truth hath said. If of my reign, prophetic writ hath told that it shall never end, so when begin. The Father in His Purpose hath decreed. He in whose hand all times and seasons roll. What if He hath decreed that I shall first be tried in humble state, and things adverse. By tribulations, injuries, insults, contempts, and scorns, and snares, and violence. Suffering. Abstaining. Quietly expecting without distrust or doubt. That He may know what I can suffer. How obey? Who best can suffer. Best can do. Best reign. Who first well hath obeyed. Just trial here I merit my exaltation, without change or end.'[276]

During our lifetime, in all that we seek and in all that we do, we must trust in God's Timing. God's Plans are to prosper us, and

275 The Holy Bible (ESV). (2016). The Book of Revelation. Chapter 12, Verses 7–9.
276 Milton, John. (Darbishire, Helen, Ed.) (1958). *The Poetical Works of John Milton*. London: Oxford University Press, p. 315.

to further our greater good on Earth. To act upon initiative and exercise our personal agency is a good idea, however, we must pray to God and seek God's Wise Counsel, in particular, when it comes to the fulfilment of consequential matters concerning our destiny.

The *Messiah* had a crystal clear purpose and vision. He came to Earth to redeem humanity of its sins. Yet, even the *Messiah* turned to God for consultation and counsel. For example, consider the profound spiritual discourse between the *Messiah* and God in the Garden of Gethsemane. Even the *Messiah* ensured that his actions were performed in God's Timing and in accordance with God's Divine Plan.

Even though this world is the Devil's kingdom, the *Messiah* reigns on Earth forever. It is only when we subdue our will, when we seek out God's Sovereign Will, only then we ascertain the true depth of God's Divine Plan for our life. The people who subjugate their will and obey God's Sovereign Will, they find an inexplicable peace on Earth. Even during times of great distress, destruction, and disturbance, those select individuals who place their reliance, hope, love, faith, wisdom, and trust in God, they overcome the numerous obstacles found along their life journey.

Nothing is impossible for that person who dares to believe in themselves. Not to mention, no person is too far gone, for God to work in their life. The combination of sincere love for God, a sincere heart towards humanity, personal responsibility, humility, repentance, commitment, dedication, compassion, benevolence, forgiveness, and sensibility, collectively promote absolution in our life. Too often, it is not the past performance of sin which holds us back with the negative emotions of grief, denial, regret, and anger. Rather, it is the guilt of sin, which holds us back from seeking absolution and moving forward with our life. Where there is love, there is redemption.

'Let that come when it comes. All hope is lost of my reception into grace. What worse? For where no hope is left, is left no fear. If there be worse, the expectation more of worse torments me than the feeling can. I would be at the worst. Worst is my port. My harbour, and my ultimate repose. The end I would attain. My final good. My error, was my error, and my crime, my crime. Whatever for itself condemned, and will alike be punished.'[277]

Throughout our lifetime, we experience tragedy, heartache, trauma, hurt, loss, suffering, injury, pain, and despair. Life is not all smooth sailing. Neither is life picture-perfect. No person on Earth runs a perfect race from start to finish. Even the *Messiah* had to contend with evil and suffering in his life. For example, consider the *Messiah* was betrayed by Judas Iscariot (one of the Twelve Apostles).[278] Not to mention, the Apostle Simon Peter denied that he knew the *Messiah* on three occasions.[279]

But despite the many struggles of the world, the *Messiah* has informed us to take heart. In the Holy Bible, within the Gospel of John, we are counselled that the *Messiah* has conquered the world, 'I have said these things to you, that in me you may have peace. In the world you will have tribulation. But take heart; I have overcome the world.'[280] Therefore, we ought to place our trust and confidence in the Son of God, so that through him, we transcend our countless worldly challenges.

We cannot always be prepared for our life's problems, issues, accidents, and tragedies. Nor is life always a pleasurable, harmonious, and joyful affair. We experience our fair share of adversity, privation, loss, and misfortune along our life journey.

---

277 Milton, John. (Darbishire, Helen, Ed.) (1958). *The Poetical Works of John Milton.* London: Oxford University Press, p. 316.

278 The Holy Bible (ESV). (2016). Gospel of Matthew. Chapter 26, Verses 14–16; 47–50.

279 The Holy Bible (ESV). (2016). Gospel of Matthew. Chapter 26, Verses 69–75.

280 The Holy Bible (ESV). (2016). Gospel of John. Chapter 16, Verse 33.

During such difficult times in our life, the Devil suggests disastrous and false thoughts in our mind. Fabricated and intrusive thoughts along the lines of: All hope is lost. God does not exist. We are guilty and condemned of sin. Last but not least, God does not love humanity.

We cannot be ignorant of the theological fact that the Devil torments us, when we are at the weakest and most vulnerable point in our life. We must not give into the Devil's manipulation, fabrication, and deception of our mind. We must not give credence to the Devil's intrusive and destructive thoughts. We must categorically reject the Devil's suggestions.

In the Devil's misplaced endeavours to advance false narratives, we must withstand the Devil's assault with God's Spiritual Armour. We must strengthen our faith, like a soldier strengthens their physical and psychological capacities. Our most powerful battles in life are spiritual in nature. In our quest to overcome evil with good, we must engage in battle with the Devil. Truth and goodness are destroyed in the world, when we silently stand by and do not confront the forces of discrimination, hate, injustice, oppression, prejudice, and evil.

It is with the remarkable power of God's Eternal Word, prayer, petition, intercession, belief, faith, love, mercy, hope, charity, community service, benevolence, forgiveness, and social justice, that good prevails over evil. Where God's Spirit is present, all things are possible. With God's Grace, Favour, Blessing, and Mercy, we transcend the countless tests, trials, troubles, and tragedies along our life journey.

'Why move thy feet so slow to what is best? Happiest, both to thyself and all the world, that thou, who worthiest art, shouldst be their king! Perhaps thou lingerest in deep thoughts detained of the enterprise so hazardous and high! No wonder. For though in thee be united. What of perfection can in man be found, or human nature can receive?'[281]

Faith is now. Faith is always in the present moment. Faith is action. We must not listen to the Devil's temptations concerning empty promises. We must be guarded, circumspect, and vigilant in our thoughts. After all, our thoughts define our worldly reality. The narrative of our life commences in our thoughts. Human nature is all too imperfect. We all have our unique and individual flaws; however, this is precisely what makes us human. We need not rely upon, let alone compare ourselves with, a fictional and mythical representation of human perfection. In our lifetime, what is more important than attaining the [unattainable] state of perfection, is to be prudent and pragmatic in our thinking.

In the exercise of human judgement, the incidence of error is inevitable, just as the coruscate of daybreak follows the pitch darkness of night. Every person on Earth is a work in progress. We need to demonstrate our enduring commitment and personal responsibility to strive and improve our character. To exercise our moral conscience. To cultivate our virtues. These positive acts strengthen the power of the spirit that resides within each and every one of us.

During our lifetime, we ought to leave the finer details of perfection to God. God is perfect in every respect. We ought to place our belief, faith, and trust in God's Grace to function

---

281 Milton, John. (Darbishire, Helen, Ed.) (1958). *The Poetical Works of John Milton*. London: Oxford University Press, p. 316.

in our life. It is by God's Grace, that we fulfil our affairs in the best possible manner, during our brief lifetime on Earth. Sooner or later, our demise in this Earthly Kingdom is inevitable.

'Best school of best experience. Quickest insight in all things that to greatest actions lead. The wisest, unexperienced, will be ever timorous, and loth, with novice modesty.'[282]

In our lifetime, we learn though the acquisition of empirical knowledge, and through direct and immediate experience. However, what we learn from our personal experience imprints a greater impression upon our senses and the faculties of our mind. Empirical knowledge is objective and impartial. The constant and universal application of empirical knowledge cannot be denied. Whereas, anecdotal experience is always subjective and personal in its nature. Practical wisdom resides in learning from both objective knowledge and subjective experience. Sometimes, our lived experience teaches us what empirical knowledge cannot.

The problem with positioning too great an emphasis on lived experience, to understand our life narrative, is that personal experience consists of countless variables. Lived experience is subject to the change of circumstance, the necessity of time, the direction of prevailing ideology, and the environment in which we were raised. Our environment includes the forces of civil society, people, culture, heritage, religion, family, language, current affairs, and national politics. There are literally an infinite quantum of variables involved in our investigation of personal experience.

---

282 Milton, John. (Darbishire, Helen, Ed.) (1958). *The Poetical Works of John Milton*. London: Oxford University Press, p. 317.

In all cases, our life experience is inherently and uniquely ours, for it is lived by us. Having said that, personal experience is undeniably defined by and subject to, countless forces that are beyond our immediate control. It is for these reasons that personal experience is the predominant guide along our life journey. On the contrary, personal experience has its limitations. Personal experience can deceive our finite human understanding of reality, and the natural world around us.

CHAPTER 16

PARADISE REGAINED: BOOK FOUR

'Where God is praised aright, and Godlike men.
The Holiest of Holies, and His Saints.
Such are from God inspired, not such from thee.
Unless where moral virtue is expressed.
By light of nature, not in all quite lost.'

MILTON

BOOK FOUR is the grand finale of *Paradise Regained*. This book reveals the inherent futility of Satan's empty promises. Herein, humanity is made privy to the eternal wisdom concerning the absolute vanity of the performance of evil in the world. Humanity must diligently strive to conform to the righteous path of moral excellence and virtuous conduct. Humanity is put to the test in this transient world. Having said that, God has provided humanity with the requisite grace, mercy, love, favour, and blessing to transcend evil with good. In the final analysis, humanity must not waver in its grand mission to advance God's Sovereign Kingdom on Earth.

Collectively, it is within the power of humanity to transform Earth into a living Heaven or Hell. This superior reality starts with how we treat each other. In fact, how we treat each other, speaks volumes about ourselves. How we treat each other, speaks volumes about our personal values, principles, beliefs, doctrines, integrity, moral conscience, and character. If humanity consciously commits to the performance of love over indifference, forgiveness over vengeance, mercy over revenge, justice over injustice, peace over war, hope over despair, education over illiteracy, prosperity over poverty, benevolence over malevolence, impartïality over discrimination, and tolerance over prejudice, then we create Heaven on Earth.

> *'Perplexed and troubled at his bad success the tempter stood. Nor had what to reply. Discovered in his fraud. Thrown from his hope. So oft, and the persuasive rhetoric that sleeked his tongue, and won so much on Eve. So little here. Nay lost. But Eve was Eve. This far his over-match. Who self-deceived and rash. Beforehand had no better weighed the strength he was to cope with, or his own. But as a man who had been matchless held in cunning. Over-reached where least he thought.'*[283]

After much rigorous debate, the Devil demonstrates intense frustration at his inability to deceive the *Messiah*. The Devil's expeditious success with tempting Eve on the path to sin was not replicated, when it came to God's faithful servant Job, or the Son of God—the *Messiah*. Much like the Biblical story of Job, the Devil failed to tempt the *Messiah* into a life of sin, falsehood, and evil.

The *Messiah's* blessed lifetime on Earth demonstrates how humanity is to resist the countless temptations of the Devil. It did not matter what temptation the Devil proffered to the *Messiah*; every possible temptation failed to move the *Messiah* from the supreme path of righteousness. When we have a noble

---

283 Milton, John. (Darbishire, Helen, Ed.) (1958). *The Poetical Works of John Milton*. London: Oxford University Press, p. 323.

mission, a grand vision, a higher vocation, a selfless cause, or a transcendental purpose in life, we must not forget to remain fixated on God's Sovereign Will and Eternal Word. If we truly perceive beyond the Self, then the Devil fails to tempt us in the flesh.

> *'But tedious waste of time. To sit and hear, so many hollow compliments and lies. Outlandish flatteries? Then proceedest to talk of the emperor. How easily subdued. How gloriously. I shall, thou sayest, expel a brutish monster: What if I withal expel a Devil who first made him such? Let his tormenter, conscience, find him out. For him I was not sent, nor yet to free.'*[284]

The Devil infiltrates our body, mind, and spirit with the time-tested methods of flattery, falsehood, fear, fantasy, and fiction. When the material dimension of our flesh is overpowering in our life, when our spirit is not nurtured, we remain exposed to the Devil's tricks, tactics, and treachery. The Devil is always able to tempt us with riches, private wealth, private property, beauty, fame, social status, influence, power, prestige, and worldly glory. That is to infer, the Devil tempts us with all the temporal phenomena of this material world. However, none of these worldly phenomena refine our character, strengthen our spirit, develop our wisdom, cultivate our virtue, or bring our spirit closer to God's Spirit.

In the world, all too often we witness humanity prepared to exchange its priceless soul for material success, personal income, private property, riches, sensual pleasures, and private wealth. The endless pursuit of these worldly ambitions and desires does not bring about a lasting satisfaction to our soul. Rather, we ought to work towards the cultivation of our virtues. We must

---

284 Milton, John. (Darbishire, Helen, Ed.) (1958). *The Poetical Works of John Milton*. London: Oxford University Press, p. 326.

enhance our natural attribute of morality. Our natural reason must become one with our moral conscience. At the end of our lifetime, all that remains is the ripening of our character, the fruit of our voluntary and conscious actions, and the cultivation of our spirit.

God has provisioned each person with the especial gifts of natural reason, intuition, perception, memory, imagination, will, and moral conscience. As rational agents, we possess the inherent moral capacity to act for the betterment or detriment of humanity. The irrational and excessive pursuit of self-interest always leads to an individual's downfall. When we act with a level of detachment from the immediate and proximate self, then we better ascertain the true worth of our voluntary and conscious actions, and their far-reaching consequences. When we act for the pursuit of communal interests and for the greater welfare of humanity, then we strengthen the spirit within us.

To the contrary, the Devil exploits our weaknesses in the flesh. The Devil deceives us. The Devil tempts us to seek out the vanity of self-interest, through the pursuit of sensual pleasure, private wealth, private property, influence, worldly glory, social status, personal income, political power, prestige, and fame. However, this worldly path is only an obstacle, a hindrance, an impediment to our primary objective in life—the union of our spirit with God's Spirit.

Being in and of the world, we must participate in many worldly pursuits and noble endeavours. Having said that, we must not permit our life to be defined by them. Our private wealth, vocation, formal education, status, personal income, employment, marriage, children, sporting accomplishments, and personal assets do not determine our identity. It is our faith which defines our identity.

'But govern ill, the nations under yoke. Peeling their provinces. Exhausted all by lust and rapine. First ambitious grown of triumph that insulting vanity. Then cruel, by their sports to blood enured, of fighting beasts, and men to beasts exposed. Luxurious by their wealth, and greedier still, and from the daily scene effeminate. What wise and valiant man would seek to free these. Thus degenerate, by themselves enslaved, or could of inward slaves make outward free?'[285]

The protracted problems of social governance, domestic politics, national interest, territorial integrity, sovereignty, defence, national security, foreign affairs, political power, and state affairs are endless. A legitimate ruler positions the best interests of their people before themselves.

Too often, the chequered course of human history has demonstrated how sovereigns, both kings and queens, diminish the economic resources and financial capital of the State, in the pursuit of extravagant pleasures and an endless indulgence of the flesh. A royal life of extravagance is destined to be unsatisfactory and worthless. When a sovereign fails to govern the nation-state in a manner that advances the hopes, dreams, and aspirations of the populace, then rebellion, internal strife, civil war, and discord is the end result.

Regardless a person be a sovereign or a subject, true freedom is only secured by living a measured, responsible, and productive life. Excess in any area of our life, diminishes our physical, emotional, psychological, and spiritual development. We must not make ourselves into a servant of the flesh. We must rise above and beyond the desires, demands, and dictates of the flesh. We must transcend the [physical] dimension of our being.

---

285 Milton, John. (Darbishire, Helen, Ed.) (1958). *The Poetical Works of John Milton.* London: Oxford University Press, p. 326.

We must not simply utilise our lifetime on Earth to exist, but to live a productive, harmonious, reasoned, and wholesome life. We ought to live our life in such a manner, that when we reflect upon it in our advanced age, we categorically affirm: That was a life well-lived. That was a meaningful and purposeful life. That was the life of a lifetime.

'Nor what I part with mean to give for naught. All these which in a moment thou beholdest. The kingdoms of the world to thee I give. For, given to me. I give, to whom I please. No trifle. Yet, with this reserve. Not else. On this condition. If thou will fall down, and worship me as thy superior Lord. Easily done, and hold them all of me. For what can less, so great a gift deserve?'[286]

We must remain circumspect against the Devil's illegitimate schemes, subterfuges, and stratagems. It is imperative to acknowledge that Milton's aforementioned literary writing concludes with the words: 'For what can less, so great a gift deserve?' The Devil is incredibly crafty, cunning, and clever, that nothing is further from the Eternal Truth.

In fact and reality, any exchange or pact with the Devil costs a person their soul. This most inferior trade witnesses a person relinquish their most precious and priceless possession, their soul, in exchange for the trivial satisfaction of temporal and worldly desires. We need to perceive through the Devil's duplicitous and treacherous misrepresentations. We need to posit this distorted question straight: What greater price can be paid, for such an inconsequential gift?

In any case, hypothetically speaking, if we secured all the kingdoms, wealth, power, glory, fame, influence, and riches of the world, such material wealth does not bequeath us with

---

286 Milton, John. (Darbishire, Helen, Ed.) (1958). *The Poetical Works of John Milton*. London: Oxford University Press, p. 327.

an everlasting peace on Earth. In our subjective assessment of the invaluable benefits of securing political power, we fail to contemplate that our assumptions surrounding political power are distorted.

Unfortunately, we do not always acknowledge or appreciate, the immense personal responsibility of wielding political power. In the exercise of sovereignty, we cannot neglect the operation of unprecedented personal responsibility for our decisions. Consequential political decisions, which inevitably impact the lives, opportunities, and destiny of millions of citizens within the nation-state. A sovereign that fails to advance the legitimate aspirations of their people has failed the litmus test of a righteous and noble ruler.

> *'The kingdoms of the world to thee were given! Permitted rather, and by thee usurped. Other donation none thou canst produce. If given, by whom, but by the King of Kings. God over all Supreme? If given to thee, by thee how fairly is the Giver now repaid! But gratitude in thee is lost long since. Were thou so void of fear or shame. As offer them to me, the Son of God. To me, my own. On such abhorred pact. That I fall down and worship thee as God? Get thee behind me! Plain thou now appears that evil one. Satan forever damned.'*[287]

Once and for all, the *Messiah* clarifies the inferior position of the Devil. Everything that the Devil claims to be in his possession, and therefore, affording the Devil an exclusive privilege to bestow to humanity, was originally bequeathed to him by God. In fact, the Devil's very existence was not permissible without God's Sovereign Act, which originally willed Lucifer into being as an Angel. Satan has forgotten the Creator's Eminence, Glory, Power,

---

287 Milton, John. (Darbishire, Helen, Ed.) (1958). *The Poetical Works of John Milton.* London: Oxford University Press, p. 327.

Love, and Honour. Not to mention, Satan has contravened God's Sovereign Will. As the *Messiah* has demonstrated, by his righteous thought, speech, and conduct, we too must resist temptation in its many forms and methods. We must never forget, that cloaked behind the dark veil of temptation is the Devil's undue influence.

'Me naught advantaged. Missing what I aimed. Therefore, let pass, as they are transitory, the kingdoms of this world. I shall no more advise thee. Gain them as thou canst, or not. And thou thyself seemest otherwise inclined. Than to a worldly crown, addicted more to contemplation and profound dispute.'[288]

The Devil finally relents and surrenders in his satanic quest to deceive the *Messiah*. We too must realise the inherent emptiness of securing the worldly crown. Such a trivial crown. A crown of this world. A crown that is not everlasting. If we determine to secure such a superficial crown, we relinquish the pursuit of what matters most in our life—the lifelong pursuit of our character, virtue, morality, love, integrity, community service, faith, mercy, social justice, benevolence, honesty, charity, and peace.

Often the allure of temptation renders it troublesome to perceive the whole Truth in a coherent manner. The Devil employs half-truths in order to misinform our reasoning and make a direct appeal to our ego. In order to correctly distinguish fact from fiction, we ought to consult God's Eternal Word. God's Eternal Word is true and righteous.

In the Holy Bible, within the Second Book of Timothy, we are made privy to Saint Paul the Apostle's exceptional example of living an honourable life. Saint Paul's example is one that is worthy of the genuine Crown. The Crown bestowed by God. This Crown is never lost, stolen, or destroyed.

---

288 Milton, John. (Darbishire, Helen, Ed.) (1958). *The Poetical Works of John Milton*. London: Oxford University Press, p. 328.

Towards the end of Saint Paul's life, he wrote the following words. Words that now constitute part of the New Testament in the Holy Bible. Saint Paul's words are a timely reminder to all of us, regarding what is eternally important: 'For I am already being poured out as a drink offering, and the time of my departure has come. I have fought the good fight. I have finished the race. I have kept the faith. Henceforth there is laid up for me the Crown of Righteousness, which the LORD, the Righteous Judge, will award to me on that day, and not only to me, but also to all who have loved His appearing.'[289]

It is such a Crown that is worth securing. A Crown that is endorsed by God. A Crown that defines a life of joy, community service, truthfulness, love, merit, integrity, virtue, and faith. A Crown that endures for eternity, for it is secured in God's Kingdom of Heaven. Now, it is through the performance of our voluntary and conscious actions in the world, that this Crown of Righteousness is either within our reach or distant to us. Thus, our destiny is determined by the cumulative effects of our intentional actions.

'As morning shows the day. Be famous then, by wisdom. As thy empire must extend. So let extend thy mind over all the world. In knowledge, all things in it comprehend.'[290]

The possession of empirical knowledge cannot grant us lasting peace on Earth. True wisdom has naught to do with securing fame, worldly glory, social status, profit, political power, riches, private property, influence, control, private wealth, pleasure, pecuniary gain, or prestige. True wisdom is living the content, good, joyous, and wholesome life.

---

289 The Holy Bible (ESV). (2016). Second Book of Timothy. Chapter 4, Verses 6–8.
290 Milton, John. (Darbishire, Helen, Ed.) (1958). *The Poetical Works of John Milton.* London: Oxford University Press, p. 328.

The history of human civilisation has demonstrated how empires rise and fall. Nothing on Earth endures for eternity. A mind infatuated with the fleeting and transient phenomena of this world is never at peace. The worldly reality of our being is unsettled, when it is in pursuit of what is subject to constant change. Logically speaking, how can we secure our lasting peace, within and through what is of this temporal, transient, and time-bound world?

Rather than becoming fixated with the trivial phenomena of this world, we ought to employ our worldly knowledge to perfect our moral conscience, to develop our character, to strengthen our sense of morality, and to cultivate our virtues. Our knowledge must be put to good use, and this includes to advance the cause of social justice, liberty, peace, the eradication of infectious diseases, human security, economic equality, respect, tolerance, and human dignity. Secular knowledge is only fit for the fulfilment of its purpose, and that underlying purpose is either good or evil in nature. Secular knowledge serves an end, it is never an end in and of itself. It is the collective responsibility of humanity, that our knowledge be employed for good purposes and noble ends.

'Of moral prudence, with delight received in brief sententious precepts. While they treat of fate, chance, and change in human life. High actions, and high passions best describing. Thence to the famous orators repair. Those ancient. Whose resistless eloquence wielded at will that fierce democracy.'[291]

Every person has a higher moral duty to aspire to righteousness. It is essential that we understand our primary non-delegable duty—to observe the higher-order principles of morality. This duty must be observed throughout the ebbs and flows of our life.

---

291 Milton, John. (Darbishire, Helen, Ed.) (1958). *The Poetical Works of John Milton*. London: Oxford University Press, p. 329.

In spite of the good and evil associated with misfortune, chance, luck, fate, or destiny, we always possess the personal agency to self-determine how we respond to the significant events in our lifetime.

We must demonstrate the requisite courage to advance the noble cause of human dignity, integrity, peace, equality, benevolence, tolerance, mercy, forgiveness, love, respect, community service, equity, and social justice. There is always the occurrence of select events and circumstances in our life, that are beyond our immediate control, however, such events and circumstances do not define our life narrative.

For the God-given power of free will to prevail against the necessity of fate, we must engage in the positive act of self-determination. It is only by the conscious exercise of our personal agency, that we decide how we respond to the uncontrollable events and change of circumstances that impact our life. It is not always the case, that what happens to us defines our life. Rather, it is our individual reaction to such events and circumstances, which defines our life.

A person's ability to respond at a time, place, and in a manner of one's own choosing—this is a freedom that only we affirm or deny to ourselves. Our conventional reality is defined as mind over matter. Alternatively, our reality is a representation of matter over mind. Which option shall we affirm?

'Till time mature thee to a kingdom's weight. These rules will render thee a king complete within thyself. Much more with empire joined.'[292]

Much like a king or queen desires to exert sovereign influence and political control upon the subjects of the sovereign nation-state, all too often we also desire to exert social control upon the

---

292 Milton, John. (Darbishire, Helen, Ed.) (1958). *The Poetical Works of John Milton.* London: Oxford University Press, p. 330.

significant people in our life. However, this erratic and irrational quest for control and influence of our immediate environment, and the important people within it, stems from a lack of internal confidence in ourselves. If we are secure in ourselves, we need not express concern for the divergent beliefs, thoughts, and actions of the significant people in our life. The more secure we are in ourselves, the less desire we have for control amongst other people, and our [immediate] environment.

Practical wisdom is found in concentrating our efforts to exert control over our life, so that we create our envisioned reality. Regrettably, all too often we demonstrate a propensity to become preoccupied in the opinions, thoughts, doctrines, principles, and ideas of the significant people in our life. Consequently, we fail to live an authentic, meaningful, and genuine life. We must ensure that we are never held hostage to the fleeting opinions of the significant people around us. We must seek our security in God's Word. For God's Word is unalterable, unshakeable, eternal, and timeless. If we are secure within ourselves, we need not search and seek security outside of ourselves.

The great Spanish mystic, Carmelite nun, and Doctor of the Church, Saint Teresa of Ávila (1515–1582) proffers timeless counsel for our spiritual self-development. Saint Teresa of Ávila, the author of the theological masterpiece, *The Interior Castle* (1577), shows us the righteous path in life. A superior path that is defined by equanimity, faith, hope, peace, spirituality, love, harmony, benevolence, compassion, and mercy.

Saint Teresa of Ávila encourages us to live our life with serious contemplation on God, coupled with the earnest application of prayer in our life. One of Ávila's many famous sayings are, 'God alone is enough. Let nothing upset you. Let nothing startle you. All things pass. God does not change. Patience wins all it seeks. Whoever has God lacks nothing. God alone is enough.' Regardless of what faith, denomination, or set of secular beliefs we subscribe to, humanity agrees that a life of authenticity, harmony, confidence, joy, social justice, prosperity, peace, and liberty is desirable.

> *'Think not but that I know these things; or think I know them not. Not therefore am I short of knowing what I ought. He who receives light from above. From the fountain of light. No other doctrine needs. Though granted true. But these are false, or little else but dreams. Conjectures. Fancies. Built on nothing firm.'*[293]

Only God's Grace enlightens us to live our life in a blessed manner. Only God's Grace provisions us with a prosperous, successful, abundant, peaceful, and joyful life on Earth. All human-made scientific doctrines and secular ideologies are inadequate to explain Creation, and our present and immediate existence within it. There are certain mysteries of the Universe that forever remain beyond the capacity of the human intellect.

Philosophy constitutes humanity's attempt to cognise the true origin of Creation within the finite boundaries of human understanding. With the sole instrument of natural reason at our disposal, we have no real possibility at attaining a successful resolution to the perennial quandary of how and why Creation came into existence.

The pioneering breakthroughs and astonishing advancements of modern science have resolved most of the problematic aspects, pertaining to the material dimension of human life on Earth. For example, consider the elimination of infectious and communicable diseases. Improvement of living standards. The management of non-communicable diseases. Novel advancements in public health measures. Greater employment opportunities through the industrialisation of the nation-state. Unprecedented progress in computer, mobile, and internet technology. Profound

---

293 Milton, John. (Darbishire, Helen, Ed.) (1958). *The Poetical Works of John Milton*. London: Oxford University Press, p. 330.

accomplishments in the field of engineering. Last but not least, a revolution in the application of antibiotics to treat and prevent bacterial infections.

Despite all this remarkable progress, the modern institution of science has no authority to venture into the timeless matters of faith. It is faith which directly impacts the spiritual dimension of the human condition. The spiritual matters of the soul are exclusively addressed through an intimate and mysterious dialogue with God.

'The first and wisest of them all professed to know this only. That he nothing knew. The next to fabling fell and smooth conceits. A third sort doubted all things. Though plain sense. Others in virtue placed felicity. But virtue joined with riches and long life. In corporal pleasure he, and careless ease. The stoic last in philosophical pride. By him called virtue, and his virtuous man. Wise. Perfect in himself, and all possessing equal to God. Oft shames not to prefer. As fearing God nor man. Condemning all wealth. Pleasure. Pain. Torment. Death and life. Which, when he lists, he leaves, or boasts he can. For all his tedious talk, is but vain boast.'[294]

The eminent Greek philosopher, Socrates expressed a profound clarity on the finite capacity of the human intellect to ascertain an objective and accurate representation of worldly reality. The unrivalled sage, Socrates understood the beginning and end of the shallow depth of natural reason. For this realisation alone, Socrates was an enlightened person. Socrates expressed a conscious awareness of his limitations, flaws, and weaknesses in understanding the vast expanse of the Universe.

---

294 Milton, John. (Darbishire, Helen, Ed.) (1958). *The Poetical Works of John Milton*. London: Oxford University Press, p. 330.

All philosophical arguments are vain attempts to rationalise the inability of our natural reason to understand the world objectively and impartially. Not to mention, the abstract and conceptual ideas of philosophy are far removed from the exigent demands and pressing problems of civil society.

Regardless, whether we examine Kant's modern philosophy, or Plato's ancient philosophy to inform our thinking, there remain inherent flaws in every person's philosophy. This is always the case, as in the end the author of any philosophical work is only human. All the renowned schools of Eastern and Western philosophical thought, such as Stoicism, Hedonism, Taoism, Materialism, Daoism, Existentialism, Epicureanism, Determinism, Utilitarianism, Legalism, Secularism, and many more, only purport to represent the natural world from a distinct and partial perspective. No ancient, contemporary, or future work of philosophy establishes irrefutable proofs of reality, but rather is subject to [valid] assumptions, which limit its ability to deduce [factual] propositions from theorems.

'Alas! What can they teach, and not mislead. Ignorant of themselves, of God much more, and how the world began, and how man fell. Degraded by himself, on grace depending? Much of the soul they talk. But all awry, and in themselves seek virtue, and to themselves all glory arrogate. To God give none. Rather accuse Him, under usual names. Fortune and fate. As one regardless quite of mortal things. Who, therefore seeks in these true wisdom, finds it not, or by delusion, far worse. Its false resemblance only meets, an empty cloud. However, many books, wise men have said, are wearisome. Who reads incessantly, and to his reading brings not a spirit and judgement equal or superior, and what he brings, what needs he elsewhere seek? Uncertain and unsettled still remains. Deep versed in books and shallow in himself.'[295]

Milton exposes the fallacy of the human ego. Each person seeks the fullness of life, and indeed the world, within and through their individual experience of being. While our focus is consumed with the materiality of our being in the world, our spirit remains detached from God. It is only by God's Grace, that we merge our spirit with God's Spirit. No matter how learned, wealthy, influential, or accomplished we become in our lifetime, at the very heart of the matter, we are ignorant of the very fact that this life is only a lease concerning our temporal existence on Earth. We, in our individual capacity, own nothing.

Life is a finite lease, for which we are truly dependent upon God's Grace for our existence. But we live our life ignorant of this Truth. We live our life with our indomitable ego at the centre of everything that we perform. Our ego is always situated at the core of our lived experience. Our ego virtually defines every aspect

---

295 Milton, John. (Darbishire, Helen, Ed.) (1958). *The Poetical Works of John Milton*. London: Oxford University Press, pp. 330–331.

of our being in the world. In fact, where there is more of our ego, there is less of God.

Too often, we fail to give God the requisite credit for our personal achievements and grand successes. We prefer to attribute the true cause of our accomplishments unto ourselves. This is the vanity of the human intellect, which remains subservient to the aims and ambitions of the unrestrained ego. Throughout our brief lifetime on Earth, our spirit remains unsettled, unfulfilled, and unsatisfied with the entirety of the human condition.

No matter the worldly riches, fame, personal income, glory, private wealth, political power, private property, prestige, social status, pecuniary gain, or influence that we acquire, it is never sufficient to satisfy our finite sense of being in the world. The acquisition of worldly phenomena momentarily gratifies our five senses and appeases our ego, before returning the ego to its original state of discontent. The materiality of worldly phenomena is incapable of permanently satisfying the immaterial dimension of our being—our soul.

The true contentment that we constantly seek, to fulfil our human condition resides beyond us. We cannot find a lasting sense of contentment situated within our inherent capacities, personal attributes, talents, skills, private wealth, expertise, empirical knowledge, formal education, private property, and positive qualities, but rather beyond them. That is to infer, contentment resides beyond the confines of the Self. No quantum of striving fulfils the inherent spiritual poverty and emptiness of the human condition.

It is only if and when we realise that God makes our life complete in every respect, then we come to a place of realisation and acceptance of reality, in the manner that God has decreed. Then we come to secure an unsurpassable peace. A peace that is everlasting. A profound peace that is done with the irrational vanity of striving against the Self. A perpetual peace that exists, emanates, and endures, despite the troubles and problems that we encounter along our life journey. A peace that is greater than any and every pleasure known to humankind. A peace that is God.

Within the Holy Bible, in the Book of Psalms, we find a Psalm of David. This particular Psalm is a timely reminder to all of us, that eternal peace is only obtained by the remembrance of God. In this Psalm, David does not let his innumerable personal challenges interfere with the divine thought of God's Goodness, 'The LORD is my shepherd. I shall not want. He makes me lie down in green pastures. He leads me beside still waters. He restores my soul. He leads me in paths of righteousness for His Name's sake. Even though I walk through the valley of the shadow of death, I will fear no evil, for You are with me. Your rod and your staff, they comfort me. You prepare a table before me in the presence of my enemies. You anoint my head with oil. My cup overflows. Surely goodness and mercy shall follow me all the days of my life, and I shall dwell in the House of the LORD forever.'[296]

David understood this principle. That it is not our pressing problems that define our life. Rather, it is what our focus, attention, time, resources, and thoughts are absorbed in, that ultimately define our life narrative. If we keep our mind on the LORD's Eternal Word, then we are protected by peace in the midst of a storm.

In the final analysis, we must remember that we are all incomplete without the illuminating Presence of God in our life. The presence and function of God's Grace is the single most important attribute to living a remarkable life. Only the Creator provisions the created with the genuine remedy to a peaceful, prosperous, and plentiful life on Earth. Therefore, let us turn our attention towards seeking a closer union with God. So that God's Spirit permeates our experience of being in the world. We must not diminish this precious and finite lifetime that we

---

296 The Holy Bible (ESV). (2016). The Book of Psalms. Chapter 23, Verses 1–6.

have on Earth, in the pursuit of trivial endeavours that are of no lasting significance or consequence. If we have faith, God leads us to victory in any situation.

The ancient Greek philosophical aphorism, often attributed to the Greek philosopher Socrates, 'to know thyself is the beginning of all wisdom,' sets the foundation stone for our lifelong quest for purpose and meaning. In our noble-minded quest for purpose and meaning, we ought to commence with the exploration of ourselves. We ought to learn more about ourselves; our thoughts, intentions, behaviour, lived experience, and unique perception of conventional reality. In learning about ourselves, we discover our unique talents, gifts, abilities, and skills. Becoming truly acquainted with ourselves, empowers us to live a fulfilling, enriching, authentic, and rewarding life.

There are many desirable and positive emotional states that are associated with our state of being. These ideal emotional states are defined by wholesome attributes and good principles, that are beyond our immediate and proximate self. These desirable emotional states that can permeate our experience of being, are obtained through our higher association with the spirit, and not through the exigencies of the flesh. If we seek to find something, first we have to search in the right place. Where are we searching to secure our lasting contentment, joy, peace, love, harmony, equanimity, and happiness? These desirable states of our being are only furthered through our association with the spirit.

'Since neither wealth, nor honour, arms, nor arts, kingdom, nor empire, pleases thee. Nor aught by me proposed in life contemplative, or active, tended on by glory, or fame. What dost thou in this world? The wilderness for thee is fittest place. I found thee there, and thither will return thee. Soon thou shall have cause, to wish thou never hadst rejected. Thus, nicely or cautiously, my offered aid, which would have set thee in short time with ease on David's Throne; or throne of all the world. Now at full age. Fullness of time. Thy season. When prophecies of thee are best fulfilled. Now contrary, if I read aught in Heaven, or Heaven write aught of fate. By what the stars voluminous, or single characters, in their conjunction met. Give me to spell. Sorrows. Labours. Opposition. Hate. Attends thee. Scorns. Reproaches. Injuries. Violence. Stripes. Lastly, cruel death.'[297]

Wholly due to the Devil's abject failure to successfully tempt the *Messiah*, the Devil reproached the *Messiah*. However, the *Messiah* remained disinterested in the trivial amusements, riches, and wealth of this world. At all times, the *Messiah* was transfixed on God's Sovereign Will. The Devil failed to conquer the *Messiah's* spirit, mind, soul, or heart. The terminal outcome of this battle between good and evil was the *Messiah* defeated the Devil.

The historical, political, legal, economic, social, religious, and cultural considerations failed to overpower the *Messiah's* formidable spirit on Earth. The *Messiah* chose the righteous path, not the most convenient or favourable path on Earth. It was of no significance, that the Devil threatened the *Messiah* with [physical] death, for the Anointed One had the blessing of Almighty God. It was God's Royal Decree, that the Anointed

---

297 Milton, John. (Darbishire, Helen, Ed.) (1958). *The Poetical Works of John Milton.* London: Oxford University Press, p. 332.

One transcend [physical] death. The Anointed One has risen, to live for eternity.

> *'Our saviour. Meek, and with untroubled mind, after his aery jaunt. Though hurried sore. Hungry and cold. Betook him to his rest. Wherever, under some concourse of shades. Whose branching arms thick intertwined might shield from dews and damps of night his sheltered head. But, sheltered. Slept in vain. For at his head the tempter watched, and soon with ugly dreams, disturbed his sleep.'[298]*

The Devil attempts to disturb our peace of mind. In the first instance, the Devil starts to unduly influence our thoughts, ideas, doctrines, principles, and beliefs. As we witnessed within the Old Testament of the Holy Bible, the Devil successfully deceived Eve, by first questioning her thoughts, ideas, principles, doctrines, and beliefs. From that point, the Devil had Eve question God's Eternal Word. Through immoral acts of betrayal and treachery, the Devil implanted the poisonous seed of doubt into Eve's mind.

Once doubt was implanted into Eve's mind, it was only a matter of time before Original Sin and the Fall of Man. Needless to say, confusion followed doubt. Temptation followed confusion. Fear followed temptation. Unbelief followed fear. Sin followed unbelief. Guilt followed sin. Punishment followed the guilt of sin. This chain reaction of disaster was only broken, when the divine power of redemption and salvation followed sin and punishment.

We must be aware, that the Devil relentlessly attempts to deceive us, precisely when we are at the most vulnerable moment in our life. It is best counsel, never to give the Devil a foothold in our thoughts. For when we entertain the Devil in our thoughts,

---

298 Milton, John. (Darbishire, Helen, Ed.) (1958). *The Poetical Works of John Milton*. London: Oxford University Press, p. 333.

we have already lost the spiritual war. Therefore, we must keep a watchful eye on our thoughts.

> *'All to the push of fate. Pursue thy way of gaining David's Throne no man knows when. For both the when and how is nowhere told. Thou shall be what thou art ordained. No doubt. For Angels have proclaimed it, but concealing the time and means? Each act is rightest done. Not when it must. But when it may be best.'*[299]

When it comes to the fulfilment of our hopes, dreams, ambitions, objectives, and endeavours, we ought to position our confidence and trust in God. God's Favour, Goodness, Blessing, Grace, and Mercy overcome all the obstacles and challenges that we confront along our life journey. There are several profound life lessons that we deduce from King David's remarkable life journey. It is important to acknowledge, that while David succeeded in his grand endeavour to secure the Throne of Israel, prior to his accession as King to the Throne of Israel, David confronted relentless opposition from his predecessor, King Saul.

In fact, King Saul plotted to take David's life on several occasions. On one of these dreadful occasions, King Saul was almost successful, 'Then a harmful spirit from the LORD came upon Saul, as he sat in his house with his spear in his hand. And David was playing the lyre. And Saul sought to pin David to the wall with the spear, but he eluded Saul, so that he struck the spear into the wall. And David fled and escaped that night.'[300]

What we understand from David's personal experience with King Saul, is that when we are subject to hostility, when there is opposition, when we have to confront adversity, then our personal values, doctrines, principles, beliefs, and moral conscience are put

---

299 Milton, John. (Darbishire, Helen, Ed.) (1958). *The Poetical Works of John Milton*. London: Oxford University Press, p. 334.
300 The Holy Bible (ESV). (2016). First Book of Samuel. Chapter 19, Verses 9–10.

to the ultimate test. The content of our character is determined, not on the basis of how we act during times of peace, prosperity, security, and liberty, but rather during times of conflict, anarchy, and war.

At no time did David seek vengeance or retribution against King Saul. Nor did David take matters into his own hands. Even when David was presented with two distinct and independent opportunities to take King Saul's life, and secure the Throne of Israel for himself, David did not engage in such an evil and callous act. On the first occasion, David and his men had King Saul surrounded, 'And the men of David said to him, "Here is the day of which the LORD said to you, 'Behold, I will give your enemy into your hand, and you shall do to him as it shall seem good to you.'" Then David arose and stealthily cut off a corner of Saul's robe. He said to his men, "The LORD forbids that I should do this thing to my Lord, the LORD's anointed, to put out my hand against him, seeing he is the LORD's anointed."'[301]

Now on the second occasion, David also spared King Saul's life, 'And David answered and said, "Here is the spear, O King! Let one of the young men come over and take it. The LORD rewards every man for his righteousness and his faithfulness, for the LORD gave you into my hand today, and I would not put out my hand against the LORD's anointed."'[302]

David's character was developed during his formative years and during turbulent times. Yet, in such challenging situations, David exercised and thereby strengthened his moral conscience. Simply because we have a vested interest in the ends of our self-interested actions, this does not grant us the requisite legitimacy of utilising any and every means possible to secure our desired ends. We require moral justification, to inform our voluntary and conscious actions. We must not rationalise or justify our

---

301 The Holy Bible (ESV). (2016). First Book of Samuel. Chapter 24, Verses 4–6.
302 The Holy Bible (ESV). (2016). First Book of Samuel. Chapter 26, Verses 22–23.

voluntary and conscious actions, after the fact that we have performed them.

What we learn through the aforementioned verses of scripture, is that instead of seeking revenge against King Saul's jealousy, envy, anger, bitterness, pride, and hatred, David kept his mind focused on God's Eternal Word. In the Holy Bible, within the Book of Psalms, we are made privy to God's Eternal Wisdom that David observed in his life, 'I hasten and do not delay to keep Your Commandments. Though the cords of the wicked ensnare me, I do not forget Your Law.'[303]

In God's Timing, David succeeded King Saul. David secured the Throne of Israel. Practical wisdom involves factoring into our consideration both the means and ends, both our actions and intentions, both the consequences and rewards pertaining to the exercise of our personal agency and free will. The dimension of morality is not excluded, when it comes to the performance of voluntary and conscious actions, that are executed in accordance with our natural reason.

---

303 The Holy Bible (ESV). (2016). The Book of Psalms. Chapter 119, Verses 60–61.

'Thou art to be my fatal enemy. Good reason. Then, if I beforehand seek to understand my adversary. Who and what he is? His wisdom. Power. Intent. By parle, or composition, truce, or league. To win him, or win from him what I can. And opportunity, I here have had. To try thee, sift thee, and confess have found thee. Proof against all temptation, as a rock. Of adamant and as a centre, firm. To the utmost of mere man, both wise and good. Not more. For honours. Riches. Kingdoms. Glory. Have been before contemned, and may again.'[304]

During the significant period of world history that the *Messiah* was in the flesh and situated on Earth, he was tested time and time again. However, the *Messiah* proved that he was immovable. We too must anchor our life upon a firm foundation, one that does not waver. We must anchor our life upon God's Sovereign Command and Eternal Word. In this manner, we definitively overcome the temptations, obstacles, and hindrances that are situated along our life journey.

We need to effectuate into practice the principles of work, righteousness, social justice, respect, joy, community service, faithfulness, mercy, benevolence, tolerance, peace, love, charity, forgiveness, human dignity, and faith, to create a better and brighter world. The construction of a better and brighter world starts with our heart. Therefore, we must all ask ourselves the question: Where is our heart at?

The power of good transcends the weakness of evil. The collective power of humanity overcomes the multitude of challenges that we confront in this world. The Love of God conquers any problem, challenge, or issue that we experience in our lifetime. When being part of any transformative political change, advancing the noble cause of social justice, or fighting a

---

304 Milton, John. (Darbishire, Helen, Ed.) (1958). *The Poetical Works of John Milton*. London: Oxford University Press, p. 336.

spiritual battle, what truly matters is our intention. We are not perfect, but we can be better.

When all is said and done, what really mattered is that we *loved* God and one another. We *worked* towards the advancement of good. Last but not least, we *hoped* for the best in the worst of times. On our journey of a lifetime, from time to time we must pause and reflect upon the following questions: How far have we come? Where are we now? What do we desire to accomplish with our remaining years? When our time on Earth is finished, let us leave the world with memories, not unfulfilled endeavours. Peace be with you.

CONCLUSION

This critique has explored the magnificent poetry of the English poet and intellectual, John Milton (1608–1674). Milton's twelve books on *Paradise Lost* and four books on *Paradise Regained*, portray a fascinating and riveting account of the Biblical narratives pertaining to Original Sin, the Fall of Man, and finally, the Redemption of Humanity. Milton, true to his intellectual and creative nature, cleverly and eloquently describes Adam and Eve's time in the Garden of Eden.

Subsequently, Milton masterfully articulates the sombre story of Satan's treacherous temptation of Eve, which led to her consumption of the Forbidden Fruit from the Tree of the Knowledge of Good and Evil. Unfortunately, Eve convinces Adam to also consume the Forbidden Fruit. Adam, loyal and faithful to his spouse, consumes the Forbidden Fruit. We witness Adam seal his fate and join his wife, Eve in their unfavourable date with destiny. Once Adam and Eve are banished from the Garden of Eden, the curse of Original Sin and the Fall of Man is forever upon humanity.

Despite Adam and Eve's justified banishment from Paradise, all hope is not lost for human civilisation. Through Milton's narrative poem, we witness the Son of God descend to Earth, in the flesh, to redeem humanity from the lasting effects of their sinful conduct. This atonement is acceptable to God. While humanity has created the problem (i.e., Original Sin and the Fall of Man), God has provided the solution (i.e., the Crucifixion and Resurrection of the Son of God).

Milton beautifully narrates how the Devil tests the *Messiah* during his blessed time on Earth. Despite the Devil literally offering the kingdom of this world to the *Messiah*, the *Messiah* remains unmoved by the Devil's worldly temptations. Finally, the Devil concedes defeat. The Devil is unable to convince the *Messiah* to follow the path of evil. The *Messiah* conquers the Devil. The *Messiah* is victorious in the epic spiritual battle between good and evil.

Milton's *Paradise Lost and Regained* is one of the greatest poems in the English-speaking world. Milton demonstrates a natural talent to employ the English language to create brilliant literary effects through the use of allusion, imagery, metaphor, irony, tone, prosody, foreshadowing, and diction. In addition, Milton's impressive use of blank verse poetry is enhanced by his originality in creating Miltonic verse; a novel approach to Milton's writing of English poetry. Miltonic verse altogether redefines the spelling and punctuation found within *Paradise Lost and Regained*. Miltonic verse creates a striking phonetic effect on Milton's ingenious poem.

Through the medium of poetry, Milton's writing truly brings out the vivid and evocative dimensions of theology to the surface. The reader cannot help but be mesmerised, with the profound discourses, messages of morality, colourful language, meaningful theology, the spiritual battles of good and evil, the tests of faith, the angelic interventions, and the many Biblical parables portrayed across these sixteen books.

This critique has examined each of the sixteen books of Milton. It has explored Milton's literary work in an accessible and uncomplicated manner. Not only has Milton succeeded in re-telling the major Biblical stories in an original style, however, he has also made reading the Biblical accounts colourful, charming, and captivating.

In the contemporary era, one that is defined by scientific progress, technological advances, unending intellectual curiosity, materialism, humanism, and secularism, Milton's poetry remains relevant to our study of the age-old theological questions concerning sin, punishment, redemption, obedience, salvation, faith, destiny, Original Sin, the Fall of Man, hope, despair, providence, fate, good, evil, mercy, free will, crucifixion, grace, agency, heaven, hell, love, disobedience, and temptation. In spite of the passage of three and a half centuries, Milton's literary writing has stood the test of time. Milton's *Paradise Lost and Regained* continues to inform, impress, and impact upon the vivid imagination of readers, from all walks of life.

BIBLIOGRAPHY

Agostini, I. (2015). Descartes' Proofs of God and the Crisis of Thomas Aquinas' Five Ways in Early Modern Thomism: Scholastic and Cartesian Debates. *The Harvard Theological Review*. Volume 108, No. 2, pp. 235–262.

Anderson, J. (2016). *Innovative Catholicism and the Human Condition*. New York: Routledge Publication.

Aristotle (W. K. C. Guthrie, Trans.) (1939). *Aristotle: On the Heavens*. (Loeb Classical Library). Cambridge, Massachusetts: Harvard University Press.

Aristotle. (1952). *Aristotle: Meteorologica*. (Loeb Classical Library). Cambridge, Massachusetts: Harvard University Press.

Aristotle. (H. Tredennick, Trans.) (1960). *Posterior Analytics*. Cambridge, Massachusetts: Harvard University Press.

Aristotle. (J. L. Ackrill and L. Judson, Eds.) (J. L. Ackrill, Trans.) (1975). *Aristotle: Categories and De Interpretatione*. New York: Oxford University Press.

Aristotle. (J. Barnes, Ed.) (1984). *The Complete Works of Aristotle. Volume I*. Princeton; New Jersey: Princeton University Press.

Aristotle. (J. Barnes, Ed.) (1984). *The Complete Works of Aristotle. Volume II*. Princeton; New Jersey: Princeton University Press.

Aristotle. (R. Smith, Trans.) (1989). *Prior Analytics*. Indianapolis: Hackett Publishing Company.

Aristotle. (H. Lawson-Tancred, Ed. and Trans.) (1992). *The Art of Rhetoric*. London: Penguin Books.

Aristotle. (R. F. Stalley, Ed.) (E. Barker, Trans.) (1995). *Politics*. New York: Oxford University Press.

Aristotle. (H. Lawson-Tancred, Trans.) (1999). *The Metaphysics*. London: Penguin Books.

Aristotle. (D. Bostock, Ed.) (R. Waterfield, Trans.) (2008). *Physics*. New York: Oxford University Press.

Aristotle. (2010). *On Sense and the Sensible*. Montana: Kessinger Publishing, LLC.

Aristotle. (2010). *On Sophistical Refutations*. Montana: Kessinger Publishing, LLC.

Aristotle. (R. C. Bartlett, and S. D. Collins Trans.) (2012). *Aristotle's Nicomachean Ethics*. London: University of Chicago Press.

Aristotle. (E. M. Edghill, Trans.) (2014). *The Categories*. California: CreateSpace Independent Publishers.

Aristotle. (2015). *Topics*. London: Aeterna Press.

Aristotle. (F. D. Miller Jr., Translator) (2018). *On the Soul: and Other Psychological Works*. New York: Oxford University Press.

Aristotle. (2018). *On Generation and Corruption*. Knutsford: A & D Publishing.

Ayer, A. J. (1949). *Language, Truth, and Logic*. London: Victor Gollancz Ltd.

Ayer, A. J. (1963). *The Concept of a Person and Other Essays*. New York: St. Martin's Press.

Ayer, A. J. (1965). *Philosophical Essays*. London: Macmillan & Co Ltd.

Ayer, A. J. (1968). *The Origins of Pragmatism*. Toronto: Macmillan Company.

Ayer, A. J. (1968). *The Humanist Outlook*. London: Pemberton, Barrie & Rockliff.

Ayer, A. J. (1971). *Russell and Moore: The Analytical Heritage*. Cambridge, Massachusetts: Harvard University Press.

Ayer, A. J. (1972). *Probability and Evidence*. New York: Columbia University Press.

Ayer, A. J. (1974). *The Central Questions of Philosophy*. New York: Holt, Rinehart, and Winston.

Ayer, A. J. (1979). *Perception and Identity*. London: Macmillan.

Ayer, A. J. (1982). *Philosophy in the Twentieth Century*. New York: Vintage Books.

Ayer, A. J. (1984). *Freedom and Morality and other Essays*. Oxford: Oxford University Press.

Ayer, A. J. (1988). *Essays on Moral Realism*. New York: Cornell University Press.

Ayer, A. J. (1988). *The Meaning of Life*. London: Orion Publishing Co.

Ayer, A. J. (1990). *The Problem of Knowledge*. New York: Penguin Books.

Banerjee, R. (2021). *India in Early Modern English Travel Writings: Protestantism, Enlightenment, and Toleration.* Boston: Brill.

Bare, A. L. (2018). Feminism Regained: Exposing the Objectification of Eve in John Milton's Paradise Lost. *English Studies.* Volume 99, No. 2, pp. 93–112.

Basevich, E. (2020). God Comes to Her: A Kantian Reflection on Evil and Religious Experience in Saint Teresa of Ávila and Simone Weil. *Cosmos and History.* Volume 16, No. 1, p. 325.

Baweja, P. (2021). *A Philosophical Treatise of Reality: Volume I.* Melbourne: Paul Baweja.

Baweja, P. (2021). *A Philosophical Treatise of Reality: Volume II.* Melbourne: Paul Baweja.

Baweja, P. (2021). *A Philosophical Treatise of Reality: Volume III.* Melbourne: Paul Baweja.

Baweja, P. (2021). *A Philosophical Treatise of Reality: Volume IV.* Melbourne: Paul Baweja.

Baweja, P. (2023). *A Commentary on Shakespeare's Plays.* Melbourne: Paul Baweja.

Bennett, R. (Director). (1980). *Hamlet.* (Film). The BBC Shakespeare Collection. London: The British Broadcasting Corporation.

Bilinkoff, J. (1989). *The Ávila of Saint Teresa: Religious Reform in a Sixteenth-century City.* Ithaca: Cornell University Press.

Billington, K. (Director). (1979). *Henry VIII.* (Film). The BBC Shakespeare Collection. London: The British Broadcasting Corporation.

Burge, S. (Director). (1984). *Much Ado About Nothing.* (Film). The BBC Shakespeare Collection. London: The British Broadcasting Corporation.

Carroll, T. (2018). *Orthodox Christian Material Culture: Of People and Things in the Making of Heaven.* London: Routledge Publication.

Cataldo, J. W. (2017). *Biblical Terror: Why Law and Restoration in the Bible depend upon Fear.* London: Bloomsbury Academic.

Chan, W., (Trans.). (1969). *A Source Book in Chinese Philosophy.* Princeton, New Jersey: Princeton University Press.

Chappel, J. (2018). *Catholic Modern: The Challenge of Totalitarianism and the Remaking of the Church.* Cambridge, Massachusetts: Harvard University Press.

Cicero, M. T. (W. A. Falconer, Ed.) (1923). *On Old Age. On Friendship. On Divination.* Cambridge, Massachusetts: Harvard University Press.

Cicero, M. T. (M. Hadas, Ed.) (1951). *The Basic Works of Cicero*. New York: Modern Library.

Cicero, M. T. (H. Rackham, Ed.) (1972). *De Natura Deorum; Academica*. Cambridge, Massachusetts: Harvard University Press.

Cicero, M. T. (M. Grant, Trans.) (1980). *On the Good Life*. London: Penguin Classics.

Cicero, M. T. (J. G. F. Powell, Ed.) (1988). *Cicero: Cato Maior de Senectute*. Cambridge: Cambridge University Press.

Cicero, M. T. (H. E. Gould, and J. L. Whiteley, Eds.) (2013). *De Amicitia*. London: Bloomsbury Publication.

Coleman, B. (Director). (1978). *As You Like It*. (Film). The BBC Shakespeare Collection. London: The British Broadcasting Corporation.

Conti, B. (2019). Milton, Jerome, and Apocalyptic Virginity. *Renaissance Quarterly*. Volume 72, Issue 1, pp. 194–230.

Cooper, K. W. (2013). Reason and Desire after the Fall of Man: A Rereading of Hobbes' Two Postulates of Human Nature. *Hobbes Studies*. Volume 26, No. 2, pp. 107–129.

Cross, R. (2017). Aquinas on Physical Impairment: Human Nature and Original Sin. *The Harvard Theological Review*. Volume 100, No. 3, pp. 317–338.

Crossley, J. G. (2016). *Harnessing Chaos: The Bible in English Political Discourse Since 1968*. London, England: Bloomsbury Academic.

Danielson, D. (1999). *The Cambridge Companion to Milton*. Second Edition. Cambridge: Cambridge University Press.

Davis, D. (Director). (1979). *Measure for Measure*. (Film). The BBC Shakespeare Collection. London: The British Broadcasting Corporation.

Dewey, J. (1894). *The Study of Ethics: A Syllabus*. Ann Arbor, Michigan: G. Wahr.

Dewey, J. (1899). *The School and Society: Being Three Lectures*. Chicago: University of Chicago Press.

Dewey, J., and Tufts, J. H. (1906). *Ethics*. New York: Henry Holt & Company.

Dewey, J. (1909). *Moral Principles in Education*. New York: Houghton Mifflin Company.

Dewey, J. (1913). *Interest and Effort in Education*. Boston: Houghton Mifflin Company.

Dewey, J. (1922). *Human Nature and Conduct*. New York: Henry Holt & Company.

Dewey, J. (1925). *Experience and Nature*. LaSalle, Illinois: Open Court Press.

Dewey, J. (1926). *Reconstruction in Philosophy*. New York: Henry Holt & Company.

Dewey, J. (1929). *The Sources of a Science of Education*. New York: Horace Liveright.

Dewey, J. (1930). *Individualism Old and New*. New York: Milton Balch & Company.

Dewey, J. (1934). *A Common Faith*. New Haven: Yale University Press.

Dewey, J. (1935). *Liberalism and Social Action*. New York: G. P. Putnam's Sons.

Dewey, J. (1938). *Experience and Education*. New York: Macmillan Co.

Dewey, J. (1938). *Logic: The Theory of Inquiry*. New York: Henry Holt & Company.

Dewey, J. (1939). *Freedom and Culture*. New York: G. P. Putnam's Sons.

Dewey, J. (J. A. Boydston., and F. Bowers., Eds.) (1969). *John Dewey: Essays and Outlines of a Critical Theory of Ethics*. Carbondale: Southern Illinois University Press.

Dewey, J. (1997). *How We Think*. New York: Dover Publications.

Dewey, J. (2004). *Reconstruction in Philosophy*. New York: Dover Publications.

Donnelly, P. J. (2009). *Milton's Scriptural Reasoning: Narrative and Protestant Toleration*. Cambridge: Cambridge University Press.

Dulles, A. (1995). *The Craft of Theology: From Symbol to System*. New York: Crossroad.

Duran, A. (2008). *A Concise Companion to Milton*. New York: John Wiley & Sons.

Durant, W. (2001). *Heroes of History: A Brief History of Civilisation from Ancient Times to the Dawn of the Modern Age*. New York: Simon & Schuster.

Durant, W. (Little, J., Ed.) (2002). *The Greatest Minds and Ideas of All Time*. New York: Simon & Schuster.

Durant, W. (2005). *The Story of Philosophy*. New York: Simon & Schuster.

Durant, W., and Durant, A. (2010). *The Lessons of History*. New York: Simon & Schuster.

Ebbeler, J. V. (2012). *Disciplining Christians: Correction and Community in Augustine's Letters*. Oxford: Oxford University Press.

Elders, L. J. (2018). *Thomas Aquinas and His Predecessors: The Philosophers and the Church Fathers in His Works*. Washington D.C.: The Catholic University of America Press.

Evans, J. H. (2013). The growing Social and Moral Conflict between Conservative Protestantism and Science. *Journal for the Scientific Study of Religion*. Volume 52, No. 2, pp. 368–385.

Fabre, C. (2021). The Law vs. The Sword: Arthur Ripstein's Account of the Morality and Law of War. *Criminal Justice Ethics*. Volume 40, No. 3, pp. 256–268.

Fodor, J., and Higton, M. (2015). *The Routledge Companion to the Practice of Christian Theology*. First Edition. London: Routledge Publication.

Ford, D. (1989). *The Modern Theologians: An Introduction to Christian Theology in the Twentieth Century*. Oxford: Basil Blackwell.

Frankl, V. E. (2006). *Man's Search for Meaning*. Boston: Beacon Press.

Gandhi, M. K. (1993). *An Autobiography: The Story of My Experiments with Truth*. Boston: Beacon Press.

Gibbon, E. (H. Trevor-Roper, Introduction) (2010). *The Decline and Fall of the Roman Empire*. Volume I—VI. New York: Knopf Doubleday Publishing Group.

Giles, D. (Director). (1979). *Henry IV: Part One*. (Film). The BBC Shakespeare Collection. London: The British Broadcasting Corporation.

Giles, D. (Director). (1979). *Henry IV: Part Two*. (Film). The BBC Shakespeare Collection. London: The British Broadcasting Corporation.

Giles, D. (Director). (1979). *Henry V*. (Film). The BBC Shakespeare Collection. London: The British Broadcasting Corporation.

Giles, D. (Director). (1984). *The Life and Death of King John*. (Film). The BBC Shakespeare Collection. London: The British Broadcasting Corporation.

Gold, J. (Director). (1980). *The Merchant of Venice*. (Film). The BBC Shakespeare Collection. London: The British Broadcasting Corporation.

Gold, J. (Director). (1983). *Macbeth*. (Film). The BBC Shakespeare Collection. London: The British Broadcasting Corporation.

Gorman, M. J. (2014). *The Death of the Messiah and the Birth of the New Covenant: A (Not So) New Model of the Atonement*. Eugene: Wipf and Stock Publishers.

Gorrie, J. (Director). (1980). *The Tempest*. (Film). The BBC Shakespeare Collection. London: The British Broadcasting Corporation.

Gorrie, J. (Director). (1980). *Twelfth Night*. (Film). The BBC Shakespeare Collection. London: The British Broadcasting Corporation.

Gray, P. (2016). *Paul as a Problem in History and Culture: The Apostle and His Critics through the Centuries*. Grand Rapids, Michigan: Baker Publishing Group.

Grogan, J. (2020). *Beyond Greece and Rome: Reading the Ancient Near East in Early Modern Europe*. Oxford: Oxford University Press.

Gurteen, S. H. (1896). *The Epic of the Fall of Man: A Comparative Study of Caedmon, Dante, and Milton*. New York: G. P. Putnam's Sons.

Hale, J. K. (1997). *Milton's languages: The impact of multilingualism on style*. Cambridge: Cambridge University Press.

Harrison, P. (1998). *The Bible, Protestantism, and the Rise of Natural Science*. New York: Cambridge University Press.

Harvey, D. (1989). *The Condition of Postmodernity, An Enquiry into the Origins of Cultural Change*. Oxford: Basil Blackwell.

Harvey, D. (2006). *A Brief History of Neoliberalism*. Oxford: Oxford University Press.

Harvey, P. (1990). *An Introduction to Buddhism: Teachings, History, and Practices*. Cambridge: Cambridge University Press.

Hays, C. B. (2014). *Hidden Riches: A Sourcebook for the Comparative Study of the Hebrew Bible and Ancient Near East*. Kentucky: Presbyterian Publishing Corporation.

Heavey, K. (2015). *The Early Modern Medea: Medea in English Literature, 1558–1688*. New York: Palgrave Macmillan.

Hobbes, T. (E. Curley, Ed.) (1994). *Leviathan: With Selected Variants from the Latin Edition of 1668*. Indiana: Hackett Publishing Company.

Hodge, C. (1960). *Systematic Theology*. Volumes I—III. Michigan: William B. Eerdmans Publication Co.

Hollinger, D. A. (2022). *Christianity's American Fate: How Religion became more conservative and Society more secular*. Princeton, New Jersey: Princeton University Press.

Horan, D. P. (2014). *Postmodernity and univocity: A critical account of radical orthodoxy and John Duns Scotus*. Minneapolis: Fortress Press.

Hovey, C., and Phillips, E. (2015). *The Cambridge Companion to Christian Political Theology*. Cambridge: Cambridge University Press.

Howell, J. (Director). (1981). *The Winter's Tale*. (Film). The BBC Shakespeare Collection. London: The British Broadcasting Corporation.

Howell, J. (Director). (1983). *Henry VI: Part One*. (Film). The BBC Shakespeare Collection. London: The British Broadcasting Corporation.

Howell, J. (Director). (1983). *Henry VI: Part Two*. (Film). The BBC Shakespeare Collection. London: The British Broadcasting Corporation.

Howell, J. (Director). (1983). *Henry VI: Part Three*. (Film). The BBC Shakespeare Collection. London: The British Broadcasting Corporation.

Howell, J. (Director). (1983). *Richard II*. (Film). The BBC Shakespeare Collection. London: The British Broadcasting Corporation.

Howell, J. (Director). (1983). *The Tragedy of Richard III*. (Film). The BBC Shakespeare Collection. London: The British Broadcasting Corporation.

Howell, J. (Director). (1985). *Titus Andronicus*. (Film). The BBC Shakespeare Collection. London: The British Broadcasting Corporation.

Hudson, H. (2014). *The Fall and Hypertime*. Oxford: Oxford University Press.

Hume, D. (1875). *Essays Moral, Political, and Liberty*. London: Longmans, Green, and Co.

Hume, D. (J. Y. T. Greig, Ed.) (1932). *The Letters of David Hume. Volume I*. New York: Oxford University Press.

Hume, D. (J. Y. T. Greig, Ed.) (1932). *The Letters of David Hume. Volume II*. New York: Oxford University Press.

Hume, D. (R. Klibansky, and E. C. Mossner, Eds.) (1954). *New Letters of David Hume*. Oxford: Clarendon Press.

Hume, D. (L.A. Selby, Ed.) (Revised by P. H. Nidditch) (1975). *A Treatise on Human Nature*. Second Edition. Oxford: Clarendon Press.

Hume, D. (R. H. Popkin, Ed.) (1980). *Dialogues Concerning Natural Religion. Of the Immortality of the Soul, of Suicide, and of Miracles*. Cambridge: Hackett Publishing Company.

Hume, D. (W. B. Todd, Ed.) (1983). *The History of England*. Indianapolis: Liberty Classics.

Hume, D. (1985). *The History of England. Volumes I—VI.* Indianapolis: Liberty Fund.

Hume, D. (E. F. Miller, Ed.) (1985). *Essays: Moral, Political, and Literary.* Indianapolis: Liberty Classics.

Hume, D. (1998). *An Enquiry concerning the Principles of Morals.* Oxford: Oxford University Press.

Hume, D. (K. Haakonssen, Ed.) (1994). *Hume: Political Essays.* Cambridge: Cambridge University Press.

Hume, D. (2000). *A Treatise of Human Nature.* Oxford: Oxford University Press.

Hume, D. (T. L. Beauchamp, Ed.) (2007). *A Dissertation on the Passions and the Natural History of Religion.* Oxford: Clarendon Press.

Hume, D. (D. Coleman, Ed.) (2007). *Dialogues Concerning Natural Religion.* Cambridge: Cambridge University Press.

Hume, D. (2008). *An Enquiry Concerning Human Understanding.* Oxford: Oxford University Press.

Hurley, T. J. (2023). The Word, the Lamb, and the World: Reflecting on Christ, Power, and Humanity with Thomas Aquinas' Commentary on John. *Logos: A Journal of Catholic Thought and Culture.* Volume 26, No. 2, pp. 33–51.

James, S. (2015). Metaphysics and Empowerment: Moore on the place of Metaphysics in Spinoza's Philosophy. *Philosophical Topics.* Volume 43, Issue 1–2, pp. 13–26.

Jeffrey, R. (1965). *The Logic of Decision.* Chicago: University of Chicago Press.

Jeffrey, R. (2004). *Subjective Probability: The Real Thing.* Cambridge: Cambridge University Press.

Jenkins, R. (2001). *Churchill: A Biography.* New York: Penguin Books.

Jennings, R. E. (1994). *The Genealogy of Disjunction.* Oxford: Oxford University Press.

Johnston, E. M. (2016). The Apostle, the Philosopher, and Friar Thomas: The Place of Aristotle in Thomas Aquinas' Dominican Vocation. *Logos: A Journal of Catholic Thought and Culture.* Volume 19, No. 4, pp. 15–46.

Jones, D. H. (Director). (1982). *The Merry Wives of Windsor.* (Film). The BBC Shakespeare Collection. London: The British Broadcasting Corporation.

Jones, D. H. (Director). (1984). *Pericles: Prince of Tyre*. (Film). The BBC Shakespeare Collection. London: The British Broadcasting Corporation.

Jones, J. C. (Director). (1983). *The Comedy of Errors*. (Film). The BBC Shakespeare Collection. London: The British Broadcasting Corporation.

Kane, R. (Ed.) (2011). *The Oxford Handbook of Free Will*. New York: Oxford University Press.

Kant, I. (T. M. Greene, and H. H. Hudson, Trans.) (1960). *Religion within the Limits of Reason Alone*. New York: Harper and Row.

Kant, I. (1987). *Critique of Judgement*. Cambridge: Hackett Publishing Company.

Kant, I. (J. M. Young, Ed.) (1992). *Lectures on Logic*. Cambridge: Cambridge University Press.

Kant, I. (1995). *Opus Postumum*. New York: Cambridge University Press.

Kant, I. (P. Guyer, and A. W. Wood, Eds. and Trans.) (1999). *Critique of Pure Reason*. New York: Cambridge University Press.

Kant, I. (M. J. Gregor, Trans.) (1999). *Practical Philosophy*. New York: Cambridge University Press.

Kant, I. (P. Guyer, and E. Matthews, Trans.) (2001). *Critique of the Power of Judgement*. New York: Cambridge University Press.

Kant, I. (2001). *Lectures on Metaphysics*. New York: Cambridge University Press.

Kant, I. (A. W. Wood, and G. di Giovanni, Eds. and Trans.) (2001). *Religion and Rational Theology*. New York: Cambridge University Press.

Kant, I. (2002). *Critique of Practical Reason*. Cambridge: Hackett Publishing Company.

Kant, I. (D. Walford, and R. Meerbote, Eds.) (2003). *Theoretical Philosophy, 1755–1770*. New York: Cambridge University Press.

Kant, I. (A. Zweig, Ed.) (2007). *Correspondence*. Cambridge: Cambridge University Press.

Kant, I. (2007). *Critique of Pure Reason*. London: Penguin Classics.

Kant, I. (P. Heath, and J. B. Schneewind, Eds.) (2010). *Lectures on Ethics*. New York: Cambridge University Press.

Kant, I. (R. B. Louden, and G. Zoller, Eds. and Trans.) (2011). *Anthropology, History, and Education*. Cambridge: Cambridge University Press.

Kant, I. (E. Watkins, Ed.) (M. Schonfeld, J. B. Edwards, O. Reinhardt, and L. W. Beck, Trans.) (2012). *Kant: Natural Science.* New York: Cambridge University Press.

Kant, I. (R. B. Louden, A. W. Wood, R. R. Clewis, and G. F. Munzel, Trans.) (2013). *Lectures on Anthropology.* New York: Cambridge University Press.

Klassen, P. E. (2011). *Spirits of Protestantism: Medicine, Healing, and Liberal Christianity.* California: University of California Press.

Krijger, T. (2019). *The Eclipse of Liberal Protestantism in the Netherlands: Religious, Social, and International Perspectives on the Dutch Modernist Movement (1870–1940).* Boston: Brill.

Lamb, M. (2022). *A Commonwealth of Hope: Augustine's Political Thought.* Princeton, New Jersey: Princeton University Press.

Last, R. (2011). What Purpose did Paul understand His Mission to Serve? *The Harvard Theological Review.* Volume 104, No. 3, pp. 299–324.

Lee, S. (1902). *Shakespeare's Comedies, Histories, and Tragedies. A supplement to the reproduction in facsimile of the First Folio Edition, 1623, from the Chatsworth copy in the possession of the Duke of Devonshire, KG. Containing a census of extant copies with some account of their history and condition.* Oxford: Clarendon Press.

Locke, J. (1689). *An Essay Concerning Human Understanding.* London: Thomas Bassett.

Locke, J. (1689). *Two Treatise of Government.* London: Awnsham Churchill.

Locke, J. (R. I. Aaron, and J. Gibb, Eds.) (1936). *An Early Draft of Locke's Essay Together with Excerpts from his Journal.* Oxford: Clarendon Press.

Locke, J. (P. Abrams, Ed.) (1967). *John Locke: Two Tracts of Government.* Cambridge: Cambridge University Press.

Locke, J. (J. L. Axtell, Ed.) (1968). *The Educational Writings of John Locke: A Critical Edition.* Cambridge: Cambridge University Press.

Locke, J. (R. Ashcraft, Ed.) (1987). *Locke's The Two Treatises of Civil Government.* London: Routledge Publication.

Locke, J. (P. Laslett, Ed.). (1988). *Locke: Two Treatises of Government.* Cambridge: Cambridge University Press.

Loewenstein, D. (2001). *Representing Revolution in Milton and His Contemporaries: Religion, Politics, and Polemics in Radical Puritanism.* Cambridge: Cambridge University Press.

Loveridge, J. (2017). Rhetorical Deliberation, Memory, and Sensation in the Thought of Thomas Aquinas. *Philosophy and Rhetoric.* Volume 50, No. 2, pp. 178–200.

Lowe, B. (2010). *Commonwealth and the English Reformation: Protestantism and the Politics of Religious Change in the Gloucester Vale, 1483–1560.* Burlington: Ashgate Publishing Company.

Lowndes, W. T. (1857). *A Bibliographer's Manual of English Literature.* First Edition. London: Henry G. Bohn.

Machiavelli, N. (Q. Skinner., and R. Price, Eds.) (1988). *Principe.* Cambridge: Cambridge University Press.

Machiavelli, N. (A. Gilbert, Ed. and Trans.). (1989). *Machiavelli: The Chief Works and Others.* Volume I. North Carolina: Duke University Press Books.

Machiavelli, N. (A. Gilbert, Ed. and Trans.). (1989). *Machiavelli: The Chief Works and Others.* Volume II. North Carolina: Duke University Press Books.

Machiavelli, N. (A. Gilbert, Ed. and Trans.). (1989). *Machiavelli: The Chief Works and Others.* Volume III. North Carolina: Duke University Press Books.

Mandela, N. (1995). *Long Walk to Freedom: The Autobiography of Nelson Mandela.* Boston: Back Bay Books.

Mann, W. E. (2014). *Augustine's Confessions: Philosophy in Autobiography.* Oxford: Oxford University Press.

Mann, W. E. (2015). *God, Modality, and Morality.* Oxford: Oxford University Press.

Mann, W. E. (2016). *God, Belief, and Perplexity.* New York: Oxford University Press.

Marshall, P. (1994). *The Catholic Priesthood and the English Reformation.* Oxford: Oxford University Press.

Marshall, P. (1997). *The Impact of the English Reformation, 1500–1640.* New York: St Martin's Press.

Maslow, A. H. (1943). A Theory of Human Motivation. *Psychological Review.* Volume 50, No. 4, pp. 370–396.

May, H. F. (1991). *The Divided Heart: Essays on Protestantism and the Enlightenment in America.* New York: Oxford University Press.

McClendon, M. C. (1999). *The Quiet Reformation: Magistrates and the Emergence of Protestantism in Tudor Norwich.* Stanford, California: Stanford University Press.

McDowell, N., and Smith, N. (Eds.) (2011). *The Oxford Handbook of Milton*. Oxford: Oxford University Press.

Milbank, J. (1997). *The Word made Strange: Theology, Language, Culture*. Cambridge, Massachusetts: Blackwell Publishers.

Milbank, J., Pickstock, C., and Ward, G. (2000). *Radical Orthodoxy? A Catholic Enquiry*. London: Routledge Publication.

Miller, J. (Director). (1980). *The Taming of the Shrew*. (Film). The BBC Shakespeare Collection. London: The British Broadcasting Corporation.

Miller, J. (Director). (1981). *Antony And Cleopatra*. (Film). The BBC Shakespeare Collection. London: The British Broadcasting Corporation.

Miller, J. (Director). (1981). *Othello*. (Film). The BBC Shakespeare Collection. London: The British Broadcasting Corporation.

Miller, J. (Director). (1981). *Timon of Athens*. (Film). The BBC Shakespeare Collection. London: The British Broadcasting Corporation.

Miller, J. (Director). (1981). *Troilus and Cressida*. (Film). The BBC Shakespeare Collection. London: The British Broadcasting Corporation.

Miller, J. (Director). (1982). *King Lear*. (Film). The BBC Shakespeare Collection. London: The British Broadcasting Corporation.

Milton, J. (H. Darbishire, Ed.) (1958). *The Poetical Works of John Milton*. London: Oxford University Press.

Minear, E. (2011). *Reverberating Song in Shakespeare and Milton: Language, Memory, and Musical Representation*. London: Routledge Publication.

Miroshnikov, I. (2018). *The Gospel of Thomas and Plato: A Study of the Impact of Platonism on the 'Fifth Gospel'*. Boston: Brill.

Moberly, R. W. L. (2000). *The Bible, Theology, and Faith: A Study of Abraham and Jesus*. Cambridge: Cambridge University Press.

Montesquieu, C. (C. J. Betts, Trans.) (1973). *Persian Letters*. New York: Penguin Classics.

Montesquieu, C. (A.M. Cohler, B.C. Miller., and H.S. Stone., Trans., and Eds.) (1989). *Montesquieu: The Spirit of the Laws*. Cambridge: Cambridge University Press.

Moore, A. W. (2019). *Language, World, and Limits: Essays in the Philosophy of Language and Metaphysics*. First Edition. Oxford: Oxford University Press.

Moore, A. W. (2023). *The Human a Priori: Essays on how we make sense in Philosophy, Ethics, and Mathematics*. Oxford: Oxford University Press.

Moore, M. S. (1993). *Act and Crime: The Philosophy of Action and its implications for Criminal Law*. New York: Oxford University Press.

Moore, M. S. (2012). The Various Relations between Law and Morality in Contemporary Legal Philosophy. *Ratio Juris*. Volume 25, No. 4, pp. 435–471.

Moore, T. W. (1982). *Philosophy of Education: An Introduction*. London: Routledge & Kegan Paul.

Morrill, B. (2019). *Sacramental Theology: Theory and Practice from Multiple Perspectives*. Basel, Switzerland: Multidisciplinary Digital Publishing Institute.

Moshinsky, E. (Director). (1981). *All's Well That Ends Well*. (Film). The BBC Shakespeare Collection. London: The British Broadcasting Corporation.

Moshinsky, E. (Director). (1981). *A Midsummer Night's Dream*. (Film). The BBC Shakespeare Collection. London: The British Broadcasting Corporation.

Moshinsky, E. (Director). (1982). *Cymbeline*. (Film). The BBC Shakespeare Collection. London: The British Broadcasting Corporation.

Moshinsky, E. (Director). (1984). *Coriolanus*. (Film). The BBC Shakespeare Collection. London: The British Broadcasting Corporation.

Moshinsky, E. (Director). (1985). *Love's Labour's Lost*. (Film). The BBC Shakespeare Collection. London: The British Broadcasting Corporation.

Moss, C. R. (2019). *Divine Bodies: Resurrecting Perfection in the New Testament and Early Christianity*. New Haven: Yale University Press.

Munoz, D. (2018). The Spiritual Force of Unleashed Love: Echoes of Saint John of the Cross in Federico Garcia Lorca's Sonnets of the Dark Love. *Spiritus*. Volume 18, No. 2, pp. 152–175.

Murphy, G. R. (1980). *Brecht and the Bible: A Study of Religious Nihilism and Human Weakness in Brecht's Drama of Morality and the City*. North Carolina: The University of North Carolina Press.

Murphy, M. C. (2011). *God and Moral Law: On the Theistic Explanation of Morality*. Oxford: Oxford University Press.

Nietzsche, F. (W. Kaufmann, Trans.) (1967). *The Birth of Tragedy and the Case of Wagner*. New York: Vintage Books.

Nietzsche, F. (W. Kaufmann, Ed.) (W. Kaufmann, and R. J. Hollingdale, Trans.) (1968). *The Will to Power.* New York: Vintage Books.

Nietzsche, F. (1974). *Nietzsche: Philosopher, Psychologist, Antichrist.* Princeton, New Jersey: Princeton University Press.

Nietzsche, F. (W. Kaufmann, Trans.) (1989). *Beyond Good and Evil: Prelude to a Philosophy of the Future.* New York: Vintage Books.

Nietzsche, F. (W. Kaufmann, Ed.) (1989). *On the Genealogy of Morals and Ecce Homo.* New York: Vintage Books.

Nietzsche, F. (1994). *The Birth of Tragedy: Out of the Spirit of Music.* London: Penguin Classics.

Nietzsche, F. (W. Kaufmann, Trans.) (1995). *Thus Spoke Zarathustra: A Book for All and None.* New York: Modern Library.

Nietzsche, F. (R. J. Hollingdale, Trans.) (1996). *Nietzsche: Human, All too Human: A Book for Free Spirits.* Cambridge: Cambridge University Press.

Nietzsche, F. (M. Clark, and B. Leiter, Eds.) (1997). *Daybreak: Thoughts on the Prejudices of Morality.* New York: Cambridge University Press.

Nietzsche, F. (M. Clark, and A. J. Swensen, Trans.) (1998). *On the Genealogy of Morality.* Indiana: Hackett Publishing.

Nietzsche, F. (1998). *On the Genealogy of Morals.* Oxford: Oxford University Press.

Nietzsche, F. (B. Williams, Ed.) (J. Nauckhoff, and A. Del Caro, Trans.) (2001). *Nietzsche: The Gay Science.* New York: Cambridge University Press.

Nietzsche, F. (2003). *Beyond Good and Evil.* London: Penguin Classics.

Nietzsche, F. (R. Bittner, and K. Sturge, Eds.) (2003). *Nietzsche: Writings from the Late Notebooks.* Cambridge: Cambridge University Press.

Nietzsche, F. (2003). *Thus Spoke Zarathustra.* London: Penguin Classics.

Nietzsche, F. (2005). *The Anti-Christ, Ecce Homo, Twilight of the Idols.* Cambridge: Cambridge University Press.

Nietzsche, F. (R. Guess., and A. Nehamas, Eds.) (L. Lob., Trans.) (2009). *Nietzsche: Writings from the Early Notebooks.* Cambridge: Cambridge University Press.

Nietzsche, F. (R. J. Hollingdale, and W. Kaufmann, Trans.) (2016). *Twilight of the Idols: How to Philosophize with a Hammer.* California: CreateSpace Independent Publishing.

Nietzsche, F. (D. Breazeale, Ed.) (1997). *Nietzsche: Untimely Meditations.* Cambridge: Cambridge University Press.

Nightingale, A. (2011). *Once out of Nature: Augustine on Time and the Body*. Chicago: University of Chicago Press.

Oakeshott, M. (1975). *Hobbes on Civil Association*. Oxford: Oxford University Press.

O'Neill, M. (2010). *The Cambridge History of English Poetry*. Cambridge: Cambridge University Press.

Orrego, C. (2010). Autonomy within the Limits of Sympathy: A Comment on Neil MacCormick's Practical Reason in Law and Morality. *Jurisprudence*. Volume 1, No. 1, pp. 137–146.

Paddock, J. A. B. (2002). The imagery of Fire, Water, and Marriage in Saint Teresa of Ávila. *Bulletin of Spanish Studies*. Volume 92, Issue 8–10, pp. 91–124.

Pagels, E. H. (2003). *Beyond Belief: The Secret Gospel of Thomas*. New York: Random House.

Parker, S. (1997). *Stories in Scripture and Inscriptions: Comparative Studies on Narratives in Northwest Semitic Inscriptions and the Hebrew Bible*. Oxford: Oxford University Press.

Pasnau, R. (2001). *Thomas Aquinas on Human Nature: A Philosophical Study of Summa Theologiae*. Cambridge: Cambridge University Press.

Patrides, C. A. (1967). *Milton's Epic Poetry: Essays on Paradise Lost and Paradise Regained*. Harmondsworth: Penguin Books.

Patterson, S. (2013). *The Gospel of Thomas and Christian Origins: Essays on the Fifth Gospel*. Boston: Brill.

Pelikan, J. (1975). *The Christian Tradition: A History of the Development of Doctrine. Volume I: The Emergence of the Catholic Tradition (100–600)*. Chicago: University of Chicago Press.

Pelikan, J. (1977). *The Christian Tradition: A History of the Development of Doctrine. Volume II: The Spirit of Eastern Christendom (600–1700)*. Chicago: University of Chicago Press.

Pelikan, J. (1980). *The Christian Tradition: A History of the Development of Doctrine. Volume III: The Growth of Medieval Theology (600–1300)*. Chicago: University of Chicago Press.

Pelikan, J. (1985). *The Christian Tradition: A History of the Development of Doctrine. Volume IV: Reformation of Church and Dogma (1300–1700)*. Chicago: University of Chicago Press.

Pelikan, J. (1991). *The Christian Tradition: A History of the Development of Doctrine. Volume V: Christian Doctrine and Modern Culture (Since 1700)*. Chicago: University of Chicago Press.

Pierce, R. B. (2006). Reading Paradise Regained Ethically. *Philosophy and Literature*. Volume 30, No. 1, pp. 208–222.

Plato. (J. M. Cooper, and D. S. Hutchinson, Eds.) (1997). *Plato Complete Works*. Cambridge: Hackett Publishing Company.

Poole, W. (2005). *Milton and the Idea of the Fall*. Cambridge: Cambridge University Press.

Powell, R. (2021). *Perception and Analogy: Poetry, Science, and Religion in the Eighteenth Century*. Manchester: Manchester University Press.

Rakoff, A. (Director). (1978). *Romeo and Juliet*. (Film). The BBC Shakespeare Collection. London: The British Broadcasting Corporation.

Rata, T. (2018). Inductive Bible Study: Observation, Interpretation, and Application through the Lenses of History, Literature, and Theology. *Journal of the Evangelical Theological Society*. Volume 61, No. 4, pp. 858–860.

Rawls, J. (1985). Justice as Fairness: Political not Metaphysical. *Philosophy and Public Affairs*. Volume 14, No. 3, pp. 223–251.

Rawls, J. (1993). *Political Liberalism*. New York: Columbia University Press.

Rawls, J. (1999). *A Theory of Justice*. Cambridge, Massachusetts: Harvard University Press.

Rawls, J. (B. Herman, Ed.) (2000). *Lectures on the History of Moral Philosophy*. Cambridge, Massachusetts: Harvard University Press.

Rawls, J. (2001). *Justice as Fairness*. Cambridge, Massachusetts: Harvard University Press.

Raymond, J. (2010). *Milton's Angels: The Early-Modern Imagination*. Oxford: Oxford University Press.

Reisner, N. (2009). *Milton and the ineffable*. Oxford: Oxford University Press.

Ritchie, A. (2012). *From Morality to Metaphysics: The Theistic Implications of our Ethical Commitments*. Oxford: Oxford University Press.

Rosenberg, R. S. (2017). *The Givenness of Desire: Concrete Subjectivity and the Natural Desire to See God*. Toronto: University of Toronto Press.

Rosenfeld, N. (2008). *The Human Satan in Seventeenth-century English Literature: From Milton to Rochester*. Vermont: Ashgate Publishing.

Rowland, C. (2007). *The Cambridge Companion to Liberation Theology*. New York: Cambridge University Press.

Rutherford, D. (2006). *The Cambridge Companion to Early Modern Philosophy*. Cambridge: Cambridge University Press.

Saint John of the Cross. (2003). *Dark Night of the Soul*. New York: Dover Publications.

Sainsbury, R. M. (1986). Degrees of Belief and Degrees of Truth. *Philosophical Papers*. Volume 15, No. 2, pp. 97–106.

Sainsbury, R. M. (1991). Is There Higher-Order Vagueness? *Philosophical Quarterly*. Volume 41, No. 163, pp. 167–182.

Sainsbury, R. M. (2009). *Paradoxes*. Third Edition. Cambridge: Cambridge University Press.

Sartre, J. P. (1949). *Reflections on Our Age*. New York: Columbia University Press.

Sartre, J. P. (K. Black, Trans.) (1960). *The Devil and the Good Lord*. New York: Knopf.

Sartre, J. P. (1968). *On Genocide*. Boston, Massachusetts: Beacon Press.

Sartre, J. P. (H. E. Barnes, Trans.) (1968). *Search for a Method*. New York: Vintage Books.

Sartre, J. P. (L. Alexander, Trans.) (1969). *Nausea*. New York: New Directions.

Sartre, J. P. (L. Alexander, Trans.) (1969). *The Wall*. New York: New Directions Paperbook.

Sartre, J. P. (F. Williams, and R. Kirkpatrick, Trans.) (1972). *The Transcendence of the Ego: An Existentialist Theory of Consciousness*. New York: Octagon Books.

Sartre, J. P. (J. Mathews, Trans.) (1974). *Between Existentialism and Marxism: Essays and Interviews, 1959–1970*. London: New Left Books.

Sartre, J. P. (P. Auster., and L. Davis., Trans.) (1977). *Life Situations: Essays Written and Spoken*. New York: Pantheon.

Sartre, J. P. (B. Frechtman, Trans.) (1981). *The Words: The Autobiography of Jean-Paul Sartre*. New York: Vintage Books.

Sartre, J. P. (1984). *Critique of Dialectical Reason. Volume I: Theory of Practical Ensembles*. London: Verso Books.

Sartre, J. P. (1988). *What is Literature? And Other Essays*. Cambridge, Massachusetts: Harvard University Press.

Sartre, J. P. (1992). *The Age of Reason: A Novel*. New York: Vintage Books.

Sartre, J. P. (D. Pellauer, Trans.) (1992). *Notebooks for an Ethics*. Chicago: University of Chicago Press.

Sartre, J. P. (S. Beauvoir, Ed.) (1992). *Witness to My Life: The Letters of Jean-Paul Sartre to Simone de Beauvoir, 1926–1939*. New York: Scribner.

Sartre, J. P. (A. Hoven, Trans.) (1992). *Truth and Existence*. Chicago: University of Chicago Press.

Sartre, J. P. (H. Barnes, Trans.) (1993). *Being and Nothingness: An Essay on Phenomenological Ontology*. New York: Washington Square Press.

Sartre, J. P. (A. Haddour, S. Brewer, and T. McWilliams, Trans.) (2001). *Colonialism and Neocolonialism*. London: Routledge Publication.

Sartre, J. P. (A. Elkaim-Sartre, Ed.) (Q. Hoare, Trans.) (2006). *Critique of Dialectical Reason*. Volume II. London: Verso Books.

Sartre, J. P. (C. Macomber, Trans.) (2007). *Existentialism is a Humanism*. New Haven: Yale University Press.

Sartre, J. P. (P. Mairet, Trans.) (2008). *Emotions: Outline of a Theory*. London: Routledge Classics.

Sartre, J. P. (A. D. Cordero, Trans.) (2009). *Wartime Diary*. Urbana: University of Illinois Press.

Sartre, J. P. (2015). *The Imaginary: A Phenomenological Psychology of the Imagination*. New York: Routledge Classics.

Sassi, M. M. (2018). *The Beginnings of Philosophy in Greece*. Princeton, New Jersey: Princeton University Press.

Savage, R. (2012). *Philosophy and Religion in Enlightenment Britain: New case studies*. Oxford: Oxford University Press.

Scaltsas, T. (1994). *Substances and Universals in Aristotle's Metaphysics*. Ithaca: Cornell University.

Schelling, F. W. J. (T. Pfau, Ed. and Trans.) (1994). *Idealism and the Endgame of Theory: Three Essays by F. W. J. Schelling*. New York: State University of New York Press.

Schelling, F. W. J. (J. M. Wirth, Trans.) (2000). *The Ages of the World*. New York: State University of New York Press.

Schelling, F. W. J. (F. Steinkamp, Trans.) (2002). *Clara: Or, on Nature's Connection to the Spirit World*. New York: State University of New York Press.

Schelling, F. W. J. (K. R. Peterson, Trans.) (2004). *First Outline of a System of the Philosophy of Nature*. New York: State University of New York Press.

Schelling, F. W. J. (J. Love and J. Schmidt, Trans.) (2007). *Philosophical Investigations into the Essence of Human Freedom*. New York: State University of New York Press.

Schelling, F. W. J. (B. Matthews, Trans.) (2008). *The Grounding of Positive Philosophy: The Berlin Lectures*. New York: State University of New York Press.

Schelling, F. W. J. (M. Richey, and M. Zisselsberger, Trans.) (2008). *Historical-Critical Introduction to the Philosophy of Mythology*. New York: State University of New York Press.

Schopenhauer, A. (E. F. J. Payne, Trans.) (1969). *The World as Will and Representation*. Volume I. New York: Dover Publications.

Schopenhauer, A. (E. F. J. Payne, Trans.) (1969). *The World as Will and Representation*. Volume II. New York: Dover Publications.

Schopenhauer, A. (1970). *Essays and Aphorisms*. London: Penguin Classics.

Schopenhauer, A. (E. F. J. Payne, Trans.) (1999). *On the Basis of Morality*. Indiana: Hackett Publishing Company.

Schopenhauer, A. (G. Zoller, and E. F. J. Payne, Eds.) (1999). *Prize Essay on the Freedom of the Will*. Cambridge: Cambridge University Press.

Schopenhauer, A. (2004). *The Wisdom of Life*. New York: Dover Publications.

Schopenhauer, A. (2010). *The Two Fundamental Problems of Ethics*. New York: Oxford University Press.

Schopenhauer, A. (D. E. Cartwright, E. E. Erdmann, and C. Janaway, Trans.) (2012). *Schopenhauer: On the Fourfold Root of the Principle of Sufficient Reason and Other Writings*. Cambridge: Cambridge University Press.

Schopenhauer, A. (S. Roehr, and C. Janaway, Trans.) (2014). *Schopenhauer: Parerga and Paralipomena. Volume I: Short Philosophical Essays*. Cambridge: Cambridge University Press.

Schopenhauer, A. (C. Janaway, Ed.). (A. D. Caro, Trans.) (2015). *Schopenhauer: Parerga and Paralipomena. Volume II: Short Philosophical Essays*. Cambridge: Cambridge University Press.

Schopenhauer, A. (Cartwright, D. E., Ed.) (Payne, E. F. J., Trans.) (1994). *On Vision and Colors: An Essay*. Oxford: Berg Publishers.

Scott, C. D. (2016). Saint Thomas Aquinas' Ontological Epistemology as clarified realism: The relating of subject to object for ontological knowledge. *South African Journal of Philosophy*. Volume 35, No. 3, pp. 249–260.

Shagan, E. H. (2019). *The Birth of Modern Belief: Faith and Judgement from the Middle Ages to the Enlightenment*. Princeton, New Jersey: Princeton University Press.

Shakespeare, W. (Condell, H., Droeshout, M., and Heminges, J., Eds.) (1623). *Mr. William Shakespeare's Comedies, Histories, and Tragedies. Published according to the true original copies. Gentle Master Shakespeare. First Folio.* London: Isaac Laggard and Ed Blount.

Shakespeare, W. (1632). *Mr. William Shakespeare Comedies, Histories, and Tragedies. Published according to the true original copies. The Second Impression.* London: Tho. Cotes, for Robert Allot.

Shakespeare, W. (1664). *Mr. William Shakespeare's Comedies, Histories, and Tragedies. Published according to the true original copies. The Third Impression.* London: Philip Chetwind.

Shakespeare, W. (1685). *Mr. William Shakespeare's Comedies, Histories, and Tragedies. Published according to the true original copies. The Fourth Folio.* London: Herringman, H., Brewster, E., Chiswell, R., and Bentley, R.

Shakespeare, W. (1978). *The Plays and Sonnets of William Shakespeare.* Seven Volumes. Pennsylvania: Franklin Library.

Shakespeare, W. (1996). *The Norton Facsimile: The First Folio of Shakespeare prepared by Charlton Hinman.* Second Edition. New York: Norton and Company.

Shakespeare, W. (2015). *The Complete Works of William Shakespeare.* New York: Barnes and Noble, Inc.

Shakespeare, W. (Jowett, J., Montgomery, W., Taylor, G., and Wells, S., Eds.) (2005). *The Oxford Shakespeare: The Complete Works.* Second Edition. Oxford: Oxford University Press.

Shakespeare, W. (J. Kerrigan, Ed.) (1999). *The Sonnets and a Lover's Complaint.* London: Penguin Classics.

Shakespeare, W. (B. A. Mowat, and P. Werstine, Eds.) (2003). *Cymbeline.* New York: Simon & Schuster.

Shakespeare, W. (B. A. Mowat, and P. Werstine, Eds.) (2004). *Julius Caesar.* New York: Simon & Schuster.

Shakespeare, W. (B. A. Mowat, and P. Werstine, Eds.) (2004). *The Merry Wives of Windsor.* New York: Simon & Schuster.

Shakespeare, W. (B. A. Mowat, and P. Werstine, Eds.) (2004). *Shakespeare's Sonnets.* New York: Simon & Schuster.

Shakespeare, W. (B. A. Mowat, and P. Werstine, Eds.) (2005). *Henry IV: Part One.* New York: Simon & Schuster.

Shakespeare, W. (B. A. Mowat, and P. Werstine, Eds.) (2005). *Love's Labour's Lost.* New York: Simon & Schuster.

Shakespeare, W. (B. A. Mowat, and P. Werstine, Eds.) (2005). *Measure for Measure*. New York: Simon & Schuster.

Shakespeare, W. (B. A. Mowat, and P. Werstine, Eds.) (2005). *Pericles, Prince of Tyre*. New York: Simon & Schuster.

Shakespeare, W. (B. A. Mowat, and P. Werstine, Eds.) (2005). *The Winter's Tale*. New York: Simon & Schuster.

Shakespeare, W. (B. A. Mowat, and P. Werstine, Eds.) (2005). *Antony and Cleopatra*. New York: Simon & Schuster.

Shakespeare, W. (B. A. Mowat, and P. Werstine, Eds.) (2005). *Titus of Andronicus*. New York: Simon & Schuster.

Shakespeare, W. (B. A. Mowat, and P. Werstine, Eds.) (2006). *Henry IV: Part Two*. New York: Simon & Schuster.

Shakespeare, W. (B. A. Mowat, and P. Werstine, Eds.) (2006). *All's Well That Ends Well*. New York: Simon & Schuster.

Shakespeare, W. (B. A. Mowat, and P. Werstine, Eds.) (2006). *The Two Gentlemen of Verona*. New York: Simon & Schuster.

Shakespeare, W. (B. A. Mowat, and P. Werstine, Eds.) (2006). *King John*. New York: Simon & Schuster.

Shakespeare, W. (B. A. Mowat, and P. Werstine, Eds.) (2006). *Timon of Athens*. New York: Simon & Schuster.

Shakespeare, W. (B. A. Mowat, and P. Werstine, Eds.) (2007). *Troilus and Cressida*. New York: Simon & Schuster.

Shakespeare, W. (B. A. Mowat, and P. Werstine, Eds.) (2007). *Henry VIII*. New York: Simon & Schuster.

Shakespeare, W. (B. A. Mowat, and P. Werstine, Eds.) (2008). *Henry VI: Part One*. New York: Simon & Schuster.

Shakespeare, W. (B. A. Mowat, and P. Werstine, Eds.) (2008). *Henry VI, Part Two*. New York: Simon & Schuster.

Shakespeare, W. (B. A. Mowat, and P. Werstine, Eds.) (2009). *Henry VI, Part Three*. New York: Simon & Schuster.

Shakespeare, W. (B. A. Mowat, and P. Werstine, Eds.) (2009). *Coriolanus*. New York: Simon & Schuster.

Shakespeare, W. (B. A. Mowat, and P. Werstine, Eds.) (2010). *The Merchant of Venice*. New York: Simon & Schuster.

Shakespeare, W. (B. A. Mowat, and P. Werstine, Eds.) (2011). *Romeo and Juliet*. New York: Simon & Schuster.

Shakespeare, W. (B. A. Mowat, and P. Werstine, Eds.) (2012). *Hamlet*. New York: Simon & Schuster.

Shakespeare, W. (B. A. Mowat, and P. Werstine, Eds) (2013). *Macbeth.* New York: Simon & Schuster.

Shakespeare, W. (B. A. Mowat, and P. Werstine, Eds.) (2014). *The Taming of the Shrew.* New York: Simon & Schuster.

Shakespeare, W. (B. A. Mowat, and P. Werstine, Eds.) (2015). *The Comedy of Errors.* New York: Simon & Schuster.

Shakespeare, W. (B. A. Mowat, and P. Werstine, Eds.) (2015). *The Tempest.* New York: Simon & Schuster.

Shakespeare, W. (B. A. Mowat, and P. Werstine, Eds.) (2015). *King Lear.* New York: Simon & Schuster.

Shakespeare, W. (B. A. Mowat, and P. Werstine, Eds.) (2016). *A Midsummer Night's Dream.* New York: Simon & Schuster.

Shakespeare, W. (B. A. Mowat, and P. Werstine, Eds.) (2016). *Richard II.* New York: Simon & Schuster.

Shakespeare, W. (B. A. Mowat, and P. Werstine, Eds.) (2017). *Othello.* New York: Simon & Schuster.

Shakespeare, W. (B. A. Mowat, and P. Werstine, Eds.) (2018). *Richard III.* New York: Simon & Schuster.

Shakespeare, W. (B. A. Mowat, and P. Werstine, Eds.) (2018). *Much Ado About Nothing.* New York: Simon & Schuster.

Shakespeare, W. (B. A. Mowat, and P. Werstine, Eds.) (2019). *As You Like It.* New York: Simon & Schuster.

Shakespeare, W. (B. A. Mowat, and P. Werstine, Eds.) (2019). *Twelfth Night.* New York: Simon & Schuster.

Shakespeare, W. (B. A. Mowat, and P. Werstine, Eds.) (2020). *Henry V.* New York: Simon & Schuster.

Shakespeare, W. (J. Roe, Ed.) (2006). *The Poems: Venus and Adonis, The Rape of Lucrece, The Phoenix and The Turtle, The Passionate Pilgrim, A Lover's Complaint.* New York: Cambridge University Press.

Shoemaker, S. J. (2004). *Ancient Traditions of the Virgin Mary's Dormition and Assumption.* Oxford: Oxford University Press.

Slade, C. (1995). *Saint Teresa of Ávila: Author of a Heroic Life.* Berkeley: University of California Press.

Snow, N. E. (2014). *Cultivating Virtue: Perspectives from Philosophy, Theology, and Psychology.* New York: Oxford University Press.

Sterba, J. (2022). *Is the God of Traditional Theism Logically Compatible with All the Evil in the World?* Basel: Multidisciplinary Digital Publishing Institute.

Stettler, C. (2023). The Resurrection of the Body. Its Place in Biblical Theology and Its Meaning for Christian Life and Witness. *European Journal of Theology*. Volume 32, No. 1, pp. 26–59.

Stone, M. E. (2013). *Adam and Eve in the Armenian Tradition: Fifth through Seventeenth Centuries*. Atlanta: Society of Biblical Literature.

Streete, A. (2009). *Protestantism and Drama in Early Modern England*. New York: Cambridge University Press.

Stuart-Buttle, Tim. (2019). *From Moral Theology to Moral Philosophy: Cicero and Visions of Humanity from Locke to Hume*. Oxford: Oxford University Press.

Taliadoros, J. (2013). Law, Theology, and Morality: Conceptions of the Rights of the Poor in the Twelfth and Thirteen Centuries. *Journal of Religious History*. Volume 37, Issue 4, pp. 474–493.

Taylor, D. (1983). *The Two Gentlemen of Verona*. (Film). The BBC Shakespeare Collection. London: The British Broadcasting Corporation.

Theokritoff, E., and Cunningham, M. B. (2008). *The Cambridge Companion to Orthodox Christian Theology*. Cambridge: Cambridge University Press.

Tillich, P. (1973). *Systematic Theology. Volume I*. Chicago: University of Chicago Press.

Tillich, P. (1975). *Systematic Theology. Volume II*. Chicago: University of Chicago Press.

Tillich, P. (1976). *Systematic Theology. Volume III*. Chicago: University of Chicago Press.

Toom, T. (2020). *The Cambridge Companion to Augustine's "Confessions"*. Cambridge: Cambridge University Press.

Tzu, L. (D. C. Lau, Ed.) (1964). *Tao Te Ching*. London: Penguin Classics.

Urban, D. V. (2015). John Milton, Paradox, and the Atonement: Heresy, Orthodoxy, and the Son's Whole-Life Obedience. *Studies in Philology*. Volume 112, No. 4, pp. 817–836.

Urban, D. V. (2022). Metagenre in Paradise Lost and Paradise Regained: Its Relevance to Milton's Presentation of the Son's Self-Sacrificial Epic Heroism. *Style*. Volume 56, No. 4, pp. 392–412.

Valkenberg, P. (2022). *A Companion to Comparative Theology*. Boston: Brill.

Vanhoozer, K. J. (2001). *The Cambridge Companion to Postmodern Theology*. Cambridge: Cambridge University Press.

Vinzent, M. (2012). *Christ's Resurrection in Early Christianity: and the Making of the New Testament*. Farnham: Routledge Publication.

Welshon, R. (2023). *Nietzsche on the Genealogy of Morality: A Guide*. New York: Oxford University Press.

Wesley, J. (1757). *The Doctrine of Original Sin according to Scripture, Reason, and Experience*. Bristol: E Farley.

White, T. J. (2013). *The Incarnate Lord: A Thomistic Study in Christology*. Washington: Catholic University of America Press.

Wise, H. (Director). (1979). *Julius Caesar*. (Film). The BBC Shakespeare Collection. London: The British Broadcasting Corporation.

Wittgenstein, L. (1974). *Philosophical Investigations*. Oxford: Basil Blackwell.

Wittgenstein, L. (1974). *Philosophical Grammar. Part I: The Proposition and its sense. Part II: On logic and mathematics*. Berkeley: University of California Press.

Wittgenstein, L. (1974). *On Certainty*. Oxford: Basil Blackwell.

Wittgenstein, L. (Winch, P., Trans.) (1980). *Culture and Value*. Second Edition. Oxford: Basil Blackwell.

Wittreich, J. (2011). Lost Paradise Regained: The Twin Halves of Milton's Epic Vision. *University of Toronto Quarterly*. Volume 80, No. 3, pp. 731–755.

Wolter, A. B. (Adams, M. M., Ed.) (1990). *The Philosophical Theology of John Duns Scotus*. Ithaca: New York: Cornell University Press.

Woodward, J. (2003). *Making Things Happen: A Theory of Causal Explanation*. New York: Oxford University Press.

Worsley, R. (1996). *Human Freedom and the Logic of Evil: Prolegomenon to a Christian Theology of Evil*. New York: St Martin's Press.

Wright, J. P. (1983). *The Sceptical Realism of David Hume*. Manchester: Manchester University Press.

Wuthnow, R. (1993). *Communities of Discourse: Ideology and Social Structure in the Reformation, the Enlightenment, and European Socialism*. Cambridge, Massachusetts: Harvard University Press.

Wyschogrod, E. (1990). *Saints and Postmodernism: Revisioning Moral Philosophy*. Chicago: University of Chicago Press.

Xenophon. (2018). *The Memorabilia*. New York: Dover Publications.

Yablo, S. (1992). Mental Causation. *Philosophical Review*. Volume 101, Issue 2, pp. 245–280.

Yablo, S. (2002). De Facto Dependence. *Journal of Philosophy*. Volume 99, Issue 3, pp. 130–148.

Yack, B. (2012). *Nationalism and the Moral Psychology of Community*. Chicago: University of Chicago Press.

Yates, F. A. (1964). *Giordano Bruno and the Hermetic Tradition*. London: Routledge Publication.

Yolton, J. (1956). *John Locke and the Way of Ideas*. Oxford: Oxford University Press.

Yolton, J. (1960). *The Philosophy of Science of A. S. Eddington*. The Hague: Martinus Nijhoff.

Yolton, J. (1970). *Locke and the Compass of Human Understanding: A Selective Commentary on the Essay*. Cambridge: Cambridge University Press.

Yolton, J. (1971). *The Two Intellectual Worlds of John Locke*. New York: Cornell University Press.

Yolton, J. (1977). *The Locke Reader: Selections from the Works of John Locke with a General Introduction and Commentary*. Cambridge: Cambridge University Press.

Yolton, J. (1983). *Thinking Matter: Materialism in Eighteenth-Century Britain*. Minneapolis: University of Minnesota Press.

Yolton, J. (1984). *Perceptual Acquaintance from Descartes to Reid*. Minneapolis: University of Minnesota Press.

Yolton, J. (1996). *The Philosophical Canon in the 17th and 18th Centuries*. New York: University of Rochester Press.

Yolton, J. (1996). *Perception and Reality: A History from Descartes to Kant*. Ithaca: Cornell University Press.

Yoshida, K., and Kamo, C. (2015). *Essays in Idleness and Hojoki*. London: Penguin Classics.

Young, A. (1997). *The Harmony of Illusions: Inventing Post-traumatic Stress Disorder*. Princeton: Princeton University Press.

Young, M., and Edis, T. (Eds.). (2006). *Why Intelligent Design Fails: A Scientific Critique of the New Creationism*. New Brunswick: Rutgers University Press.

Yourgrau, P. (1991). *The Disappearance of Time*. Cambridge: Cambridge University Press.

Zachhuber, J. (2020). *The Rise of Christian Theology and the End of Ancient Metaphysics: Patristic Philosophy from the Cappadocian Fathers to John of Damascus*. Oxford: Oxford University Press.

Zack, Naomi (Ed.) (2017). *The Oxford Handbook of Philosophy and Race*. New York: Oxford University Press.

Zagzebski, L. T. (2004). *Divine Motivation Theory*. Cambridge: Cambridge University Press.

Zak, P. J. (2012). *The Moral Molecule: The Source of Love and Prosperity*. New York: Dutton.

Zaner, R. M. (2004). *Conversations on the Edge: Narratives of Ethics and Illness*. Washington D.C.: Georgetown University Press.

Zeman, J. J. (1973). *Modal Logic: The Lewis-Modal Systems*. Oxford: Clarendon Press.

Zhuang, Z. (Watson, B. Trans.) (1968). *The Complete Works of Chuang Tzu*. New York: Columbia University Press.

Zilsel, E. (1945). The Genesis of the Concept of Scientific Progress. *Journal of the History of Ideas*. Volume 6, No. 3, pp. 325–349.

Ziman, J. (1960). *Electrons and Phonons: The Theory of Transport Phenomena in Solids*. Oxford: Oxford University Press.

Ziman, J. (1964). *Principles of the Theory of Solids*. Cambridge: Cambridge University Press.

Ziman, J. (1968). *Public Knowledge: An Essay Concerning the Social Dimension of Science*. Cambridge: Cambridge University Press.

Ziman, J. (1969). *Elements of Advanced Quantum Theory*. Cambridge: Cambridge University Press.

Ziman, J. (1976). *The Force of Knowledge: The Scientific Dimension of Society*. Cambridge: Cambridge University Press.

Ziman, J. (1977). The International Scientific Community: Ideas Move Around Inside People. *Minerva*. Volume 15, No. 1, (Spring 1977), pp. 83–93.

Ziman, J. (1978). *Reliable Knowledge: An Exploration of the Grounds for Belief in Science*. Cambridge: Cambridge University Press.

Ziman, J. (1979). *Models of Disorder: The Theoretical Physics of Homogeneously Disordered Systems*. Cambridge: Cambridge University Press.

Ziman, J. (1980). *Teaching and Learning about Science and Society*. Cambridge: Cambridge University Press.

Ziman, J. (1981). *Puzzles, Problems, and Enigmas: Occasional Pieces on the Human Aspects of Science*. Cambridge: Cambridge University Press.

Ziman, J. (1984). *An Introduction to Science Studies: The Philosophical and Social Aspects of Science and Technology*. Cambridge: Cambridge University Press.

Ziman, J. (1986). *The World of Science and the Rule of Law: A Study of the Observance and Violations of the Human Rights of Scientists in the Participating States of the Helsinki Accords.* Oxford: Oxford University Press.

Ziman, J. (1987). *Knowing Everything about Nothing: Specialisation and Change in Research Careers.* Cambridge: Cambridge University Press.

Ziman, J. (1995). *Of One Mind: The Collectivisation of Science.* New York: American Institute of Physics Press.

Ziman, J. (2000). *Technological Innovation as an Evolutionary Process.* Cambridge: Cambridge University Press.

Ziman, J. (2000). *Real Science: What it is, and What it Means.* Cambridge: Cambridge University Press.

Zimmer, C. (2006). *Evolution: The Triumph of an Idea.* New York: Harper Perennial.

Zimmer, C. (2012). *A Planet of Viruses.* Chicago: University of Chicago Press.

Zupanov, I. G. (2019). *The Oxford Handbook of the Jesuits.* Oxford: Oxford University Press.

Zynda, L. (2000). Representation Theorems and Realism about Degrees of Belief. *Philosophy of Science.* Volume 67, No. 1, pp. 45–69.

INDEX

www.ingramcontent.com/pod-product-compliance
Lightning Source LLC
Chambersburg PA
CBHW051123300726
48981CB00022B/525/J